19/12

WITHDRAWN

WHAT SHOULD I BELIEVE?

WHAT SHOULD
I BELIEVE?

Philosophical Essays
for
Critical Thinking

Paul Gomberg

broadview press

Library and Archives Canada Cataloguing in Publication

Gomberg, Paul
        What should I believe? : philosophical essays for critical thinking / Paul Gomberg.

Includes bibliographical references and index.
ISBN 978-1-55481-013-0

        1. Belief and doubt. 2. Critical thinking. 3. Philosophy.
I. Title.

BD215.G64 2011   121'.6   C2010-907287-1

Broadview Press is an independent, international publishing house, incorporated in 1985.

We welcome comments and suggestions regarding any aspect of our publications— please feel free to contact us at the addresses below or at broadview@broadviewpress.com / www.broadviewpress.com.

North America

PO Box 1243
Peterborough, Ontario
Canada K9J 7H5
2215 Kenmore Ave.
Buffalo, New York
USA 14207
tel: (705) 743-8990
fax: (705) 743-8353
customerservice
@broadviewpress.com

UK, Europe, Central Asia, Middle East, Africa, India and Southeast Asia

Eurospan Group
3 Henrietta St., London
WC2E 8LU, UK
tel: 44 (0) 1767 604972
fax: 44 (0) 1767 601640
eurospan
@turpin-distribution.com

Australia and New Zealand

NewSouth Books
c/o TL Distribution,
15-23 Helles Ave.
Moorebank, NSW
Australia 2170
tel: (02) 8778 9999
fax (02) 8778 9944
orders@tldistribution.com.au

Edited by Robert M. Martin.

Book design by Michel Vrana.

This book is printed on paper containing 100% post-consumer fibre.

Printed in Canada

CONTENTS

ACKNOWLEDGEMENTS

WHEN, FIVE YEARS AGO, I RESUMED TEACHING CRITICAL THINKING, trying to make the course more philosophical, Arthur Fine encouraged me and suggested my inclusion of Feyerabend in the curriculum to challenge complacency about the desirability and definability of critical thinking. He also thought there would be interest in an anthology such as the present one. My former colleague Mahesh Ananth also encouraged me and suggested the selection from Gould; at one time we even planned to edit an anthology together, but in the end, I sought a more narrowly epistemological anthology and proceeded on my own.

Allen Wood was another early interlocutor on the issues of critical belief. Our discussions have improved the essay on trust and modesty as well as much of the editorial material.

Abe Roth suggested both the Wolterstorff selection and the Anscombe essay.

My essay on evolution has benefited from criticism by Laurie Walter and Elliott Sober. The paper on miracles has been helped by criticism

viii ACKNOWLEDGEMENTS

from my Broadview editor Greg Janzen, Robert Martin, Elliott Sober (who read it twice in different versions), and Arthur Fine; Janzen in particular formulated some of the arguments to which I replied. Robert Moran and Adam Elga read the paper on trust and modesty; Robert offered encouragement as did Adam, who also made criticisms which improved it.

Arthur Fine helped me write the editorial material on Feyerabend to make that piece accessible to beginning students. An anonymous reviewer for Broadview made many criticisms of my essays and editorial materials; these greatly improved the manuscript. Alex Sager at Broadview was an early advocate of the project before Greg Janzen took over. Finally I have been fortunate to have Robert Martin as my "copy-editor"; that term does not do justice to Bob's many criticisms, both stylistic and philosophical. I believe the manuscript has benefited greatly from his work on it.

I thank all of you for your help.

PREFACE

TO THE
INSTRUCTOR:
MAKING
CRITICAL THINKING
CLASSES
MORE PHILOSOPHICAL

AS A FRESHMAN IN COLLEGE, I TOOK A PHILOSOPHY CLASS TAUGHT BY John Searle. As we read Descartes, Hume, Berkeley, and Ayer, Searle was disputing their views. I realized that, whatever my limitations at that time, I was expected to think about the disagreements and develop my own ideas. I was thrilled. Philosophy was a subject where there were questions, not one where there were answers that everyone had to accept.

The purpose of this book is to facilitate turning our critical thinking classes into real philosophy classes such as the one Searle taught. Many of us teach classes that are required for the general education curriculum or that fulfill a humanities requirement. This is our opportunity to expose students to the joys of philosophical thinking and to invite them into further study of philosophy. The purpose of this anthology is to turn critical thinking (or other) classes into invitations to philosophical conversation. Textbooks often fail to do that.

The best of the critical thinking textbooks help students to analyze difficult passages in order to discover how the author intends statements to be connected (Monroe Beardsley's arrow diagramming technique popularized by Stephen Thomas is very useful here). The texts often contain helpful instruction in classical logic or modern symbolic logic and useful results from probability theory. Texts may instruct students in distinctions from philosophy of language or philosophy of logic; they may analyze the force of scientific reasoning. Even when texts do these things well, they don't engage students in the serious questions about which philosophers disagree. They give answers more than they raise questions.

Here are two questions about which people may disagree but which most critical thinking classes do not engage: Is it always good to think critically? Can critical thinking be defined clearly? While critical thinking classes are supposed to encourage students to think critically, they may not encourage students to *think critically about critical thinking*. If students are not encouraged to grapple with the difficult philosophical questions about whether critical thinking can be defined or clearly applied in many contexts (including scientific ones), or about whether critical thinking is always a desirable approach to deciding what to believe, then students are not being encouraged to think critically in the most important philosophical meaning of that phrase.

At the core of this anthology is the issue of critical belief. I assume that you can't think critically and at the same time believe just any old thing that may pop into your mind. But if not, then is it possible to say what critical belief is? The topic of critical belief raises questions such as these: What makes an idea worthy of belief? How do we decide what to believe and what not to believe (assuming this is a matter for decision, which it may not always be)? Does being a critical thinker imply giving up belief in God? We sometimes believe what other people say in both religious and scientific contexts, but does believing others play a different role in the two contexts? Is critical thinking desirable in all situations or only in some? Is there such a thing as scientific method or scientific rationality? Is science objective or does it only inscribe the political and social prejudices of scientists? This anthology is for philosophers who want to introduce students to the difficult philosophical *questions* that surround critical thinking, moving away from dogmatism to philosophical dialogue. In developing these discussions the anthology introduces students to issues in the philosophy of science, epistemology, and philosophy of religion.

The readings are at different levels of difficulty. Some students will find the selections from Peirce, Feyerabend, Anscombe, and James extremely difficult. I give help where I can, but these selections will inevitably be challenging to beginning students. Other selections—including my essays as well as some of the popular science, parts of Clifford, and some others—are much easier. You should use your own discretion in deciding which essays to assign, and trial and error may be necessary for your particular students.

The anthology grows out of my own teaching of critical thinking. The editorial materials I have added highlight issues I ask my students to address. I hope the instructor finds these materials useful, and, if so, my vision of the issues will help you to develop and frame your own. From this process—and sharing what we have learned—we can become better teachers and better philosophers.

INTRODUCTION

THE PHILOSOPHICAL PROBLEMS RAISED BY CRITICAL THINKING

THE DISCUSSION OF THE WAR IN AFGHANISTAN WAS BECOMING HEATED. "Well, I have a right to my belief!" a student said. Let's think about that remark. What does it mean? In context it might mean, "I don't want to continue this discussion." Surely no one could dispute the student's right to her belief.

Perhaps that last thought is wrong. Someone could seriously say, "You have no right to an opinion until you have some knowledge of the matter." That remark makes sense as a judgment about what is required to form opinions or beliefs in a responsible way: first you must inquire and study the issue at hand, understand different points of view, and then make a careful assessment of how strongly each possible view is supported by evidence. By "critical belief" I will mean belief formed carefully from evidence or argument, belief that, when questioned by those who doubt it, can be supported and defended or, as I will also call it, belief that can withstand scrutiny.

At least two difficult questions arise: First, can we define clearly what it means to be "formed carefully from evidence or argument"? If not, then the demand that our beliefs be critical may be empty. Second, while perhaps all of us would agree that *some* beliefs should be formed in that way, we might think that not all beliefs need to be. For example, suppose we are workers in a blood lab. It seems wrong to form a belief about whether this patient has anemia without performing the appropriate test. But do all beliefs have to meet the same standard? Can I follow the religious faith of my parents without having to justify my beliefs to someone who does not share my beliefs? Many would answer that question "yes"; they may believe that while critical belief is appropriate to laboratory and scientific contexts, in religious contexts belief does not have to meet the same standards. In this sense, many believe that we need not always strive to think critically.

The purpose of this anthology is to address this question: how we should decide what is worthy of belief? There are, as the previous paragraph sketched, two major areas of concern. First, how does critical thinking apply to belief? What beliefs are acceptable to a critical thinker, what beliefs are not? Is there a *method* of critical thinking for belief? (Some believe this is scientific method—if there is such a thing as a single scientific method, which I doubt.) Second, supposing that there is a critical thinking standard for arriving at beliefs, should we always follow that standard, or is it better, overall and from a human point of view, sometimes to have beliefs that do not meet the standards of critical thinking?

The anthology is divided into four major sections and an epilogue. The first section contains two classical defenses of critical belief by Charles Sanders Peirce and William Clifford. Both argue that belief should be supported by evidence. The second section explores natural science as a method of arriving at beliefs. This section includes essays pointing out social influences on scientific thought and essays questioning whether there is a single scientific method and even whether it is always a good idea, for the progress of science, to follow scientific rationality. The third section explores a fundamental fact about how we arrive at beliefs: we get our beliefs from other people. Is there a right way to do this, and if so, how do we know what it is? Is there a difference here between scientific and religious contexts? The last major section is about religious belief. The section contains both criticisms of religious belief and defense of beliefs that go beyond what evidence can support. The anthology closes with some final thoughts about religion and belief.

The purpose of the anthology is to invite you the student into philosophical conversation. Philosophy courses don't work well if the students do not themselves begin to become philosophers. What I mean is that you must begin to develop your own point of view. But having a point of view doesn't mean that you are thinking philosophically. Philosophical thinking requires us to think about our own point of view and defend it to others who may disagree. It is not an easy subject, but I hope you will find it as exciting and interesting to think about these things as I have.

One final word: I have written some editorial material to help you to understand the readings and the issues they raise. But just as I do not expect you to believe any of the authors that are selected here on the ground that they said it, I don't expect you to believe me either (see the section of my paper "Trust and Modesty" about philosophical method for my point here). What I am hoping you will do is use the readings and editorial materials here to work out what makes sense to you.

SECTION I

TWO DEFENSES
OF
CRITICAL BELIEF

INTRODUCTION

One question that this anthology addresses is whether we should always strive to think critically and specifically whether *all* our beliefs should be critical beliefs. Critical beliefs, as I will use the phrase, are beliefs formed from argument (reasoning) and evidence; they can be defended to those who may doubt them.

This section contains two classic defenses of critical belief. In his essay "The Fixation of Belief" Charles Sanders Peirce points out that the purpose of reasoning and inquiry is to find the truth; he then argues that, when we are in doubt, we need a method of resolving that doubt and "fixing" (that is, settling on a) belief. He reviews four methods of resolving doubt.

The first he calls the method of tenacity. Imagine people who believe what they want to believe because they want to believe it, and that ends the matter for them. They hold on to their beliefs regardless of what other people say or what the evidence shows; in fact, once they have settled on a belief, they do not reflect on it further. These people are following what Peirce calls the method of tenacity. One example he gives is of people who believe that they will live after death; he says it gives "a cheap pleasure which will not be followed by the least disappointment." His thought here is that even if death is annihilation, the person who believes in an afterlife will not be disappointed to find out she is wrong; after she dies she won't exist.

Still, he thinks the method of tenacity has a tendency to give way to a second method, which he calls the method of authority. Here imagine people who always follow their parents' beliefs or the doctrine of a church or those of a favorite teacher or whatever the science textbook says. They resolve doubt by asking that authority. Peirce is thinking of a state that imposes beliefs on its citizens, thus creating uniform belief among the citizenry—as at one time European states (the English, French, and Spanish states, for example) imposed religions on their people. This is the method of authority.

The third method he calls the *a priori* method. We arrive at our beliefs by the *a priori* method when we decide what to believe based on what seems true to us, apart from observation and experience. This method has some similarity to the method of tenacity, but involves reflecting on one's beliefs and asking "what makes sense?" or "what is reasonable?" For example, many believe that every event (everything that happens) has a cause or a reason why it happens. Why believe this is true? To some people, when they reflect on it, it just seems that it must be true, that the idea of something occurring without cause makes no sense. This is to arrive at one's belief by what Peirce calls the *a priori* method, believing what seems agreeable to our reason.

Peirce's fourth method he calls the method of science. Only the last method lets external things—the facts themselves—determine belief, and only it can give us any assurance that our beliefs conform to the facts. Peirce admits that other methods of arriving at belief can provide their own satisfactions; as you read, try to be clear about what he thinks the pluses and minuses are for each method. But in the end he supports the method of science: he concludes that "to avoid looking into the support of any belief from a fear that it may turn out rotten is quite as immoral as it is disadvantageous."

Here are some problems you may wish to think about as you read later selections: Does the method of science consist just in experiment or observation without asking what theory makes the best sense of what we observe? If the method of science does ask that question, is this the same as the *a priori* method? Peirce seems to believe that the method of science allows us to resolve disagreement, but don't scientists disagree about what the evidence shows?

William Clifford agrees with Peirce about the immorality of not inquiring into the source of a belief when there is reason to doubt it. He writes that it is wrong if we believe anything which is not supported by enough evidence. His classic essay begins with the story of a ship-owner sending an old ship to sea without having checked to determine whether it is still seaworthy. Clifford argues that what is wrong with the shipowner's act is that it derives from an unjustified belief. Thus he develops his argument for what is called Clifford's Principle: all belief is wrong if not supported by sufficient evidence. His main target is religious faith.

Do you think Clifford's examples support his conclusion about how to arrive at belief? Some of my students have pressed this point with me: there are different standards for belief, depending on how much is at stake. If there is no harm that could come from believing something (some hold that this is true of religious belief), then belief may not always have to meet Clifford's standard. Clifford seems aware of this possible objection and tries to reply to it. He writes, "But forasmuch as no belief held by one man, however seemingly trivial the belief, and however obscure the believer, is ever actually insignificant or without its effect on the fate of mankind, we have no choice but to extend our judgment to all cases of belief whatever." When we believe responsibly we "knit society together" while when we are irresponsible in our belief (believe beyond what the evidence shows) we "rend it in pieces." So Clifford thinks that irresponsible belief always does harm. Does he make that case? When we do not try to dissuade others from their various different religious beliefs (none of which, perhaps, can be proven or even justified to those who don't share them), are we "rending society to pieces"?

Clifford gives other arguments that believing beyond evidence does harm. He writes that it "weakens our powers of self-control" and encourages us to be "credulous," thus making us worse people. You should try to decide whether these arguments make his point that believing beyond the evidence always does harm. One question you might consider is how he would establish the harm done by believing beyond the evidence. Clifford asserts that believing beyond the evidence always does harm; does this assertion itself go beyond the evidence?

From "The Fixation of Belief"[1]
Charles S. Peirce

...[DOUBT AND BELIEF]

We generally know when we wish to ask a question and when we wish to pronounce a judgment, for there is a dissimilarity between the sensation of doubting and that of believing.

But this is not all which distinguishes doubt from belief. There is a practical difference. Our beliefs guide our desires and shape our actions.... The feeling of believing is a more or less sure indication of there being established in our nature some habit which will determine our actions. Doubt never has such an effect.

Nor must we overlook a third point of difference. *Doubt is an uneasy and dissatisfied state from which we struggle to free ourselves and pass into the state of belief; while the latter is a calm and satisfactory state which we do not wish to avoid, or to change to a belief in anything else.* On the contrary, we cling tenaciously, not merely to believing, but to believing just what we do believe.

Thus, both doubt and belief have positive effects upon us, though very different ones. Belief does not make us act at once, but puts us into such a condition that we shall behave in some certain way, when the occasion arises. Doubt has not the least such active effect, but stimulates us to inquiry until it is destroyed. This reminds us of the irritation of a nerve and the reflex action produced thereby; while for the analogue of belief, in the nervous system, we must look to what are called nervous associations—for example, to that habit of the nerves in consequence of which the smell of a peach will make the mouth water.

[INQUIRY IS THE STRUGGLE TO ATTAIN BELIEF]

The irritation of doubt causes a struggle to attain a state of belief. I shall term this struggle *inquiry*, though it must be admitted that this is sometimes not a very apt designation.

The irritation of doubt is the only immediate motive for the struggle to attain belief. It is certainly best for us that our beliefs should be such as may truly guide our actions so as to satisfy our desires; and this

---

1   This article was originally published in *Popular Science Monthly* 12 (November 1877), pp. 1-15. It is reprinted here with some sections removed.

reflection will make us reject every belief which does not seem to have been so formed as to insure this result. But it will only do so by creating a doubt in the place of that belief. With the doubt, therefore, the struggle begins, and with the cessation of doubt it ends. Hence, the sole object of inquiry is the settlement of opinion. We may fancy that this is not enough for us, and that we seek, not merely an opinion, but a true opinion. But put this fancy to the test, and it proves groundless; for as soon as a firm belief is reached we are entirely satisfied, whether the belief be true or false. And it is clear that nothing out of the sphere of our knowledge can be our object, for nothing which does not affect the mind can be the motive for mental effort. The most that can be maintained is, that we seek for a belief that we shall *think* to be true. But we think each one of our beliefs to be true, and, indeed, it is mere tautology to say so.

[THE METHOD OF TENACITY]

If the settlement of opinion is the sole object of inquiry, and if belief is of the nature of a habit, why should we not attain the desired end, by taking as answer to a question any we may fancy, and constantly reiterating it to ourselves, dwelling on all which may conduce to that belief, and learning to turn with contempt and hatred from anything that might disturb it?... [A]steady and immovable faith yields great peace of mind. It may, indeed, give rise to inconveniences, as if a man should resolutely continue to believe that fire would not burn him, or that he would be eternally damned if he received his *ingesta* otherwise than through a stomach-pump. But then the man who adopts this method will not allow that its inconveniences are greater than its advantages. He will say, "I hold steadfastly to the truth, and the truth is always wholesome." And in many cases it may very well be that the pleasure he derives from his calm faith overbalances any inconveniences resulting from its deceptive character. Thus, if it be true that death is annihilation, then the man who believes that he will certainly go straight to heaven when he dies, provided he have fulfilled certain simple observances in this life, has a cheap pleasure which will not be followed by the least disappointment. A similar consideration seems to have weight with many persons in religious topics, for we frequently hear it said, "Oh, I could not believe so-and-so, because I should be wretched if I did." When an ostrich buries its head in the sand as danger approaches, it very likely takes the happiest course. It hides the danger, and then calmly says there is no danger; and, if it feels perfectly sure there is none, why should it raise its head to see? A man may go through life, systematically keeping out of view all that might cause a change in his opinions, and if he only succeeds ... I do not see what can be said against his doing so. It would be an egotistical impertinence to object that his procedure is irrational, for that only amounts to saying that his method of settling belief is not ours. He does not propose to himself to be rational, and, indeed, will often talk with scorn of man's weak and illusive reason. So let him think as he pleases.

[THE METHOD OF AUTHORITY]

But this method of fixing belief, which may be called the method of tenacity, will be unable to hold its ground in practice. The social impulse is against it. The man who adopts it will find that other men think differently from him, and it will be apt to occur to him, in some saner moment, that their opinions are quite as good as his own, and this will shake his confidence in his belief. This conception, that another man's thought or sentiment may be equivalent to one's own, is a distinctly new step, and a highly important one. It arises from an impulse too strong in man to be suppressed, without danger of destroying the human species. Unless we make ourselves hermits, we shall necessarily influence each other's opinions; so that the problem becomes how to fix belief, not in the individual merely, but in the community.

Let the will of the state act, then, instead of that of the individual. Let an institution be created which shall have for its object to keep correct doctrines before the attention of the people, to reiterate them perpetually, and to teach them to the young; having at the same time power to prevent contrary doctrines from being taught, advocated, or expressed. Let all possible causes of a change of mind be removed from men's apprehensions. Let them be kept ignorant, lest they should learn of some reason to think otherwise than they do. Let their passions be enlisted, so that they may regard private and unusual opinions with hatred and horror. Then, let all men who reject the established belief be terrified into silence. Let the people turn out and tar-and-feather such men, or let inquisitions be made into the manner of thinking of suspected persons, and when they are found guilty of forbidden beliefs, let them be subjected to some signal punishment. When complete agreement could not otherwise be reached, a general massacre of all who have not thought in a certain way has proved a very effective means of settling opinion in a country. If the power to do this be wanting, let a list of opinions be drawn up, to which no man of the least independence of thought can assent, and let the faithful be required to accept all these propositions, in order to segregate them as radically as possible from the influence of the rest of the world.

This method has, from the earliest times, been one of the chief means of upholding correct theological and political doctrines, and of preserving their universal or catholic[2] character.... [W]herever there is a priesthood—and no religion has been without one—this method has been more or less made use of. Wherever there is an aristocracy, or a guild, or any association of a class of men whose interests depend, or are supposed to depend, on certain propositions, there will be inevitably found some traces of this natural product of social feeling. Cruelties always accompany this system; and when it is consistently carried out, they become atrocities of the most horrible kind in the eyes of any rational man. Nor should this occasion surprise, for the officer of a society does not feel justified in surrendering the interests of that society for the sake of mercy, as he might his own private interests. It is natural, therefore, that sympathy and fellowship should thus produce a most ruthless power.

In judging this method of fixing belief, which may be called the method of authority, we must, in the first place, allow its immeasurable mental and moral superiority to the method of tenacity. Its success is proportionately greater; and, in fact, it has over and over again worked the most majestic results. The mere structures of stone which it has caused to be put together—in Siam, for example, in Egypt, and in Europe—have many of them a sublimity hardly more than rivaled by the greatest works of Nature. And, except the geological epochs, there are no periods of time so vast as those which are measured by some of these organized faiths. If we scrutinize the matter closely, we shall find that there has not been one of their creeds which has remained always the same; yet the change is so slow as to be imperceptible during one person's life, so that individual belief remains sensibly fixed. For the mass of mankind, then, there is perhaps no better method than this. If it is their highest impulse to be intellectual slaves, then slaves they ought to remain.

---

2 [Here "catholic" does not refer to the Roman Catholic Church, but simply means "universal." PG]

[THE A PRIORI METHOD]

But no institution can undertake to regulate opinions upon every subject. Only the most important ones can be attended to, and on the rest
men's minds must be left to the action of natural causes. This imperfec-
tion will be no source of weakness so long as men are in such a state of
culture that one opinion does not influence another—that is, so long
as they cannot put two and two together. But in the most priest-ridden
states some individuals will be found who are raised above that condition. These men possess a wider sort of social feeling; they see that
men in other countries and in other ages have held to very different
doctrines from those which they themselves have been brought up to
believe; and they cannot help seeing that it is the mere accident of their
having been taught as they have, and of their having been surrounded
with the manners and associations they have, that has caused them to
believe as they do and not far differently. Nor can their candour resist
the reflection that there is no reason to rate their own views at a higher
value than those of other nations and other centuries; thus giving rise
to doubts in their minds.

They will further perceive that such doubts as these must exist in their
minds with reference to every belief which seems to be determined by
the caprice either of themselves or of those who originated the popular
opinions. The willful adherence to a belief, and the arbitrary forcing
of it upon others, must, therefore, both be given up. A different new
method of settling opinions must be adopted, that shall not only produce an impulse to believe, but shall also decide what proposition it is
which is to be believed. Let the action of natural preferences be unim-
peded, then, and under their influence let men, conversing together
and regarding matters in different lights, gradually develop beliefs in
harmony with natural causes. This method resembles that by which
conceptions of art have been brought to maturity. The most perfect
example of it is to be found in the history of metaphysical philosophy.
Systems of this sort have not usually rested upon any observed facts, at
least not in any great degree. They have been chiefly adopted because
their fundamental propositions seemed "agreeable to reason." This is
an apt expression; it does not mean that which agrees with experience,
but that which we find ourselves inclined to believe. Plato, for example,
finds it agreeable to reason that the distances of the celestial spheres
from one another should be proportional to the different lengths of
strings which produce harmonious chords. Many philosophers have
been led to their main conclusions by considerations like this; but this

is the lowest and least developed form which the method takes, for it is clear that another man might find Kepler's theory, that the celestial spheres are proportional to the inscribed and circumscribed spheres of the different regular solids, more agreeable to *his* reason. But the shock of opinions will soon lead men to rest on preferences of a far more universal nature. Take, for example, the doctrine that man only acts selfishly—that is, from the consideration that acting in one way will afford him more pleasure than acting in another. This rests on no fact in the world, but it has had a wide acceptance as being the only reasonable theory.

[THE METHOD OF SCIENCE]

This [a priori] method is far more intellectual and respectable from the point of view of reason than either of the others which we have noticed. But its failure has been the most manifest. It makes of inquiry something similar to the development of taste; but taste, unfortunately, is always more or less a matter of fashion, and accordingly metaphysicians have never come to any fixed agreement, but the pendulum has swung backward and forward between a more material and a more spiritual philosophy, from the earliest times to the latest. And so from this, which has been called the *a priori* method, we are driven, in Lord Bacon's phrase, to a true induction.[3] We have examined into this *a priori* method as something which promised to deliver our opinions from their accidental and capricious element. But development, while it is a process which eliminates the effect of some casual circumstances, only magnifies that of others. This method, therefore, does not differ in a very essential way from that of authority. The government may not have lifted its finger to influence my convictions; I may have been left outwardly quite free to choose, we will say, between monogamy and polygamy, and, appealing to my conscience only, I may have concluded that the latter practice is in itself licentious. But when I come to see that the chief obstacle to the spread of Christianity among a people of as high culture as the Hindoos has been a conviction of the immorality of our way of treating women, I cannot help seeing that, though governments do not interfere, sentiments in their development will be very greatly determined by accidental causes. Now, there are some people,

---

3 [Induction is most commonly understood as inference of a general truth from particular cases, as, for example, the inference that fires are hot from the observation that particular fires are hot. PG]

among whom I must suppose that my reader is to be found, who, when they see that any belief of theirs is determined by any circumstance extraneous to the facts, will from that moment not merely admit in words that that belief is doubtful, but will experience a real doubt of it, so that it ceases to be a belief.

To satisfy our doubts, therefore, it is necessary that a method should be found by which our beliefs may be determined by nothing human, but by some external permanency—by something upon which our thinking has no effect. Some mystics imagine that they have such a method in a private inspiration from on high. But that is only a form of the method of tenacity, in which the conception of truth as something public is not yet developed. Our external permanency would not be external, in our sense, if it was restricted in its influence to one individual. It must be something which affects, or might affect, every man. And, though these affections are necessarily as various as are individual conditions, yet the method must be such that the ultimate conclusion of every man shall be the same. Such is the method of science. Its fundamental hypothesis, restated in more familiar language, is this: There are Real things, whose characters are entirely independent of our opinions about them; those Reals affect our senses according to regular laws, and, though our sensations are as different as are our relations to the objects, yet, by taking advantage of the laws of perception, we can ascertain by reasoning how things really and truly are; and any man, if he have sufficient experience and he reason enough about it, will be led to the one True conclusion. The new conception here involved is that of Reality. It may be asked how I know that there are any Reals. If this hypothesis is the sole support of my method of inquiry, my method of inquiry must not be used to support my hypothesis. The reply is this: 1. If investigation cannot be regarded as proving that there are Real things, it at least does not lead to a contrary conclusion; but the method and the conception on which it is based remain ever in harmony. No doubts of the method, therefore, necessarily arise from its practice, as is the case with all the others. 2. The feeling which gives rise to any method of fixing belief is a dissatisfaction at two repugnant propositions. But here already is a vague concession that there is some *one* thing which a proposition should represent. Nobody, therefore, can really doubt that there are Reals, for, if he did, doubt would not be a source of dissatisfaction. The hypothesis, therefore, is one which every mind admits. So that the social impulse does not cause men to doubt it. 3. Everybody uses the scientific method about a great many things, and only ceases to use it when he does not know how to apply it. 4. Experience of the method has not led us to doubt it, but, on the contrary, scientific investigation has had the most wonderful triumphs in the way of settling opinion. These afford the explanation of my not doubting the method or the hypothesis which it supposes; and not having any doubt, nor believing that anybody else whom I could influence has, it would be the merest babble for me to say more about it. If there be anybody with a living doubt upon the subject, let him consider it....

This [method of science] is the only one of the four methods which presents any distinction of a right and a wrong way. If I adopt the method of tenacity, and shut myself out from all influences, whatever I think necessary to doing this, is necessary according to that method. So with the method of authority: the state may try to put down heresy by means which, from a scientific point of view, seem very ill-calculated to accomplish its purposes; but the only test *on that method* is what the state thinks; so that it cannot pursue the method wrongly. So with the *a priori* method. The very essence of it is to think as one is inclined to think. All metaphysicians will be sure to do that, however they may be inclined to judge each other to be perversely wrong. The Hegelian system recognizes every natural tendency of thought as logical, although it be certain to be abolished by counter-tendencies. Hegel thinks there is a regular system in the succession of these tendencies, in consequence of which, after drifting one way and the other for a long time, opinion will at last go right. And it is true that metaphysicians do get the right ideas at last; Hegel's system of Nature represents tolerably the science of his day; and one may be sure that whatever scientific investigation shall have put out of doubt will presently receive *a priori* demonstration on the part of the metaphysicians. But with the scientific method the case is different. I may start with known and observed facts to proceed to the unknown; and yet the rules which I follow in doing so may not be such as investigation would approve. The test of whether I am truly following the method is not an immediate appeal to my feelings and purposes, but, on the contrary, itself involves the application of the method. Hence it is that bad reasoning as well as good reasoning is possible; and this fact is the foundation of the practical side of logic.

It is not to be supposed that the first three methods of settling opinion present no advantage whatever over the scientific method. On the contrary, each has some peculiar convenience of its own. The *a priori* method is distinguished for its comfortable conclusions. It is the nature of the process to adopt whatever belief we are inclined to, and there are certain flatteries to the vanity of man which we all believe by nature, until we are awakened from our pleasing dream by rough facts. The method of authority will always govern the mass of mankind; and those who wield the various forms of organized force in the state will never be convinced that dangerous reasoning ought not to be suppressed in some way. If liberty of speech is to be untrammeled from the grosser forms of constraint, then uniformity of opinion will be secured by a moral terrorism to which the respectability of society will give its thorough approval. Following the method of authority is the path of peace. Certain non-conformities are permitted; certain others (considered unsafe) are forbidden. These are different in different countries and in different ages; but, wherever you are, let it be known that you seriously hold a tabooed belief, and you may be perfectly sure of being treated with a cruelty less brutal but more refined than hunting you like a wolf. Thus, the greatest intellectual benefactors of mankind have never dared, and dare not now, to utter the whole of their thought; and thus a shade of *prima facie* doubt is cast upon every proposition which is considered essential to the security of society. Singularly enough, the persecution does not all come from without; but a man torments himself and is oftentimes most distressed at finding himself believing propositions which he has been brought up to regard with aversion. The peaceful and sympathetic man will, therefore, find it hard to resist the temptation to submit his opinions to authority. But most of all I admire the method of tenacity for its strength, simplicity, and directness. Men who pursue it are distinguished for their decision of character, which becomes very easy with such a mental rule. They do not waste time in trying to make up their minds what they want, but, fastening like lightning upon whatever alternative comes first, they hold to it to the end, whatever happens, without an instant's irresolution. This is one of the splendid qualities which generally accompany brilliant, unlasting success. It is impossible not to envy the man who can dismiss reason, although we know how it must turn out at last.

Such are the advantages which the other methods of settling opinion have over scientific investigation. A man should consider well of them; and then he should consider that, after all, he wishes his opinions to coincide with the fact, and that there is no reason why the results of those three first methods should do so. To bring about this effect is the prerogative of the method of science. Upon such considerations he has to make his choice—a choice which is far more than the adoption of any intellectual opinion, which is one of the ruling decisions of his life, to which, when once made, he is bound to adhere. The force of habit will sometimes cause a man to hold on to old beliefs, after he is in a condition to see that they have no sound basis. But reflection upon the state of the case will overcome these habits, and he ought to allow reflection its full weight. People sometimes shrink from doing this, having an idea that beliefs are wholesome which they cannot help feeling rest on nothing. But let such persons suppose an analogous though different case from their own. Let them ask themselves what they would say to a reformed Mussulman[4] who should hesitate to give up his old notions in regard to the relations of the sexes; or to a reformed Catholic who should still shrink from reading the Bible. Would they not say that these persons ought to consider the matter fully, and clearly understand the new doctrine, and then ought to embrace it, in its entirety? But, above all, let it be considered that what is more wholesome than any particular belief is integrity of belief, and that to avoid looking into the support of any belief from a fear that it may turn out rotten is quite as immoral as it is disadvantageous. The person who confesses that there is such a thing as truth, which is distinguished from falsehood simply by this, that if acted on it should, on full consideration, carry us to the point we aim at and not astray, and then, though convinced of this, dares not know the truth and seeks to avoid it, is in a sorry state of mind indeed.

From "The Ethics of Belief"[5]
William K. Clifford

THE DUTY OF INQUIRY

A shipowner was about to send to sea an emigrant-ship. He knew that she was old, and not overwell built at the first; that she had seen many seas and climes, and often had needed repairs. Doubts had been suggested to him that possibly she was not seaworthy. These doubts preyed upon his mind, and made him unhappy; he thought that perhaps he ought to have her thoroughly overhauled and refitted, even though

---

4   [As with Peirce's earlier use of "Hindoos" rather than "Hindus," his use of "Mussulman" where we would say "Muslim" was common at the time he wrote. PG]
5   This article was originally published in *Contemporary Review*, 1877. It was reprinted in *Lectures and Essays* (1879), and is currently in print in *The Ethics of Belief and Other Essays* (Amherst, NY: Prometheus Books, 1999). It is reprinted here with some sections removed.

this should put him at great expense. Before the ship sailed, however, he succeeded in overcoming these melancholy reflections. He said to himself that she had gone safely through so many voyages and weathered so many storms that it was idle to suppose she would not come safely home from this trip also. He would put his trust in Providence, which could hardly fail to protect all these unhappy families that were leaving their fatherland to seek for better times elsewhere. He would dismiss from his mind all ungenerous suspicions about the honesty of builders and contractors. In such ways he acquired a sincere and comfortable conviction that his vessel was thoroughly safe and seaworthy; he watched her departure with a light heart, and benevolent wishes for the success of the exiles in their strange new home that was to be; and he got his insurance-money when she went down in mid-ocean and told no tales.

What shall we say of him? Surely this, that he was verily guilty of the death of those men. It is admitted that he did sincerely believe in the soundness of his ship; but the sincerity of his conviction can in no wise help him, because he had no right to believe on such evidence as was before him. He had acquired his belief not by honestly earning it in patient investigation, but by stifling his doubts. And although in the end he may have felt so sure about it that he could not think otherwise, yet inasmuch as he had knowingly and willingly worked himself into that frame of mind, he must be held responsible for it.

Let us alter the case a little, and suppose that the ship was not unsound after all; that she made her voyage safely, and many others after it. Will that diminish the guilt of her owner? Not one jot. When an action is once done, it is right or wrong for ever; no accidental failure of its good or evil fruits can possibly alter that. The man would not have been innocent, he would only have been not found out. The question of right or wrong has to do with the origin of his belief, not the matter of it; not what it was, but how he got it; not whether it turned out to be true or false, but whether he had a right to believe on such evidence as was before him....

It may be said, however, that it is not the belief which is judged to be wrong, but the action following upon it. The shipowner might say, "I am perfectly certain that my ship is sound, but still I feel it my duty to have her examined, before trusting the lives of so many people to her."...

In the first place, let us admit that, so far as it goes, this view of the case is right and necessary; right, because even when a man's belief is so fixed that he cannot think otherwise, he still has a choice in the action suggested by it, and so cannot escape the duty of investigating on the ground of the strength of his convictions; and necessary, because those who are not yet capable of controlling their feelings and thoughts must have a plain rule dealing with overt acts.

But this being premised as necessary, it becomes clear that it is not sufficient, and that our previous judgment is required to supplement it. For it is not possible so to sever the belief from the action it suggests as to condemn the one without condemning the other. No man holding a strong belief on one side of a question, or even wishing to hold a belief on one side, can investigate it with such fairness and completeness as if he were really in doubt and unbiased; so that the existence of a belief not founded on fair inquiry unfits a man for the performance of this necessary duty.

Nor is it that truly a belief at all which has not some influence upon the actions of him who holds it. He who truly believes that which prompts him to an action has looked upon the action to lust after it, he has committed it already in his heart. If a belief is not realized immediately in open deeds, it is stored up for the guidance of the future. It goes to make a part of that aggregate of beliefs which is the link between sensation and action at every moment of all our lives, and which is so organized and compacted together that no part of it can be isolated from the rest, but every new addition modifies the structure of the whole. No real belief, however trifling and fragmentary it may seem, is ever truly insignificant; it prepares us to receive more of its like, confirms those which resembled it before, and weakens others; and so gradually it lays a stealthy train in our inmost thoughts, which may someday explode into overt action, and leave its stamp upon our character for ever.

And no one man's belief is in any case a private matter which concerns himself alone. Our lives are guided by that general conception of the course of things which has been created by society for social purposes. Our words, our phrases, our forms and processes and modes of thought, are common property, fashioned and perfected from age to age; an heirloom which every succeeding generation inherits as a precious deposit and a sacred trust to be handed on to the next one, not unchanged but enlarged and purified, with some clear marks of its proper handiwork. Into this, for good or ill, is woven every belief of every man who has speech of his fellows. An awful[6] privilege, and an

---

6   [Here "awful" is used to mean literally awe-inspiring. PG]

awful responsibility, that we should help to create the world in which posterity will live.

In the supposed cases which have been considered, it has been judged wrong to believe on insufficient evidence, or to nourish belief by suppressing doubts and avoiding investigation. The reason of this judgment is not far to seek: it is that the belief held by one man was of great importance to other men. But forasmuch as no belief held by one man, however seemingly trivial the belief, and however obscure the believer, is ever actually insignificant or without its effect on the fate of mankind, we have no choice but to extend our judgment to all cases of belief whatever. Belief, that sacred faculty which prompts the decisions of our will, and knits into harmonious working all the compacted energies of our being, is ours not for ourselves but for humanity. It is rightly used on truths which have been established by long experience and waiting toil, and which have stood in the fierce light of free and fearless questioning. Then it helps to bind men together, and to strengthen and direct their common action. It is desecrated when given to unproved and unquestioned statements, for the solace and private pleasure of the believer; to add a tinsel splendour to the plain straight road of our life and display a bright mirage beyond it; or even to drown the common sorrows of our kind by a self-deception which allows them not only to cast down, but also to degrade us. Whoso would deserve well of his fellows in this matter will guard the purity of his beliefs with a very fanaticism of jealous care, lest at any time it should rest on an unworthy object, and catch a stain which can never be wiped away.

It is not only the leader of men, statesmen, philosopher, or poet, that owes this bounden duty to mankind. Every rustic who delivers in the village alehouse his slow, infrequent sentences, may help to kill or keep alive the fatal superstitions which clog his race. Every hard-worked wife of an artisan may transmit to her children beliefs which shall knit society together, or rend it in pieces. No simplicity of mind, no obscurity of station, can escape the universal duty of questioning all that we believe.

It is true that this duty is a hard one, and the doubt which comes out of it is often a very bitter thing. It leaves us bare and powerless where we thought that we were safe and strong. To know all about anything is to know how to deal with it under all circumstances. We feel much happier and more secure when we think we know precisely what to do, no matter what happens, than when we have lost our way and do not know where to turn. And if we have supposed ourselves to know all about anything, and to be capable of doing what is fit in regard to it, we naturally do not like to find that we are really ignorant and powerless, that we have to begin again at the beginning, and try to learn what the thing is and how it is to be dealt with—if indeed anything can be learnt about it. It is the sense of power attached to a sense of knowledge that makes men desirous of believing, and afraid of doubting.

This sense of power is the highest and best of pleasures when the belief on which it is founded is a true belief, and has been fairly earned by investigation. For then we may justly feel that it is common property, and hold good for others as well as for ourselves. Then we may be glad, not that I have learned secrets by which I am safer and stronger, but that we men have got mastery over more of the world; and we shall be strong, not for ourselves but in the name of Man and his strength. But if the belief has been accepted on insufficient evidence, the pleasure is a stolen one. Not only does it deceive ourselves by giving us a sense of power which we do not really possess, but it is sinful, because it is stolen in defiance of our duty to mankind. That duty is to guard ourselves from such beliefs as from pestilence, which may shortly master our own body and then spread to the rest of the town. What would be thought of one who, for the sake of a sweet fruit, should deliberately run the risk of delivering a plague upon his family and his neighbours?

And, as in other such cases, it is not the risk only which has to be considered; for a bad action is always bad at the time when it is done, no matter what happens afterwards. Every time we let ourselves believe for unworthy reasons, we weaken our powers of self-control, of doubting, of judicially and fairly weighing evidence. We all suffer severely enough from the maintenance and support of false beliefs and the fatally wrong actions which they lead to, and the evil born when one such belief is entertained is great and wide. But a greater and wider evil arises when the credulous character is maintained and supported, when a habit of believing for unworthy reasons is fostered and made permanent. If I steal money from any person, there may be no harm done from the mere transfer of possession; he may not feel the loss, or it may prevent him from using the money badly. But I cannot help doing this great wrong towards Man, that I make myself dishonest. What hurts society is not that it should lose its property, but that it should become a den of thieves, for then it must cease to be society. This is why we ought not to do evil, that good may come; for at any rate this great evil has come, that we have done evil and are made wicked thereby. In like manner, if I let myself believe anything on insufficient evidence, there may be no great harm done by the mere belief; it may be true after all, or I may never have occasion to exhibit it in outward acts. But I cannot help doing this great wrong towards Man, that I make myself credulous. The danger to society is not merely that it should believe wrong things, though that is great enough; but that it should become credulous, and lose the habit of testing things and inquiring into them; for then it must sink back into savagery.

The harm which is done by credulity in a man is not confined to the fostering of a credulous character in others, and consequent support of false beliefs. Habitual want of care about what I believe leads to habitual want of care in others about the truth of what is told to me. Men speak the truth of one another when each reveres the truth in his own mind and in the other's mind; but how shall my friend revere the truth in my mind when I myself am careless about it, when I believe things because I want to believe them, and because they are comforting and pleasant? Will he not learn to cry, "Peace," to me, when there is no peace? By such a course I shall surround myself with a thick atmosphere of falsehood and fraud, and in that I must live. It may matter little to me, in my cloud-castle of sweet illusions and darling lies; but it matters much to Man that I have made my neighbours ready to deceive. The credulous man is father to the liar and the cheat; he lives in the bosom of this his family, and it is no marvel if he should become even as they are. So closely are our duties knit together, that whoso shall keep the whole law, and yet offend in one point, he is guilty of all.

To sum up: it is wrong always, everywhere, and for anyone, to believe anything upon insufficient evidence....

Inquiry into the evidence of a doctrine is not to be made once for all, and then taken as finally settled. It is never lawful to stifle a doubt; for either it can be honestly answered by means of the inquiry already made, or else it proves that the inquiry was not complete.

"But," says one, "I am a busy man; I have no time for the long course of study which would be necessary to make me in any degree a competent judge of certain questions, or even able to understand the nature of the arguments."

Then he should have no time to believe.

SECTION II

UNCERTAINTY
AND
SCRUTINY
IN SCIENCE

INTRODUCTION

This section has several purposes: to inquire into what science is and what makes it different from religious belief, to think about particular examples of scientific reasoning and what makes them persuasive (if we find them persuasive), and to consider challenges to the objectivity of scientific thought.

Using examples from natural history, this section develops the argument that scientific beliefs are ones that are constantly tested against challenges. Because scientists establish their worth to the community partly by examining prior results and seeking faults with what others have accepted and better ways of understanding and explaining available data, there is a constant scrutiny of scientific ideas.

What are we to believe when there is an important hypothesis but the evidence for it is insufficient? What should we believe when there are competing hypotheses, but there is no overwhelming margin of evidence in favor of one over another? In this second case, scientists specializing in the area should, presumably, review the competing views and acknowledge that there is insufficient evidence to embrace any view with certainty. But they often act differently, staking their careers or at least a few years of them in developing one of the hypotheses, hoping to contribute a key advance in our understanding. The same would hold in the first case when there is a single hypothesis insufficiently supported by evidence: presumably we should withhold judgment or give the hypothesis only tentative acceptance, but researchers in the area may bet their careers on trying to show it is right (or wrong).

While individual scientists can be as dogmatic as anyone, scientists often contribute to the community by finding flaws in the work of others. (This view of the scientific community was developed in 1942 by the sociologist Robert K. Merton.) This organized skepticism strengthens confidence in scientific conclusions; if people are trying to show an idea wrong, but their experiments produce further evidence that the idea is right, we gain confidence in that idea. While science is conflictual in this way it is also profoundly cooperative; the investigations of one person build on others' work, and scientists have to trust the work of others.

The first selection, my essay on miracles and science, seeks to clarify one thing that is distinctive about science: it does not assume or imply any particular religious outlook, even something as general as belief in a single God; nor does it imply disbelief. By "miracle" I mean a supernatural intervention in the natural order to cause things to happen that would not happen naturally. I argue that belief in miracles in this sense tends to make it impossible to investigate nature: how do we distinguish natural events from supernatural interventions without assuming that we already know the course of nature? From a scientific viewpoint unexplained phenomena are just that—unexplained. If we suppose that they are explained by miraculous intervention, we are less likely to look for natural causes where we do not now find them, but that process of looking for undiscovered causes is helpful to scientific and medical progress. In the course of making this argument I review how and why science became independent of religious faith.

The next three selections all concern the history of life on earth. For many students inquiry in this area seems to challenge beliefs that come from their faith traditions.

In the selection by Tyson and Goldsmith, after reviewing various theories of the origin of life on earth, the evidence for them, and the limits of that evidence, they conclude that no theory is certainly correct. They write, "the outcome of our finest research, as so often occurs in science, proves unsettling to those who seek certainty." This interesting remark recommends that scientists have a tolerance for uncertainty, even in situations where they would like to know the truth. Such readiness to withhold judgment when evidence is insufficient to lead to a conclusion seems central to critical belief. As you read this selection, I propose that you ask yourself: do I know how life began? do I have beliefs about its beginning? how do I decide what to believe about a question such as this? Tyson and Goldsmith seem not to have a belief about how life began. Do you think they should? If so, why?

Stephen Jay Gould, in his essay on the extinction of dinosaurs, develops the contrast between, on the one hand, scientific hypotheses which lead to further investigation and, on the other, silly speculations that lead nowhere because they cannot be investigated and either confirmed or disconfirmed. The influence of Karl Popper's philosophy of science is evident here: scientific ideas must be open to evidence that could show them wrong—they must be falsifiable. If there is no conceivable evidence that could show an idea wrong, then it is not science. But, as Feyerabend argues in a later selection, it is not always obvious what counts as falsifying evidence. Evidence may be taken by some to falsify a view while its proponents interpret the evidence differently. Now many philosophers of science would reject Popper's "falsificationism" entirely in favor of a more naturalistic view of science (I would be one of these, although I am not a philosopher of science).

In "Are We Related to Other Life?" I present a non-technical introduction to evolution, addressing especially why it makes sense to suppose that we are biologically related to other life. I distinguish the question of whether relatedness makes sense from the question of whether it should be believed to be true (questions to which I return in my essay on trust and modesty). I argue that relatedness makes sense based on principles that all of us already accept. Part of my purpose is to be clear that evolutionary accounts explain phenomena as the result of natural (as opposed to supernatural) processes. Another purpose is to encourage students—even those who disagree with evolution—to grapple with the reasons for accepting that view of life. I point out that you can acknowledge that evolution makes sense of things without believing that it is a true account of what happened. However, then you should think about how you do decide what to believe, if not based on what makes the best sense. In answering that question you may get

clearer about what critical belief is and whether you think it is always
good to hold your beliefs in that critical spirit.

This paper's style of argument for evolution may suggest that I am
using what Peirce called "the *a priori* method" (what makes sense to
us), not the method of science, which depends on investigating the
world. Instead, I believe it shows how much argument in science still
depends on what makes sense; what makes science distinctive is that
it tries to make sense of *the details* of what we discover through investigation, for example, the similarities in mammalian forelimbs or in
primate hands. Since the paper is non-technical and intended for
the general student it does not go into further detail; it does not discuss, for example, detailed similarities in DNA across species (genera,
families, and even phyla). Evolutionary thought tries to make sense of
these details.

The first four essays of this section all explore how scientific explanation works and why scientific ideas are believable. The next three
selections raise problems with scientific thought or at least with scientific practice.

Eighteenth-century philosophers (for example, William Paley) popularized an ancient argument for the existence of God, usually called
"the teleological argument" or "the argument from design." One version of the argument is this: "If, while walking across a field, you were
to find a watch, you would conclude that the watch must have been
the product of intelligence. The adjustment of its parts to a common
purpose, to enable the watch to indicate the time, display the work
of intelligent planning. But, by the same reasoning, the anatomy of
the eye, the way that the iris, lens, viscous fluid, and retinal nerves
work together to make vision possible, shows the design of a much
greater intelligence, called God." This argument was extended across
the natural world, which tended to be viewed as a complex machine
with every part having a function or purpose in the whole. This view of
God and nature is called *deism*. The view that everything in nature has
a function is called *functionalism*, and it influenced Darwin, who tried
to explain the *appearance* of function in the biological world as the
outcome of natural selection. Still, many evolutionists (Stephen Gould
is the best known) have rejected the Darwinian analogue of functionalism; this is called *adaptationism*, the view that all characteristics of
organisms arise as adaptations which advance survival and reproduction. (Darwin himself was not an adaptationist.) The issue is important because functionalism in natural science and adaptationism in

biology may be holdovers from the earlier deistic view of the universe that everything in nature has a purpose.

Our next selection illustrates this rejection of adaptationism in evolutionary thought. Specifically the sensitivity of the clitoris in the human female and its role in female sexual pleasure do not seem to be explained as adaptations. In 2005, on Australian National Radio's show *All in the Mind*, Natasha Mitchell interviewed philosopher of science Elisabeth Lloyd about her writings on female orgasm. While the preceding essay on our biological relationship to other life left out the theory of natural selection, that concept is central to the Mitchell/Lloyd discussion: when a trait is affected by natural selection organisms that have that trait are more likely to survive and reproduce than organisms that lack it; hence the ones that have it become more common while the ones that lack it tend to disappear. Thus, over time, the population of organisms changes. Lloyd argues that female orgasm does not seem to be a product of natural selection and hence needs another kind of explanation. Her research reveals marvelous examples of gender bias and other irrationality in science. It shows how bad science can have pernicious social effects.

As you read this conversation, I suggest that you ask what makes Lloyd's arguments persuasive, provided that you find them persuasive. One part seems clear enough: Mitchell and Lloyd trace out the consequences of the view that female orgasm is an adaptation, and Lloyd argues that the expected consequences of that theory are not found in nature. For other parts of her argument it may not be as clear what makes the reasoning persuasive, but try to think about what makes something a persuasive argument.

Nancy Krieger and Mary Bassett's "The Health of Black Folk" argues that social assumptions can distort scientific explanation and impede scientific progress. Written from a Left point of view (roughly meaning socialist or anti-capitalist), they argue that science that seeks both genetic and environmental causes of poorer black health (compared to white) ignores the role that social inequality plays in the ill-health of people identified as black. While their essay was written in the mid-1980s, recent research, for example, Michael Marmot's *The Status Syndrome*, confirms their idea that inequality itself, and especially being under the control of others at work, is an important cause of mortality and morbidity.

The selection from Paul Feyerabend's *Against Method* requires me to give the reader more help. Of course, a background in physics and the

history of seventeenth-century science helps, but there is little in the
selection that all of us cannot understand. Let's start with Feyerabend's
epigram "Anything goes." He is arguing here against philosophers
who will tell us what scientific method is. Feyerabend believes that the
progress of science requires that science have no single fixed method.
Essentially he is arguing that there is no such thing as critical belief or
at least that there is no way of identifying what it is (if so, then critical
thinking classes that say, "To think critically you have to think like ..."
may be a waste of time).

The selections I have included from Feyerabend concern how Galileo
Galilei defended Copernican astronomy—especially the hypothesis of
the Earth's daily rotation on its axis—against an objection, the tower
argument. The physics that Renaissance Europe inherited from the
ancient world—especially Aristotle—was based on the assumption of
an Earth-centered universe. In that universe there were four Earthly
elements—earth, water, air, and fire—and a fifth element—the ether—
of which the heavens were composed. Each of the Earthly elements had
a natural place, earth at the center of the universe, water above earth,
air above water, and fire above air. Each element's natural motion was
to seek its natural place. The things of common life were often compounds of these elements; paper, for example, could be understood
as a compound of earth and fire. By setting a match to the paper we
release the fire that was in it—which seeks its natural place above the
air—while the earthly part, the ash, returns to Earth, its natural place.
The ether's natural place was the heavens and its natural motion was
circular; thus all the objects we see in the sky naturally move in circles
about the Earth. In this view of the universe there is absolute space,
with the Earth at the center of it, and absolute motion in space.

Copernicus proposed that we understand the universe as sun-centered and the Earth as a planet orbiting the sun and rotating on its
axis. Copernicus assumed that the orbits of all planets were circular
and that the speed of both orbital and rotational motions was constant.
As a result of these assumptions (rejected by Kepler and many who
came after him), there were problems with Copernicus's astronomy: it
could not explain the observed motions of the planets (anything that
moved against the background of fixed stars) any more accurately or
simply than the older Earth-centered Ptolemaic astronomy. Even more
important, the assumption that the Earth was a rotating planet did not
fit with the physics of natural places and motions that Europeans had
inherited from the ancients. Thus Galileo and others had to develop a

new physics that would allow for the Earth to be a rotating planet. (This process culminated in the physics of Isaac Newton.)

As the Gould selection evidences, philosophy of science often supposes that theories must be tested against observational evidence. What Feyerabend tries to show in this selection is that the idea of what counts as observational evidence is, at least sometimes, open to dispute. As a consequence it may sometimes be impossible to apply the principle that theories must be falsifiable.

In Feyerabend's view the Copernican hypothesis of a rotating Earth simply did not fit the observations, *as those observations were understood in Galileo's time.* The tower argument is simply this: imagine a stone dropped from the top of a tower; if the Earth was in motion, then the tower, moving along with the Earth, should move over a thousand feet as the stone falls (the Earth is roughly 25,000 miles in circumference; hence at the equator the Earth rotates at roughly 1500 feet per second); hence the stone should land a good distance from the base of the tower; but it doesn't; it lands at the base of the tower; therefore, the Earth does not move, and our observations prove it (the Copernican hypothesis of a rotating Earth is falsified). Feyerabend believes the argument was logically correct at the time it was made. The observations simply did not fit the Copernican theory.

Hence, for Feyerabend, Galileo's reply to the tower argument (which you will read, since Feyerabend quotes important parts of it) simply involves *reinterpreting the observations to fit the theory.* Feyerabend calls Galileo's method *counterinduction.* Instead of requiring that our theory fit the observational evidence, we reinterpret the observational evidence to fit our theory. Of course, Feyerabend does not think he can recommend this as a *general* method in science. But, he argues, in Galileo's case it worked and allowed physics to progress. Scientific progress required that Galileo and his followers expand the scope of rationality in order to make the theory work. But eventually we acquire enough evidence in this way that we now have a physics that works better than the alternative view. Because counterinduction worked for Galileo but won't always work, the only "method" Feyerabend can recommend is *anything goes.* If counterinduction sometimes works, if anything goes, then a philosophy of science that says our theories must be falsifiable is mistaken.

I should add a bit more. Feyerabend thinks *observations* are not simply sensations but are sensations combined with entrenched physical theories. If the physical theories assumed in our observations (assumed in

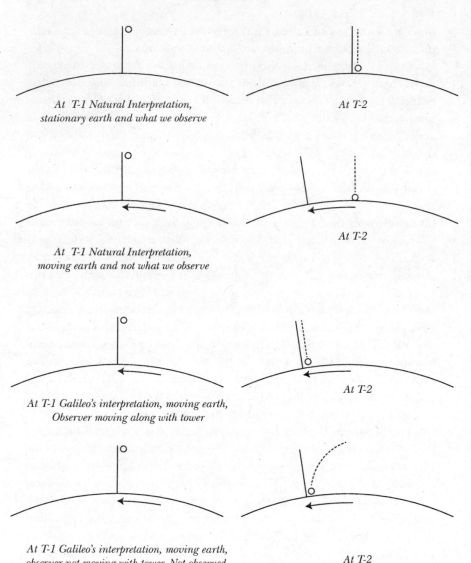

At T-1 Natural Interpretation,
stationary earth and what we observe

At T-2

At T-1 Natural Interpretation,
moving earth and not what we observe

At T-2

At T-1 Galileo's interpretation, moving earth,
Observer moving along with tower

At T-2

At T-1 Galileo's interpretation, moving earth,
observer not moving with tower. Not observed.

At T-2

common sense) are wrong, then the only way we can expose those bad
theories is by assuming the correctness of our theory and seeing how
we would have to reinterpret what we see to make it fit the theory. This
is the method Galileo follows, according to Feyerabend, and it worked.

Feyerabend believes that the observations of seventeenth-century European observers encoded a conception of absolute space and absolute

motion.[1] But it is not obvious that they did. When Galileo responds to the tower argument, he demonstrates that common sense must recognize relative motion; for example, did my cell phone move during my plane trip from Chicago to San Francisco? Well, it didn't move from my pocket, but it moved, along with me, from Chicago to San Francisco. And seventeenth-century folks were familiar with the same relativity of motion. So should we understand the motion of the stone from the top of the tower to its base in the same relativistic spirit, as not implying anything about absolute space and motion? Galileo thought so. He assumed, we could say, a *unity* of scientific thought: if relativity of motion is recognized in some contexts, it should be recognized in all; hence, if the Earth rotates on its axis uniformly (no change in speed of rotation), we should apply the same principles of relative motion to its rotation as we would in contexts where an assemblage of things move together uniformly in a straight line. So if on a ship that moves straight ahead with no change of speed, a stone, dropped from the top of its mast, lands at the base of the mast, then the stone dropped from the top of a tower on a uniformly rotating Earth should land at the base of the tower. In contrast, we could say that Feyerabend assumes the *disunity* of scientific thought. He asserts that common sense concepts of motion and place are (or were in the seventeenth-century) absolute ones. But does he argue adequately for this disunity any better than Galileo argues for the unity? That is something that you, the reader, should try to work out.

All of the essays in this section—with the exception of Feyerabend's—illustrate science as a social activity which is both cooperative and conflictual. They all show how scrutiny and criticism in science are part of a process of doing better science. Even the essay by Krieger and Bassett and the discussion by Elisabeth Lloyd, both of which show how social and other assumptions can distort scientific work, are in the scientific spirit of doing better science by criticizing the work of others. The selection from Feyerabend is the outlier. His purpose is to show that there is no adequate account of scientific method. So if to think critically is to think scientifically, Feyerabend is arguing that *we can't even say what critical thinking is.*

---

1   Absolute space would be implied by an Earth-centered universe (but also by a sun-centered universe); in modern cosmology—read Tyson and Goldsmith's very accessible book for an introduction to the subject—the Earth is at no special place in the universe *nor is anything else;* that is, there are no special places in the universe. The authors call this the Copernican principle, and it does seem foundational to contemporary astrophysics and cosmology.

Miracles and Scientific Research
Paul Gomberg

WHAT IS A MIRACLE: THE NATURAL AND THE SUPERNATURAL

As I will define the word "miracle" a miracle is a supernatural (or divine) intervention in the natural order. In a miracle, so defined, we assume *there is a natural order*, that is, we assume that *there is a course of events that would have occurred had not God intervened*. A miracle occurs in this sense when God *intervenes* in nature to cause something to happen that would not have happened naturally. It is miracles *in this sense* that create problems for scientific research.

The central miracles of Christian faith are the Resurrection and Ascension of Jesus Christ. There are thought also to be miracles of a more everyday sort; for example, the rapid healing of a severe case of eczema, the recovery of a patient from a "terminal" (the scare-quotes suggest that it is called "terminal" even if it may not be) cancer, the return of heartbeat to a patient who has flat-lined (no detectable heartbeat) for a considerable time, and a person's survival of an "unsurvivable" automobile wreck are sometimes thought to be due to God's intervention in the natural order.

Our concept of a miracle presupposes a distinction between the natural and the supernatural. How we think about the natural has changed as modern science became secular. Between the Renaissance and the twentieth century scientific activity became—and continues to be—independent of any religious faith.

In medieval and Renaissance Europe our modern distinction between the natural and the supernatural was not made. The universe was conceived as having the four sublunary elements—earth, water, air, and fire—at the center of the universe. Earth itself did not move. The heavens were composed of ether, which moved in circular paths. Planets orbited the Earth: the moon, Mercury, Venus, the Sun, Mars, Jupiter, and Saturn. Beyond Saturn was a sphere of the fixed stars, which orbited the Earth from east to west every 23 hours 56 minutes, with the stars never changing their relationship to one another. The planets, by contrast, moved about the Earth from east to west but moving westerly more slowly than the stars (the Sun, for example, takes 24 hours to return to a midday position from the same position the previous day while the stars take 23 hours 56 minutes to return to the same position in the sky relative to the horizon), moved usually from

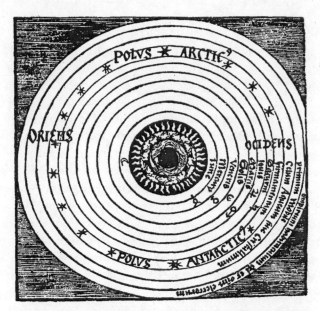

FIGURE 1. This illustration is from a woodcut published in 1508. It
represents a common medieval/renaissance view of the world. At
the center are the four Earthly elements, earth, water, air, and fire.
Beyond them are the moon, Mercury, Venus, the Sun, Mars, Jupiter,
and Saturn (the visible "planets" in the ancient sense of that word).
Beyond the planets were the stars and the prime mover. At the edge
of the universe was heaven, where God and the elect resided.

west to east against the background of the stars. Beyond the stars were
the angels and the elect, living with God. God caused everything in the
universe to move. Heaven was a place in the universe.

This science was literally Christian science. Observations of the heavens were combined with a belief in a Christian God who lived in Heaven
at the edge of the universe; by contrast, Satan lived in Hell, at the center
of the Earth. This was, for believers, a single, coherent scheme of belief.
Could science still be done today in this way? Perhaps, if human history
had taken a different course. That is, we could imagine each religious
group having its own physics, chemistry, biology, and so forth. For each
group research and faith would be woven together into a single system
of belief. But science developed differently.

These days an astronomer or physicist would not include statements
about God in an essay about planetary motion. Why not? Between 1500
and 1900 science and religion became separate. The separation did
not happen all at once. The physics of Isaac Newton (his *Principia* was

published in 1687) was a crowning achievement of early modern science. Nevertheless, in the 31st Query at the end of his *Opticks* (4th edition, 1730) Newton mixes discussions of God's role in the universe with discussion of physical principles.

We no longer do that. While there may be many reasons for this change (some others will be discussed in the objections and replies), I will emphasize one. During the eighteenth and particularly the nineteenth centuries, science became secular in the process of becoming universal. Scientists were recruited from outside Christianity and even outside European or Western religions. For example, the British recruited people from India into the study of science but did not insist on their conversion to Christianity. In Europe Jews and non-believers became part of scientific communities. Research communities in astronomy, physics, chemistry, biology, and other sciences became universal in the sense that they included people of diverse faiths and no faith at all. Science came to belong to everyone.[2] As a consequence of this openness it became independent of faith. There is no such thing as Christian chemistry or Hindu physics.

If anyone of any faith (or no faith at all) could participate in scientific work, science had to become secular. Imagine a team of chemists investigating a process in the laboratory. The team includes a Baptist, a Buddhist, a Jew, and an atheist. Chemistry is universal. One does not have to adhere to a particular faith to participate in research in chemistry. But they work together and cooperate in their research. How is that possible if they do not agree about God? In cooperating as scientists, they leave their faith out of their shared work. That does not mean that they stop having their religious beliefs. It just means that, because the work is shared in a community of scientists who do not share a common faith, each person's faith (or disbelief) cannot be assumed in their shared work. They have to stick to what they have in common. But what is that? It is the study of chemical processes, of the natural world—as *we* have come to understand "the natural." Their activity is secular: they exclude from their shared activity the beliefs that divide them.

Theistic beliefs could no longer be integral to science because no such beliefs were shared in the community. Because science is secular, miracles cannot be part of science. Our conception of the natural—the

---

2   Science belongs to everyone in this limited sense of having no religious qualification to participate in the scientific community. It does not belong to all social classes; rather, in class-divided societies, it tends to belong to the elite.

subject matter of the natural sciences—has changed as science came to be done in this secular way.[3]

THE INCOMPATIBILITY OF MIRACLES
(AS INTERVENTIONS IN NATURE) WITH SCIENTIFIC RESEARCH

How do you collect data for scientific research? As a scientist you are studying natural phenomena. Science developed as a secular social activity open to everyone. If science included the study of miracles, it would no longer be open to everyone because not everyone believes that there are gods who intervene in the natural order. So science, if it is to represent what is shared by all, can only study the *natural*, and the natural does not include miracles.

Natural history is the study of the *natural* history of life. Natural history tries to explain the evidence in the fossil record by the workings of natural processes, to explain how life forms change over time by these processes. This is evolution in the broadest sense, without any assumptions about what those processes are. In one way the Darwinian revolution is philosophical: it expanded our conception of science with its argument that history itself is natural.[4] It thus excluded the view that changes in life were the effect of supernatural events.

The exclusion of supernatural interventions—the assumption that the phenomena to be explained are natural—becomes universal in science as it becomes secular. We mix two chemicals in a beaker, apply heat, and a reaction occurs. Chemistry tries to explain such reactions. But to study them *as chemists* we have to assume these are natural events; we have to assume that the reaction is *not* the result of supernatural intervention. Chemistry cannot study supernatural interventions, only the natural. This assumption that the phenomena studied are natural is everywhere in science, but we notice it mostly in natural history.

Of course, for the theist, the natural universe itself is a "miracle" *in a different sense*—not in the sense of a divine *intervention* in nature but in the sense that God is the Author of nature. In this sense, the natural can be understood as supernatural. In discussing miracles and science, I am not discussing this view, which tends to reconcile belief in God with the study of science. When I say "the natural," I mean only the phenomena

3   While the categories "the natural" and "the supernatural" may be metaphysical, our understanding of them is affected by the social organization of science.
4   While the idea of natural history is older than Darwin, natural history is consolidated as part of science with the Darwinian revolution.

that the natural sciences study in a spirit that does not imply commitment to theism, atheism, or any philosophy about religious matters.
Even the theist who understands the natural as supernatural recognizes
that she shares with the non-theist a study of nature, and that this study,
while compatible with her theistic belief, does not assume it.

In this section I am arguing that *one cannot study the course of nature if
miraculous interventions occur that affect the phenomena under study.*[5] Let us
return to four examples of supposed miracles with which I began; they
were of (1) sudden clearing of severe eczema, (2) recovery from a "terminal" illness, say pancreatic cancer that has reached an advanced stage,
(3) resumption of heart function after flat-lining for a period of time,
and (4) survival of an "unsurvivable" automobile accident. Consider
possible research projects.

1. You are a dermatologist researching the causes and progression
   of eczema. You are assembling a database of cases to investigate
   what has led to the condition, what caused it to clear up, and
   how long recovery took. Do you include an unusual case where
   the condition cleared up abruptly, in a matter of hours?
2. You are an oncologist who wants to understand the natural
   progression of pancreatic cancer once it has reached a particular
   stage of development. You survey all of the cases in the literature
   on this cancer. Do you include in your database the one or two
   cases where patients recovered after their cancer reached this
   stage?
3. You are a heart specialist studying what happens to patients who
   flat-line for various periods of time. You survey the literature on
   this topic. You find one or two cases—out of thousands, let us
   suppose—of resumption of heart function after flat-lining for ten
   minutes. Do these cases enter the database for your study?
4. You are an automotive safety engineer studying the effect of automobile design and the type of crash on survivability of the car's
   occupants. In one or two cases occupants survived a particularly
   severe high speed crash. Do these cases enter your database?

---

5   But didn't Newton do exactly that—imply miraculous intervention in nature—at
the same time he was developing the science of his time? My point is that our idea
of natural science has changed since Newton's time and that we cannot study the
course of nature as *we* understand nature if miracles occur affecting the phenomena
we study.

As a scientist you are trying to determine through study and investigation *what the course of nature is.* Suppose that miraculous interventions occur so that some of the phenomena are natural and others the result of supernatural intervention. As scientists we must exclude the supernatural cases from our database because they go against the course of nature, and science studies only nature. Now either we know which cases are miraculous interventions, or we do not.

Suppose there is no way to know which ones are miraculous interventions. Then there is no way of gathering data to study the course of nature because we don't know which events are natural and which are supernatural interventions. Without data we cannot study the course of nature.

Suppose, on the other hand, that you do know which ones are supernatural interventions. But how would you know that? Presumably you know that because you know the course of nature and you know that these ones go against the course of nature.[6] If you already know what the course of nature is and you use that belief to decide which phenomena to include in your database (the natural occurrences) and which phenomena to exclude (the miraculous interventions), then your study cannot tell you anything about the course of nature. Why not? Because the database for your study was constructed based on an assumed knowledge of the course of nature.

Research, if successful, expands knowledge; it takes us from ignorance to knowledge. But if we know which events are miraculous, then we already know the course of nature, and knowledge cannot expand. For this reason belief in miraculous intervention *tends to be* incompatible with doing scientific research.[7] This is not an argument that miracles do not occur, only that, if they occur, they make it impossible to study nature.

The argument of the last two paragraphs is easier to understand if we take an example. Suppose there is a particularly virulent form of cancer. Only a tiny fraction of the patients diagnosed with this cancer survive a

6   The argument assumes that we cannot know which ones are miracles unless we already know the course of nature. If, as part of natural science, we could have a way of knowing which ones are miracles and which ones are natural which does not assume that you know the course of nature, then my argument in this paragraph is not correct. However, I cannot imagine what way of knowing which ones were miracles would be part of science.

7   I write "tends to be" because a scientist can acknowledge miracles outside a particular area of investigation and carry out research in areas where she believes miracles do *not* occur.

year. What are we to say about why these patients survived? Are they to be counted in a study of the natural progression of the cancer, or are these cases to be excluded on the ground that these patients recovered because there was divine intervention in the natural progression of the disease, on the ground that, *naturally*, everyone dies and anyone who survives does so only as a result of a miracle? If we exclude these cases, we must do so because we *already know* the natural progression of the disease. But if we already know the natural progression of the disease before we study how the disease progresses, then we cannot expand our knowledge through scientific research. For this reason belief in miracles is incompatible with scientific research.

Science is grounded in epistemic modesty—modesty about what we know: we don't know much, and we must investigate to know anything. I have argued that science studies the natural, and that the modern conception of the natural has to be limited to what is shared by all faiths and by non-believers as well. But then for the scientist, when something is unexplained, *there is only ignorance.* The three most important words in science are "I don't know." When we acknowledge our ignorance, we make it possible to know more in the future. When we believe in miracles, we close off advances in understanding nature. If we wish to know more, to expand knowledge and its uses in health care and else-where, then we should reject miracles.[8]

I wrote that scientific research tends to be incompatible with belief in miracles. I hope to have persuaded you that this is true. If you do research and believe that miracles occur in the domain you are studying, you will corrupt your data with unwarranted assumptions about the course of nature. Science requires modesty.

SOME OBJECTIONS AND REPLIES

I have argued that science studies only nature, excluding supernatural interventions as part of what science can study. I argued further that the reason for that exclusion is that the scientific community is inclusive of people of different faiths and no faith at all. Hence it cannot include in science the idea of a miracle, which assumes the universe includes supernatural events, an assumption that is part of a religious tradition.

---

8   But if we reject miracles, aren't we being epistemically immodest, thinking that we know that miracles do not occur? How could we know that? In reply: we don't know that the phenomena are natural (unaffected by divine intervention); we assume it in order to do science.

One reader was unconvinced of my account of why science limits itself to naturalistic methods. He wrote, "even though contemporary science is committed to methodological naturalism, this commitment isn't *a priori* [independent of the facts]. Rather, since methodological naturalism tends to yield such terrific scientific results, we should assume this methodological stance. So we should assume the stance on *a posteriori* grounds [that is, based on the factual evidence], not on dogmatic *a priori* grounds."

Let us assume for the moment, in agreement with the objection, that methodological naturalism yields good scientific results (later I will argue that the assumption is one-sided). Let me grant from the start that many people become enthusiastic about naturalistic methods and about science because of the intellectual satisfaction that comes from making sense of things. What are we to conclude from this success of naturalistic methods? Two distinct conclusions seem possible: (1) all phenomena are natural, and there are no supernatural beings or occurrences (this view is called materialism or naturalism); (2) science should limit itself to the study of natural phenomena. The success of science supports (1) better than it supports (2). After all, if methodological naturalism yields such terrific results, we should extend it to all of our thinking. But many practicing scientists and even more people engaged in applied science (engineering, drug research, etc.) believe in God and in God's activity in the world; they do not follow methodological naturalism throughout their lives, but primarily in their scientific work (they compartmentalize their lives). They exclude belief in miracles from their scientific practice. How is that to be explained? If we limit ourselves to the explanation that naturalistic assumptions lead to so much success, we are left with the puzzle of why they continue to believe that God intervenes in the natural world. The success of science as a form of knowledge seems a reason to abandon *other* ways of arriving at belief, ways which do not have the same success. What needs to be explained is why individuals who do *not* follow naturalistic ways of thinking in other matters do follow them when doing science. My explanation—the inclusive nature of the scientific community—fits and explains scientific practice.

A related objection is that, if the facts were otherwise than as they are, there could be a science of miracles. One reader writes, "Imagine a world in which statistically significant correlations between being prayed for and being suddenly cured are discovered. Suppose, further, that scientists begin inquiring into the connection, if any, between

prayer and cure and discover a very intimate one, namely, that people
who are cured always have properties a, b, and c, and have been prayed
for by people who always have properties x, y, and z. Also suppose that
scientists, in this world, are able to predict that anyone who has certain
properties and is prayed for by someone who has certain properties
will be cured. What I've described here is, arguably, a science of occurrences that are not natural—assuming, of course, that the 'miraculous'
cures can't be explained except by reference to prayer." The reader
concludes that the reason we do not allow miracles in scientific research
is that phenomena such as these do not occur, not that miracles are
ruled out by the very nature of scientific practice (again, the proscrip-
tion of miracles is *a posteriori* [based on the factual evidence], not *a
priori* [based on the nature of science]).

I disagree. I will grant, at least for the sake of argument, that we have
an explanation of why the patient was cured: she had characteristics
a, b, and c and she was prayed for by someone with characteristics x,
y, and z. And we can call this science; it certainly is a correlation, and
if correlation in this case indicates causation, then you have a causal
explanation of why the patient is cured. So far we have said nothing
about a miracle. But like any other scientific explanation it leads to further questions: why does the praying for a patient with a, b, and c by a
person with x, y, and z lead to the patient's cure? If asked in a scientific
spirit, there is only one epistemically modest answer: we don't know.

If you say you do know, if you think the explanation is divine intervention, you are doing what many have been doing for centuries: noting
phenomena they can't explain and saying "God did it." In short, given
certain unexplained phenomena some will suppose divine intervention,
a move that I have characterized as insufficiently epistemically modest.
So we are back to the argument of the essay: science is able to expand
our knowledge because it assumes that unexplained phenomena may
eventually be explained by investigating nature. Belief in miracles,
divine interventions in nature, stops that process of inquiry. And when
we suppose divine intervention, we are not doing science.

Finally, I should say something about the assertion that scientific
naturalism (exclusion of miracles as a cause) yields such good results. I
said I thought it was one-sided. An example will help. As I will argue in
my essay below about whether we are related to other life, the theory
that life is related to life by common ancestry makes sense of similarities
between organisms that we have no other way of understanding. That's
the "good results" side of the issue. The other side is that the theory

generates a huge array of puzzles. In fact it raises many more questions than it answers. It mostly gives us a way of asking questions and looking for answers. What makes science "successful" is the problems it raises, as much as the solutions it offers to those problems. Thus it stimulates human curiosity and rewards inquiry by allowing us to solve puzzles. But with each solution, new puzzles arise. Science appeals to us because of its process of inquiry and investigation as much as because of its results. Those with different habits of mind find it more intellectually satisfying to think that the explanation is that God did it. (This "explains" everything, and, of course, it explains nothing.) They don't like puzzles and unresolved questions. So while I agree that we have learned a lot by assuming naturalism and investigating nature in that way, some people do not like lots of unresolved questions.

From "The Origin of Life on Earth"[9]
Neil deGrasse Tyson and Donald Goldsmith

The search for life in the universe begins with a deep question: What is life? Astrobiologists will tell you honestly that this question has no simple or generally accepted answer. Not much use to say that we'll know it when we see it. No matter what characteristic we specify to separate living from nonliving matter on Earth, we can always find an example that blurs or erases this distinction. Some or all living creatures grow, move, or decay, but so too do objects that we would never call alive. Does life reproduce itself? So does fire. Does life evolve to produce new forms? So do certain crystals that grow in watery solutions. We can certainly say that you can tell some forms of life when you see them—who could fail to see life in a salmon or an eagle?—but anyone familiar with life in its diverse forms on Earth will admit that many creatures will remain entirely undetected until the luck of time and the skill of an expert reveal their living nature.

Since life is short, we must press onward with a rough-and-ready, generally appropriate criterion for life. Here it is: Life consists of sets of objects that can both reproduce and evolve. We shall not call a group of objects alive simply because they make more of themselves. To qualify

---

9   From *Origins: Fourteen Billion Years of Cosmic Evolution* (New York: Norton, 2004) by Neil deGrasse Tyson and Donald Goldsmith. Used by permission of W.W. Norton and Company.

as life, they must also evolve into new forms as time passes. This definition therefore eliminates the possibility that any single object can be
judged to be alive. Instead, we must examine a range of objects in space
and follow them through time. This definition of life may yet prove too
restrictive, but for now we shall employ it....

The origin of life on Earth remains locked in murky uncertainty. Our
ignorance about life's beginnings stems in large part from the fact that
whatever events made inanimate matter come alive occurred billions
of years ago and left no definitive traces behind. For times more than 4
billion years in the past, the fossil and geological record of Earth's history does not exist. Yet the interval in solar system history between 4.6
and 4 billion years ago—the first 600 million years after the Sun and its
planets had formed—includes the era when most paleobiologists, spe-
cialists in reconstructing life that existed during long-vanished epochs,
believe that life first appeared on our planet.

The absence of all geological evidence from epochs more than 4
billion years ago arises from motions of Earth's crust, familiarly called
continental drift but scientifically known as plate tectonics. These
motions, driven by heat that wells up from Earth's interior, continually
force pieces of our planet's crust to slide, collide, and ride by or over
one another. Plate tectonic motions have slowly buried everything that
once lay on Earth's surface. As a result, we possess few rocks older than
2 billion years, and none more than 3.8 billion years in age. This fact,
together with the reasonable conclusion that the most primitive forms
of life had little chance of leaving behind fossil evidence, has left our
planet devoid of any reliable record of life during Earth's first 1 or 2 billion years. The oldest definite evidence we have for life on Earth takes
us back "only" 2.7 billion years into the past, with indirect indications
that life did exist more than 1 billion years before then.

Most paleobiologists believe that life must have appeared on Earth
at least 3 billion years ago, and quite possibly more than 4 billion years
ago, within the first 600 million years after Earth formed. Their conclusion relies on a reasonable supposition about primitive organisms. At
times a bit less than 3 billion years ago, significant amounts of oxygen
began to appear in Earth's atmosphere. We know this from Earth's geological record independently of any fossil remains: oxygen promotes
the slow rusting of iron-rich rocks, which produces lovely red tones
like those of the rocks in Arizona's Grand Canyon. Rocks from the pre-
oxygen era show neither any such colors nor other telltale signs of the
element's presence.

The appearance of atmospheric oxygen was the greatest pollution ever to occur on Earth. Atmospheric oxygen does more than combine with iron; it also takes food from the (metaphorical) mouths of primitive organisms by combining with all the simple molecules that could otherwise have provided nutrients for early forms of life. As a result, oxygen's appearance in Earth's atmosphere meant that all forms of life had to adapt or die—and that if life had not appeared by that time, it could never do so thereafter, because the would-be organisms would have nothing to eat, for their potential food would have rusted away. Evolutionary adaptation to this pollution worked well in many cases, as all oxygen-breathing animals can testify. Hiding from the oxygen also did the trick. To this day, every animal's stomach, including our own, harbor billions of organisms that thrive in the anoxic[10] environment that we provide, but would die if exposed to air.

What made Earth's atmosphere relatively rich in oxygen? Much of it came from tiny organisms floating in the seas, which released oxygen as part of their photosynthesis. Some oxygen would have appeared even in the absence of life, as UV from sunlight broke apart some of the H_2O molecules at the ocean surfaces, releasing hydrogen and oxygen atoms into the air. Wherever a planet exposes significant amounts of liquid water to starlight, that planet's atmosphere should likewise gain oxygen, slowly but surely, over hundreds of millions or billions of years. There too, atmospheric oxygen would prevent life from originating by combining with all possible nutrients that could sustain life. Oxygen kills! Not what we usually say about this eighth element on the periodic table, but for life throughout the cosmos, this verdict appears accurate. Life must begin early in a planet's history, or else the appearance of oxygen in its atmosphere will put the kibosh on life forever.

By a strange coincidence, the epoch missing from the geological record that includes the origin of life also includes the so-called era of bombardment, which covers those critical first few hundred million years after Earth had formed. All portions of Earth's surface must then have endured a continual rain of objects. During those several hundred thousand millennia, infalling objects as large as the one that made the Meteor Crater in Arizona must have struck our planet several times in every century, with much larger objects, each several miles in diameter, colliding with Earth every few thousand years. Each one of the large impacts would have caused a local remodeling of the surface, so

---

10   [An anoxic environment is one where no oxygen is present. PG]

a hundred thousand impacts would have produced global changes in our planet's topography.

How did these impacts affect the origin of life? Biologists tell us that they might have triggered both the appearance and the extinction of life on Earth, not once but many times. Much of the infalling material during the era of bombardment consisted of comets, which are essentially large snowballs laden with tiny rocks and dirt. Their cometary "snow" consists of both frozen water and frozen carbon dioxide, familiarly called dry ice. In addition to their snow, grit, and rocks rich in minerals and metals, the comets that bombarded Earth during its first few hundred million years contained many different types of small molecules, such as methane, ammonia, methyl alcohol, hydrogen cyanide, and formaldehyde. These molecules, along with water, carbon monoxide, and carbon dioxide, provide the raw materials for life. They all consist of hydrogen, carbon, nitrogen, and oxygen, and they all represent the first steps in building complex molecules.

Cometary bombardment therefore appears to have provided Earth with some of the water for its oceans and with material from which life could begin. Life itself might have arrived in these comets, though their low temperatures, typically hundreds of degrees below zero Fahrenheit, argue against the formation of truly complex molecules. But whether or not life arrived with the comets, the largest objects to strike during the era of bombardment might well have destroyed life that had arisen on Earth. Life might have begun, at least in its most primitive forms, in fits and starts many times over, with each new set of organisms surviving for hundreds of thousands or even millions of years, until a collision with a particularly large object wreaked such havoc on Earth that all life perished, only to appear again, and to be destroyed again, after the passage of a similar amount of time.

We can gain some confidence in the fits-and-starts origin of life from two well-established facts. First, life appeared on our planet sooner rather than later, during the first third of Earth's lifetime. If life could and did arise within a billion years, perhaps it could do so in far less time. The origin of life might require no more than a few million, or a few tens of millions, of years. Second, we know that collisions between large objects and Earth have, at intervals of time measured in tens of millions of years, destroyed most of the species alive on our planet. The most famous of these, the Cretaceous-Tertiary extinction 65 million years ago, killed all the non-avian dinosaurs, along with enormous numbers of other species. Even this mass extinction fell short of the most extensive one, the Permian-Triassic mass extinction, that destroyed nearly 90 percent of all species of marine life and 70 percent of all terrestrial vertebrate species, 252 million years ago, leaving fungi as the dominant forms of life on land.

The Cretaceous-Tertiary and Permian-Triassic mass extinctions arose from the collisions of Earth with objects one or two dozen miles across. Geologists have found an enormous 65-million-year-old impact crater, coincident in time with the Cretaceous-Tertiary extinction, that stretches across the northern Yucatán Peninsula and the adjoining seabed. A large crater exists with the same age as the Permian-Triassic extinction, discovered off the northwest coast of Australia, but this mass dying might have arisen from something in addition to a collision, perhaps from sustained volcanic eruptions. Even the single example of the Cretaceous-Tertiary dinosaur extinction reminds us of the immense damage to life that the impact of a comet or asteroid can produce. During the era of bombardment, Earth must have reeled not only from this sort of impact, but also from the much more serious effects of collisions with objects 50, 100, or even 250 miles in diameter. Each of these collisions must have cleared the decks of life, either completely or so thoroughly that only a tiny percentage of living organisms managed to survive, and they must have occurred far more often than collisions with ten-mile-wide objects do now. Our present knowledge of astronomy, biology, chemistry, and geology points toward an early Earth ready to produce life, and a cosmic environment ready to eliminate it. And wherever a star and its planets have recently formed, intense bombardment by debris left over from the formation process may even now be eliminating all forms of life on those planets.

More than 4 billion years ago, most of the debris from the solar system's formation either collided with a planet or moved into orbits where collisions could not occur. As a result, our cosmic neighborhood gradually changed from a region of continual bombardment to the overall calm that we enjoy today, broken only at multi-million-year intervals by collisions with objects large enough to threaten life on Earth. You can compare the ancient and ongoing threat from impacts whenever you look at the full moon. The giant lava plains that create the face of the "man in the Moon" are the result of tremendous impacts some 4 billion years ago, as the era of bombardment ended, whereas the crater named Tycho, fifty-five miles across, arose from a smaller, but still highly significant, impact that occurred soon after the dinosaurs disappeared from Earth.

We do not know whether life already existed 4 billion years ago, having survived the early impact storm, or whether life arose on Earth only after relative tranquility began. These two alternatives include the possibility that incoming objects seeded our planet with life, either during the era of bombardment or soon afterward. If life began and died out repeatedly while chaos rained down from the skies, the processes by which life originated seem robust, so that we might reasonably expect them to have occurred again and again on other worlds similar to our own. If, on the other hand, life arose on Earth only once, either as home-grown life or as the result of cosmic seeding, its origin may have occurred here by luck.

In either case, the crucial question of how life actually began on Earth, either once or many times over, has no good answer, though speculation on the subject has acquired a long and intriguing history. Great rewards lie in store for those who can resolve this mystery. From Adam's rib to Dr. Frankenstein's monster, humans have answered the question by invoking a mysterious *élan vital* that imbues otherwise inanimate matter with life.

Scientists seek to probe more deeply, with laboratory experiments and examinations of the fossil record that attempt to establish the height of the barrier between inanimate and animate matter, and to find how nature breached this dike. Early scientific discussions about the origin of life imagined the interaction of simple molecules, concentrated in pools or tide ponds, to create more complex ones. In 1871, a dozen years after the publication of Charles Darwin's marvelous book *The Origin of Species*, in which he speculated that "probably all of the organic beings which have ever lived on this Earth have descended from some one primordial form," Darwin wrote to his friend Joseph Hooker that

> It is often said that all the conditions for the first production of a living organism are now present, which could ever have been present. But if (and oh! what a big if!) we could conceive in some warm little pond, with all sorts of ammonia and phosphoric salts, light, heat, electricity, &c., present, that a proteine [*sic*] compound was chemically formed ready to undergo still more complex changes, at the present day such matter would be instantly absorbed, which would not have been the case before living creatures were found.

In other words, when Earth was ripe for life, the basic compounds necessary for metabolism might have existed in surplus, with nothing in existence to eat them (and, as we have discussed, no oxygen to combine with them and spoil their chances to serve as food).

From a scientific perspective, nothing succeeds like experiments that can be compared with reality. In 1953, seeking to test Darwin's conception of the origin of life in ponds or tide pools, Stanley Miller, who was then a US graduate student working at the University of Chicago with the Nobel laureate Harold Urey, performed a famous experiment that duplicated the conditions within a highly simplified and hypothetical pool of water on the early Earth. Miller and Urey partly filled a laboratory flask with water and topped the water with a gaseous mixture of water vapor, hydrogen, ammonia, and methane. They heated the flask from below, vaporizing some of the contents and driving them along a glass tube into another flask, where an electrical discharge simulated the effect of lightning. From there the mixture returned to the original flask, completing a cycle that would be repeated over and over during a few days, rather than a few thousand years. After this entirely modest time interval, Miller and Urey found the water in the lower flask to be rich in "organic gunk," a compound of numerous complex molecules, including different types of sugar, as well as two of the simplest amino acids, alanine and guanine.

Since protein molecules consist of twenty types of amino acids arranged into different structural forms, the Miller-Urey experiment takes us, in a remarkably brief time, a significant part of the way from the simplest molecules to the amino-acid molecules that form the building blocks of living organisms. The Miller-Urey experiment also made some of the modestly complex molecules called nucleotides, which provide the key structural element for DNA, the giant molecule that carries instructions for forming new copies of an organism. Even so, a long path remains before life emerges from experimental laboratories. An enormously significant gap, so far unbridged by human experiment or invention, separates the formation of amino acids— even if our experiments produced all twenty of them, which they do not—and the creation of life. Amino-acid molecules have also been found in some of the oldest and least altered meteorites, believed to have remained unchanged for nearly the entire 4.6-billion-year history of the solar system. This supports the general conclusion that natural processes can make amino acids in many different situations. A balanced view of the experimental results finds nothing totally surprising: The simpler molecules found in living organisms form quickly in many situations, but life does not. The key question still remains: How does a collection of molecules, even one primed for life to appear, ever generate life itself?

Since the early Earth had not weeks but many million years in which to bring forth life, the Miller-Urey experimental results seemed to support the tide-pool model for life's beginnings. Today, however, most scientists who seek to explain life's origin consider the experiment to have been significantly limited by its techniques. Their shift in attitude arose not from doubting the test's results, but rather from recognizing a potential flaw in the hypotheses underlying the experiment. To understand this flaw, we must consider what modern biology has demonstrated about the oldest forms of life.

Evolutionary biology now relies on careful study of the similarities and differences between living creatures in their molecules of DNA and RNA, which carry the information that tells an organism how to function and how to reproduce. Careful comparison of these relatively enormous and complex molecules has allowed biologists, among whom the great pioneer has been Carl Woese, to create an evolutionary tree of life that records the "evolutionary distances" between various life forms, as determined by the degrees to which these life forms have nonidentical DNA and RNA.

The tree of life consists of three great branches, Archaea, Bacteria, and Eucarya, that replace the biological "kingdoms" formerly believed to be fundamental. The Eucarya includes every organism whose individual cells have a well-defined center or nucleus that contains the genetic material governing the cells' reproduction. This characteristic makes Eucarya more complex than the other two types, and indeed every form of life familiar to the non-expert belongs to this branch. We may reasonably conclude that Eucarya arose later than Archaea or Bacteria. And because Bacteria lie farther from the origin of the tree of life than the Archaea do—for the simple reason that their DNA and RNA has changed more—the Archaea, as their name implies, almost certainly represent the oldest forms of life. Now comes a shocker: Unlike the Bacteria and Eucarya, the Archaea consist mainly of "extremophiles," organisms that love to live, and live to love, in what we now call extreme conditions: temperatures near or above the boiling point of water, high acidity, or other situations that would kill other forms of life. (Of course, if the extremophiles had their own biologists, they would classify themselves as normal and any life that thrives at room temperature as an extremophile.) Modern research into the tree of life tends to suggest that life began with the extremophiles, and only later evolved into forms of life that benefit from what we call normal conditions.

In that case, Darwin's "warm little pond," as well as the tide pools duplicated in the Miller-Urey experiment, would evaporate into the mist of rejected hypotheses. Gone would be the relatively mild cycles of drying and wetting. Instead, those who seek to find the places where life may have begun would have to look to locales where extremely hot water, possibly laden with acids, surges from Earth.

The past few decades have allowed oceanographers to discover just such places, along with the strange forms of life they support. In 1977, two oceanographers piloting a deep sea submersible vehicle discovered the first deep sea vents, a mile and a half beneath the calm surface of the Pacific Ocean near the Galápagos Islands. At these vents, Earth's crust behaves locally like a household cooker, generating high pressure inside a heavy-duty pot with a lockable lid and heating water beyond its ordinary boiling temperature without letting it reach an actual boil. As the lid partially lifts, the pressurized, superheated water spews out from below Earth's crust into the cold ocean basins.

The superheated seawater that emerges from these vents carries dissolved minerals that quickly collect and solidify to surround the vents with giant, porous rock chimneys, hottest in their cores and coolest at the edges that make direct contact with seawater. Across this temperature gradient live countless life forms that have never seen the Sun and care nothing for solar heating, though they do require the oxygen dissolved in seawater, which in turn comes from the existence of solar-driven life near the surface. These hardy bugs live on geothermal energy, which combines heat left over from Earth's formation with heat continuously produced by the radioactive decay of unstable isotopes such as aluminum-26, which lasts for millions of years, and potassium-40, which lasts for billions.

Near these vents, far below the depths to which any sunlight can penetrate, the oceanographers found tube worms as long as a man, thriving amidst large colonies of bacteria and other small creatures. Instead of drawing their energy from sunlight, as plants do with photosynthesis, life near deep sea vents relies on "chemosynthesis," the production of energy by chemical reactions, which in turn depend on geothermal heating.

How does this chemosynthesis occur? The hot water gushing from the deep sea vents emerges laden with hydrogen-sulfur and hydrogen-iron compounds. Bacteria near the vents combine these molecules with the hydrogen and oxygen atoms in water molecules, and with the carbon and oxygen atoms of the carbon dioxide molecules dissolved in sea water. These reactions form larger molecules—carbohydrates—from carbon, oxygen, and hydrogen atoms. Thus the bacteria near deep sea vents mimic the activities of their cousins far above, which likewise make carbohydrates from carbon, oxygen, and hydrogen. One set of microorganisms draws the energy to make carbohydrates from sunlight, and the other from chemical reactions at the ocean floors. Close by the deep sea vents, other organisms consume the carbohydrate-making bacteria, profiting from their energy in the same way that animals eat plants, or eat plant-eating animals.

In the chemical reactions near deep sea vents, however, more goes on than the production of carbohydrate molecules. The iron and sulfur atoms, which are not included in the carbohydrate molecule, combine to make compounds of their own, most notably crystals of iron pyrite, familiarly called "fool's gold," known to the ancient Greeks as "fire stone" because a good blow from another rock will strike sparks from it. Iron pyrite, the most abundant of all the sulfur-bearing minerals found on Earth, might have played a crucial role in the origin of life by encouraging the formation of carbohydratelike molecules. This hypothesis sprang from the mind of a German patent attorney and amateur biologist, Günter Wächtershäuser, whose profession hardly excludes him from biological speculation, any more than Einstein's work as a patent attorney barred him from insights into physics. (To be sure, Einstein had an advanced degree in physics, while Wächtershäuser's biology and chemistry are mainly self-taught.)

In 1994, Wächtershäuser proposed that the surfaces of iron pyrite crystals, formed naturally by combining iron and sulfur that surged from deep sea vents early in Earth's history, would have offered natural sites where carbon-rich molecules could accumulate, acquiring new carbon atoms from the material ejected by the nearby vents. Like those who hypothesize that life began in ponds or tide pools, Wächtershäuser has no clear way to pass from the building blocks to living creatures. Nevertheless, with his emphasis on the high-temperature origin of life, he may prove to be on the right track, as he firmly believes. Referring to the highly ordered structure of iron pyrite crystals, on whose surfaces the first complex molecules for life might have formed, Wächtershäuser has confronted his critics at scientific conferences with the striking statement that "Some say that the origin of life brings order out of chaos—but I say, 'order out of order out of order!'" Delivered with German brio, this claim acquires a certain resonance, though only time can tell how accurate it may be.

So which basic model for life's origin is more likely to prove correct—tide pools at the ocean's edge, or superheated vents on the ocean floors? For now, the betting is about even. Experts on the origin of life have challenged the assertion that life's oldest forms lived at high temperatures, because current methods for placing organisms at different points along the branches of the tree of life remain the subject of debate. In addition, computer programs that trace out how many compounds of different types existed in ancient RNA molecules, the close cousins of DNA that apparently preceded DNA in life's history, suggest that the compounds favored by high temperatures appeared only after life had undergone some relatively low-temperature history.

Thus the outcome of our finest research, as so often occurs in science, proves unsettling to those who seek certainty. Although we can state approximately when life began on Earth, we don't know where or how this marvelous event occurred. Paleobiologists have recently given the elusive ancestor of all Earthlife the name LUCA, for the last universal common ancestor. (See how firmly these scientists' minds have remained fixed to our planet: they should call life's progenitor LECA, for the last Earthly common ancestor.) For now, naming this ancestor— a set of primitive organisms that all shared the same genes—mainly underscores the distance that we still must travel before we can pierce the veil that separates life's origin from our understanding.

More than a natural curiosity as to our own beginnings hinges on the resolution of this issue. Different origins for life imply different possibilities for its origin, evolution, and survival both here and elsewhere in the cosmos. For example, Earth's ocean floors may provide the most stable ecosystem on our planet. If a jumbo asteroid slammed into Earth and rendered all surface life extinct, the oceanic extremophiles would almost certainly continue undaunted in their happy ways. They might even evolve to repopulate Earth's surface after each extinction episode. And if the Sun were mysteriously plucked from the center of the solar system and Earth drifted through space, this event would hardly merit attention in the extremophile press, as life near deep sea vents might continue relatively undisturbed. But in 5 billion years, the Sun will become a red giant as it expands to fill the inner solar system. Meanwhile, Earth's oceans will boil away and Earth itself will partially vaporize. Now that would be news for any form of Earthlife.

The ubiquity of extremophiles on Earth leads us to a profound question: Could life exist deep within many of the rogue planets or plan-
etesimals that were ejected from the solar system during its formation?
Their "geo"thermal reservoirs could last for billions of years. What
about the countless planets that were forcibly ejected by every other
solar system that ever formed? Could interstellar space be teeming with
life—formed and evolved deep within these starless planets? Before
astrophysicists recognized the importance of extremophiles, they envi-
sioned a "habitable zone" surrounding each star, within which water or
another substance could maintain itself as a liquid, allowing molecules
to float, interact, and produce more complex molecules. Today, we
must modify this concept, so that far from being a tidy region around a
star that receives just the right amount of sunlight, a habitable zone can
be anywhere and everywhere, maintained not by starlight heating but
by localized heat sources, often generated by radioactive rocks. So the
Three Bears' cottage was, perhaps, not a special place among fairy tales.
Anybody's residence, even one of the Three Little Pigs', might contain
a bowl of food at a temperature that is just right.

What a hopeful, even prescient fairy tale this may prove to be. Life,
far from being rare and precious, may be almost as common as planets
themselves. All that remains is for us to go find it.

From "Sex, Drugs, Disasters, and the Extinction of Dinosaurs"[11]

Stephen Jay Gould

Science, in its most fundamental definition, is a fruitful mode of inquiry,
not a list of enticing conclusions. The conclusions are the consequence,
not the essence.

My greatest unhappiness with most popular presentations of science
concerns their failure to separate fascinating claims from the methods
that scientists use to establish the facts of nature. Journalists, and the
public, thrive on controversial and stunning statements. But science is,
basically, a way of knowing—in P.B. Medawars's apt words, "the art of the
soluble." If the growing corps of popular science writers would focus on

---

how scientists develop and defend those fascinating claims, they would make their greatest possible contribution to public understanding.

Consider three ideas, proposed in perfect seriousness to explain that greatest of all titillating puzzles—the extinction of dinosaurs. Since these three notions invoke the primally fascinating themes of our culture—sex, drugs, and violence—they surely reside in the category of fascinating claims. I want to show why two of them rank as silly speculation, while the other represents science at its grandest and most useful.

Science works with testable proposals. If, after much compilation and scrutiny of data, new information continues to affirm a hypothesis, we may accept if provisionally and gain confidence as further evidence mounts. We can never be completely sure that a hypothesis is right, though we may be able to show with confidence that it is wrong. The best scientific hypotheses are also generous and expansive: they suggest extensions and implications that enlighten related, and even far distant, subjects. Simply consider how the idea of evolution has influenced virtually every intellectual field.

Useless speculation, on the other hand is restrictive. It generates no testable hypothesis, and offers no way to obtain potentially refuting evidence. Please note that I am not speaking of truth or falsity. The speculation may well be true; still, if it provides, in principle, no material for affirmation or rejection, we can make nothing of it. It must simply stand forever as an intriguing idea. Useless speculation turns in on itself and leads nowhere; good science, containing both seeds for its potential refutation and implications for more and different testable knowledge, reaches out. But, enough preaching. Let's move on to dinosaurs, and the three proposals for their extinction.

1. SEX: Testes function only in a narrow range of temperatures (those of mammals hang externally in a scrotal sac because internal body temperatures are too high for their proper function). A worldwide rise in temperature at the close of the Cretaceous period caused the testes of dinosaurs to stop functioning and led to their extinction by sterilization of males.

2. DRUGS: Angiosperms (flowering plants) first evolved toward the end of the dinosaurs' reign. Many of these plants contain psychoactive agents, avoided by mammals today as a result of their bitter taste. Dinosaurs had neither means to taste the bitterness nor livers effective enough to detoxify the substances. They died of massive overdoses.

3. DISASTERS: A large comet or asteroid struck the Earth some 65
million years ago, lofting a cloud of dust into the sky and block-
ing sunlight, thereby suppressing photosynthesis and so drasti-
cally lowering world temperatures that dinosaurs and hosts of
other creatures became extinct.

Before analyzing these three tantalizing statements, we must establish a basic ground rule often violated in proposals for the dinosaurs'
demise. *There is no separate problem of the extinction of dinosaurs.* Too often
we divorce specific events from their wider contexts and systems of
cause and effect. The fundamental fact of dinosaur extinction is its
synchrony with the demise of so many other groups across a wide range
of habitats, from terrestrial to marine.

The history of life has been punctuated by brief episodes of mass
extinction. A recent analysis by University of Chicago paleontologists
Jack Sepkoski and Dave Raup, based on the best and most exhaustive
tabulation of data ever assembled, shows clearly that five episodes of
mass dying stand well above the "background" extinctions of normal
times (when we consider all mass extinctions, large and small, they
seem to fall in a regular 26-million-year cycle...). The Cretaceous deba-
cle, occurring 65 million years ago and separating the Mesozoic and
Cenozoic eras of our geological time scale, ranks prominently among
the five. Nearly all the marine plankton (single-celled floating creatures)
died with geological suddenness; among marine invertebrates, nearly 15
percent of all families perished, including many previously dominant
groups, especially the ammonites (relatives of squids in coiled shells).
On land, the dinosaurs disappeared after more than 100 million years
of unchallenged domination.

In this context, speculations limited to dinosaurs alone ignore the
larger phenomenon. We need a coordinated explanation for a system
of events that includes the extinction of dinosaurs as one component.
Thus it makes little sense, though it may fuel our desire to view mammals as inevitable inheritors of the Earth, to guess that dinosaurs died
because small mammals ate their eggs (a perennial favorite among
untestable speculations). It seems most unlikely that some disaster
peculiar to dinosaurs befell these massive beasts—and that the deba-
cle happened to strike just when one of history's five great dyings had
enveloped the Earth for completely different reasons.

The testicular theory, an old favorite from the 1940s, had its root in an
interesting and thoroughly respectable study of temperature tolerances

in the American alligator, published... in 1946 by three experts on living and fossil reptiles—E.H. Colbert, my own first teacher in paleontology; R.B. Cowles; and C.M. Bogert.

The first sentence of their summary reveals a purpose beyond alligators: "This report describes an attempt to infer the reactions of extinct reptiles, especially the dinosaurs, to high temperatures as based upon reactions observed in the modern alligator." They studied, by rectal thermometry, the body temperatures of alligators under changing conditions of heating and cooling. (Well, let's face it, you wouldn't want to try sticking a thermometer under a 'gator's tongue.) The predictions under test go way back to an old theory first stated by Galileo in the 1630s—the unequal scaling of surfaces and volumes. As an animal, or any object, grows (provided its shape doesn't change), surface areas must increase more slowly than volumes—since surfaces get larger as length squared, while volumes increase much more rapidly, as length cubed. Therefore, small animals have high ratios of surface to volume, while large animals cover themselves with relatively little surface.

Among cold-blooded animals lacking any physiological mechanism for keeping their temperatures constant, small creatures have a hell of a time keeping warm—because they lose so much heat through their relatively large surfaces. On the other hand, large animals, with their relatively small surface, may lose heat so slowly that, once warm, they may maintain effectively constant temperatures against ordinary fluctuations in climate. (In fact, the resolution of the "hot-blooded dinosaur" controversy that burned so brightly a few years back may simply be that, while large dinosaurs possessed no physiological mechanism for constant temperature, and were not therefore warm-blooded in the technical sense, their large size and relatively small surface area kept them warm.)

Colbert, Cowles, and Bogert compared the warming rates of small and large alligators, As predicted, the small fellows heated up (and cooled down) more quickly. When exposed to a warm sun, a tiny 50-gram (1.76 ounce) alligator heated up one degree Celsius every minute and a half, while a large alligator, 260 times bigger at 13,000 grams (28.7 pounds), took seven and a half minutes to gain a degree. Extrapolating up to an adult 10-ton dinosaur, they concluded that a one-degree rise in body temperature would take eighty-six hours. If large animals absorb heat so slowly (through their relatively small surfaces), they will also be unable to shed any excess heat gained when temperatures rise above a favorable level.

The authors then guessed that large dinosaurs lived at or near their optimum temperatures; Cowles suggested that a rise in global temperatures just before the Cretaceous extinction caused the dinosaurs to heat up beyond their optimal tolerance—and, being so large, they couldn't shed the unwanted heat. (In a most unusual statement within a scientific paper, Colbert and Bogert then explicitly disavowed this speculative extension of their empirical work on alligators.) Cowles conceded that this excess heat probably wasn't enough to kill or even to enervate the great beasts, but since testes often function only within a narrow range of temperatures, he proposed that this global rise might have sterilized all the males, causing extinction by natural contraception.

The overdose theory has recently been supported by UCLA psychiatrist Ronald K. Siegel. Siegel has gathered, he claims, more than 2,000 records of animals who, when given access, administer various drugs to themselves—from a mere swig of alcohol to massive doses of the big H. Elephants will swill the equivalent of twenty beers at a time, but do not like alcohol in concentrations greater than 7 percent. In a silly bit of anthropocentric speculation, Siegel states that "elephants drink, perhaps, to forget ... the anxiety produced by shrinking rangeland and the competition for food."

Since fertile imagination can apply almost any hot idea to the extinction of dinosaurs, Siegel found a way. Flowering plants did not evolve until late in the dinosaurs' reign. These plants also produced an array of aromatic, amino-acid-based alkaloids—the major group of psychoactive agents. Most mammals are "smart" enough to avoid these potential poisons. The alkaloids simply don't taste good (they are bitter); in any case, we mammals have livers happily supplied with the capacity to detoxify them. But, Siegel speculates, perhaps dinosaurs could neither taste the bitterness nor detoxify the substances once ingested. He recently told members of the American Psychological Association: "I'm not suggesting that all dinosaurs OD'd on plant drugs, but it certainly was a factor." He also argued that death by overdose may help explain why so many dinosaur fossils are found in contorted positions. (Do not go gentle into that good night.)

Extraterrestrial catastrophes have long pedigrees in the popular literature of extinction, but the subject exploded again in 1979, after a long lull, when the father-son, physicist-geologist team of Luis and Walter Alvarez proposed that an asteroid, some 10 km in diameter, struck the Earth 65 million years ago (comets, rather than asteroids have since gained favor for [good] reasons.... Good science is self-corrective).

The force of such a collision would be immense, greater by far than the megatonnage of all the world's nuclear weapons.... In trying to reconstruct a scenario that would explain the simultaneous dying of dinosaurs on land and so many creatures in the sea, the Alvarezes proposed that a gigantic dust cloud, generated by particles blown aloft in the impact, would so darken the Earth that photosynthesis would cease and temperatures drop precipitously.... The single-celled photosynthetic oceanic plankton, with life cycles measured in weeks, would perish outright, but land plants might survive through the dormancy of their seeds (land plants were not much affected by the Cretaceous extinction, and any adequate theory must account for the curious pattern of differential survival). Dinosaurs would die by starvation and freezing; small, warm-blooded mammals, with more modest requirements for food and better regulation of body temperature, would squeak through....

All three theories, testicular malfunction, psychoactive overdosing, and asteroidal zapping, grab our attention mightily. As pure phenomenology, they rank about equally high on any hit parade of primal fascination. Yet one represents expansive science, the others restrictive and untestable speculation. The proper criterion lies in evidence and methodology; we must probe behind the superficial fascination of particular claims.

How could we possibly decide whether the hypothesis of testicular frying is right or wrong? We would have to know things that the fossil record cannot provide. What temperatures were optimal for dinosaurs? Could they avoid the absorption of excess heat by staying in the shade, or in caves? At what temperatures did their testicles cease to function? Were late Cretaceous climates ever warm enough to drive the internal temperatures of dinosaurs close to this ceiling? Testicles simply don't fossilize, and how could we infer their temperature tolerances even if they did? In short, Cowles's hypothesis is only an intriguing speculation leading nowhere. The most damning statement against it appeared right in the conclusion of Colbert, Cowles, and Bogert's paper, when they admitted: "It is difficult to advance any definite arguments against this hypothesis." My statement may seem paradoxical—isn't a hypothesis really good if you can't devise any arguments against it? Quite the contrary. It is simply untestable and unusable.

Siegel's overdosing has even less going for it. At least Cowles extrapolated his conclusion from some good data on alligators. And he didn't completely violate the primary guideline of siting dinosaur extinction in the context of a general mass dying—for rise in temperature could be the root cause of a general catastrophe, zapping dinosaurs by testicular malfunction and different groups for other reasons. But Siegel's speculation cannot touch the extinction of ammonites or oceanic plankton (diatoms make their own food with good sweet sunlight; they don't OD on the chemicals of terrestrial plants). It is simply a gratuitous, attention-grabbing guess. It cannot be tested, for how can we know what dinosaurs tasted and what their livers could do? Livers don't fossilize any better than testicles.

The hypothesis doesn't even make any sense in its own context. Angiosperms were in full flower for ten million years before dinosaurs went the way of all flesh. Why did it take so long? As for the pains of a chemical death recorded in contortions of fossils, I regret to say (or rather I'm pleased to note for the dinosaur's sake) that Siegel's knowledge of geology must be a bit deficient: muscles contract after death and geological strata rise and fall with motions of the Earth's crust after burial—more than enough reason to distort a fossil's pristine appearance.

The impact story, on the other hand, has a sound basis in evidence. It can be tested, extended, refined and, if wrong, disproved. The Alvarezes did not just construct an arresting guess for public consumption. They proposed their hypothesis after laborious geochemical studies with Frank Asaro and Helen Michael had revealed a massive increase of iridium in rocks deposited right at the time of extinction. Iridium, a rare metal of the platinum group, is virtually absent from indigenous rocks of the Earth's crust; most of our iridium arrives on extraterrestrial objects that strike the Earth.

The Alvarez hypothesis bore immediate fruit. Based originally on evidence from two European localities, it led geochemists throughout the world to examine other sediments of the same age. They found abnormally high amounts of iridium everywhere—from continental rocks of the western United States to deep sea cores from the South Atlantic.

Cowles proposed his testicular hypothesis in the mid-1940s. Where has it gone since then? Absolutely nowhere, because scientists can do nothing with it. The hypothesis must stand as a curious appendage to a solid study of alligators. Siegel's overdose scenario will also win a few press notes and fade into oblivion. The Alvarezes' asteroid falls into a different category altogether, and much of the popular commentary has missed this essential distinction by focusing on the impact and its attendant results, and forgetting what really matters to a scientist—the iridium. If you talk just about asteroids, dust, and darkness, you tell stories no better and no more entertaining than fried testicles or terminal trips. It is the iridium—the source of testable evidence—that counts and forges the crucial distinction between speculation and science.

The proof, to twist a phrase, lies in the doing. Cowles's hypothesis has generated nothing in thirty-five years. Since its proposal in 1979, the Alvarez hypothesis has spawned hundreds of studies, a major conference, and attendant publications. Geologists are fired up. They are looking for iridium at all other extinction boundaries. Every week exposes a new wrinkle in the scientific press. Further evidence that the Cretaceous iridium represents extraterrestrial impact and not indigenous volcanism continues to accumulate. As I revise this essay in November 1984 (this paragraph will be out of date when the book is published), new data include chemical "signatures" of other isotopes indicating unearthly provenance, glass spherules of a size and sort produced by impact and not by volcanic eruptions, and high-pressure varieties of silica formed (so far as we know) only under the tremendous shock of impact.

My point is simply this: Whatever the eventual outcome (I suspect it will be positive), the Alvarez hypothesis is exciting, fruitful science because it generates tests, provides us with things to do, and expands outward. We are having fun, battling back and forth, moving toward a resolution, and extending the hypothesis beyond its original scope....

As just one example of the unexpected, distant cross-fertilization that good science engenders, the Alvarez hypothesis made a major contribution to a theme that has riveted public attention in the past few months—the so-called nuclear winter.... In a speech delivered in April 1982, Luis Alvarez calculated the energy that a ten-kilometer asteroid would release on impact. He compared such an explosion with a full nuclear exchange and implied that all-out atomic war might unleash similar consequences.

This theme of impact leading to massive dust clouds and falling temperatures formed an important input to the decision of Carl Sagan and a group of colleagues to model the climatic consequences of nuclear holocaust. Full nuclear exchange would probably generate the same kind of dust cloud and darkening that may have wiped out the dinosaurs. Temperatures would drop precipitously and agriculture might become impossible. Avoidance of nuclear war is fundamentally an ethical and political imperative, but we must know the factual consequences to make firm judgments. I am heartened by a final link across disciplines and deep concerns—another criterion, by the way, of science at its best: A recognition of the very phenomenon that made our

evolution possible by exterminating the previously dominant dinosaurs
and clearing a way for the evolution of large mammals, including us,
might actually help to save us from joining those magnificent beasts in
contorted poses among the strata of the Earth.

Are We Related to Other Life?
Paul Gomberg

This short paper is about evolution, particularly whether we humans
share common ancestry with other life. It is intended to introduce students to evolutionary thought and address some of the misunderstand-
ings that typically arise. Most important, it is intended to explain the
simple reasons for thinking we are related to other life. Whether you
choose to believe that we are related is a more complex issue.

WHAT IS EVOLUTION?

For well over a hundred and fifty years geologists have been aware
that the Earth's crust contains the remains of life that no longer exists.
These remains are called "fossils." Fossils are minerals in the shape of
living things. While everything that lives dies, most things disappear
without a trace, the living material often being consumed by predators
and scavengers and the remains dissolving as a result of the action of
micro-organisms. In some circumstances, however, there is insufficient
oxygen to support micro-organisms, and in those cases, through the
action of water, minerals can replace the organic material, particularly
teeth and bones, which disintegrate more slowly, but rarely some softer
tissue as well. This can lead to fossilization, particularly of aquatic life,
but occasionally of terrestrial and arboreal life as well.

Moreover, since the crust exists in layers and since, in most instances,
lower layers represent older life forms than higher layers (this idea is
called "the principle of superposition"), geologists have been aware
that there was a long history of life, older life forms disappearing from
the fossil record, newer life forms appearing only to disappear later.
Figure 2 is a representation of the geologic time scale.

The numerical values under the headings "Era," "Period," and
"Epoch" indicate the approximate ages of the various periods in millions
of years before the present. So, for example, the end of the Pliocene
and beginning of the Pleistocene was 1.6 million years ago, while the
origin of the Earth was 4,600 million (4.6 billion) years before the

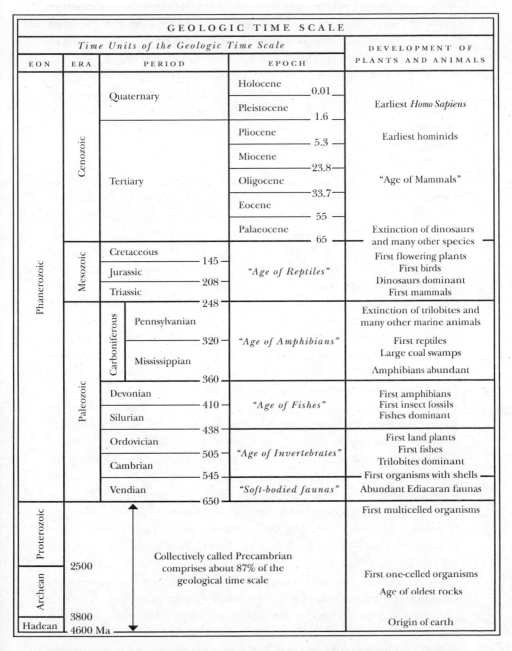

GEOLOGIC TIME SCALE					
Time Units of the Geologic Time Scale				DEVELOPMENT OF PLANTS AND ANIMALS	
EON	ERA	PERIOD	EPOCH		
Phanerozoic	Cenozoic	Quaternary	Holocene — 0.01 —	Earliest *Homo Sapiens*	
			Pleistocene — 1.6 —		
		Tertiary	Pliocene — 5.3 —	Earliest hominids	
			Miocene —23.8—	"Age of Mammals"	
			Oligocene —33.7—		
			Eocene — 55 —		
			Palaeocene — 65 —	Extinction of dinosaurs and many other species	
	Mesozoic	Cretaceous — 145 —	"Age of Reptiles"	First flowering plants First birds Dinosaurs dominant First mammals	
		Jurassic — 208 —			
		Triassic — 248 —			
	Paleozoic	Carboniferous — Pennsylvanian — 320 —	"Age of Amphibians"	Extinction of trilobites and many other marine animals First reptiles Large coal swamps Amphibians abundant	
		Mississippian — 360 —			
		Devonian — 410 —	"Age of Fishes"	First amphibians First insect fossils Fishes dominant	
		Silurian — 438 —			
		Ordovician — 505 —	"Age of Invertebrates"	First land plants First fishes Trilobites dominant First organisms with shells	
		Cambrian — 545 —			
		Vendian — 650 —	"Soft-bodied faunas"	Abundant Ediacaran faunas	
	Proterozoic	2500	Collectively called Precambrian comprises about 87% of the geological time scale	First multicelled organisms	
	Archean			First one-celled organisms Age of oldest rocks	
	Hadean	3800 4600 Ma		Origin of earth	

FIGURE 2. Geologic Time Scale, copyright Evolution for Teaching Website Project, Faculty of Science and Engineering, University of Waikato (New Zealand); reproduced with permission.

present. These ages are derived from dating techniques grounded in physical chemistry. Because some elements are radioactive, the rates of decay of radioisotopes or other such regular physical events can serve as a measure of time. The dates are approximate because the techniques are just that, techniques that give an estimate of a past time. When a number of dating techniques, tests, and samples converge on similar dates, we grow more confident in the accuracy of these dates. Recognition of the history of life is *not the same as evolution.* No one who seriously studies the fossil evidence denies that there has been a long history of life on Earth.

In the broadest sense the "theory of evolution" is really an area of study: how can the changes that we observe in Earth's life, as evidenced in fossils, be explained as the effects of natural processes, many of those processes still at work today? As an area of scientific study, evolution in this very broad sense is based on the assumption that changes can be explained by natural processes. The idea of evolution thus stands in contrast to the idea that a supernatural God *intervenes* in natural processes to cause things to happen that otherwise would not happen. The study of evolution is *not* incompatible with belief in God (for example, as Creator of the natural universe) but only with belief that God *intervenes* in the natural order to cause changes in life forms over time. This makes the study of evolution *exactly like every other natural science.* For example, we could not engage in the chemical study of reactions in test tubes unless we assume that we are studying natural reactions. If we believe that God *intervenes* in the processes we are observing so as to make things happen that would not happen by natural chemical processes alone, then we believe that those processes are beyond what chemistry, as a *natural* science, can study. So evolution, like every other natural science, assumes that there is a natural process to study and that there is no supernatural intervention in the phenomena studied.

Some may be puzzled that the study of evolution is criticized in a way that chemistry and physics are not. Why? Perhaps because Darwin and others revolutionized our conception of natural science. During Darwin's lifetime biology, chemistry, and physics were understood as studying only *contemporary* processes. Darwin's studies (and those of others), have led us to think of science in a different way: we can understand *long term change* from the way things were at one time to the way they were at a later time as a result of natural processes.[12] Science comes

12   The "others" are especially Karl Marx, a rough contemporary of Darwin, who proposed that the history of human society could be studied as a natural process,

to include *natural history*. This is a very profound change in our conception of natural science.

DOES EVOLUTION MAKE SENSE?

In this section I will explain why evolution (including the idea that
living things are related by common ancestry), makes sense to me and
should make sense to you. I will not at this point address whether you
should believe that living things share common ancestry. That can be
considered a separate question. Here I will only consider why the idea
makes sense. Consider the mammalian forelimbs depicted in figure 3.

These line drawings depict the bones in the forelimbs of seven mam-
mal species. In each species the bones occur in the same sequence, and
anatomists have given them the same names. Yet the shape and size of
the bones are very different in different species. How are both the differences and similarities to be understood?

This much should be clear: the different sizes and configurations of
these bones enable the forelimbs of these mammals to be used in ways
that these limbs are needed in the lives of the animals. For example,
the size and shape of the elephant's forelimb enable the elephant to
walk and support its bulk; bones shaped like those in a bat's forelimbs,
regardless of their size, could not support the weight of an elephant.
Nor would the bones of any of the other mammals' forelimbs enable
a bat to fly. So the bony anatomy of these mammals' forelimbs is well
suited for the use these animals make of their forelimbs. In that sense,
their bony anatomy is well *adapted*. In this way it makes sense that these
bones are different.

But how are we to understand the *similarities*? Why should all these
species have the same bones in the same sequence? Consider this *possibility*: suppose that 200 million years ago there was a small population (a
gene pool, a group of organisms that reproduced with one another) of
mammals and that all modern mammals are descendants of this ancestral population. Would it make sense to you that their descendants 200
million years later would share similarities yet be very different?

---

and Edwin Hubble, whose discovery of the red shift of light from distant galaxies in
the 1920s led to a change in our understanding of the subject matter of astrophysics: long term changes in the natural universe could be understood as the result of
natural processes; most of us know this idea through the prevailing theory of the
earliest universe, "big bang" cosmology.

BAT

MOLE

TREE SHREW

Fulcrom

HUMAN

WOLF

ELEPHANT

SEA LION

Scapula (*a*)   Carpals (*e*)
Humerus (*b*)   Metacarpals (*f*)
Radius (*c*)   Phalanges (*g*)
Ulna (*d*)

Fatty pad

FIGURE 3. Mammalian Forelimbs. Drawings from Adrienne Zihlman, *The Human Evolution Coloring Book*: Copyright 2000 2nd edition, Harper/Collins. Reproduced by
permission of Adrienne Zihlman.

Consider what we know about sexual reproduction: when sexually
reproducing organisms mate and produce offspring, their offspring are
like their parents, but not exactly like them. Given that sexual reproduction preserves similarities, it makes sense that distant descendants
would still share some similarities. Given that sexual reproduction
allows differences to emerge, it makes sense that distant descendants
could be very different from one another. Thus the hypothesis of common ancestry makes sense of the similarities we observe in mammalian
forelimbs and allows for their differences.[13]

13   The present paper is only an introduction to evolutionary thought. Darwin
proposed that the ways that the parts of organisms enhance their survival and reproduction might be explained as an effect of *natural selection*, analogous to the artificial
selection used in animal husbandry and in creating new plant cultivars. Natural

Is there another way of understanding why the mammalian forelimbs would be similar? Here I suggest that if you think there is, you try out your ideas and see if your explanation makes sense of why these particular animals would share anatomical structures despite the very different specifics of bone shape and size and the very different ways in which these animals use their forelimbs. Insect wings enable flight through very different structures. The wings of birds, like bat's wings, are based on a bony structure, but they do not involve the same bony anatomy as the mammals share. Why would mammalian bony anatomy be more similar than that of birds and bats? I would conclude that the supposition of common ancestry makes sense of why mammalian forelimbs are similar and that no other hypothesis can make sense of it—at least none makes sense of it *to me*. You must decide for yourself whether this supposition makes sense of it *to you*.

Someone may agree that the hypothesis of common ancestry among mammals makes sense but still not think it is *true* that we share common ancestry. I acknowledge this possibility.

Even an introductory exposition should say more about how common ancestry makes sense of relatedness. Consider the primate hands represented in figure 4:

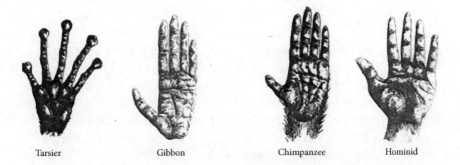

| Tarsier | Gibbon | Chimpanzee | Hominid |

FIGURE 4. Primate Hands. Copyright 1981 Luba D. Gudz from *Lucy: The Beginnings of Humankind* (D.C. Johanson and M.A. Edey). Reproduced by permission of Luba D. Gudz.

---

selection is simply the idea that, in natural conditions, some variants within a population would give the organisms that had those variants an advantage in the struggle to survive and reproduce. To explain the origin of *species*, yet other hypotheses are needed, specifically that populations become sufficiently reproductively isolated that speciation can occur. This reproductive isolation could occur for geographic reasons. There is a lot more to evolutionary theory than the small part I explain in this paper.

These are hands of a tarsier, gibbon, chimpanzee, and hominid (humans and similar species—modern humans are the only surviving hominids). While our hands share certain similarities with paws of a dog or cat—the common mammalian bony structure of metacarpals and phalanges as well as nails of a sort—our hands are more similar to the hand of a gibbon (a small ape of Asia superbly adapted to swinging through trees by its arms) than to the paw of a dog and even more similar to the hand of chimpanzee. And the fingernails are also quite similar. Why would that be? If we shared common ancestry with a gibbon which was much more recent than our common ancestry with a dog, the relative recentness (perhaps within the last 15-20 million years) of common ancestry with a gibbon would make sense of our greater similarity. And if our common ancestry with a chimpanzee was yet more recent (perhaps 7 million years ago), that would explain why we are more like chimpanzees than we are like gibbons. So the idea of common ancestry —and of how recent common ancestry might be—allows us to make sense of greater and lesser *degrees* of similarity.

What is true of visible similarities is also true at a molecular level. We share enormous genetic similarity with chimpanzees—98% of the genetic material is identical. We share lesser degrees of genetic similarity with organisms that we appear less like. All of these degrees of similarity in both apparent and molecular characteristics can be understood in terms of more recent and more remote common ancestry: we are more like the organisms with which we share more recent common ancestry. This makes sense of what we can observe.

When I say that the hypotheses of common ancestry of organisms that are similar and of more recent common ancestry of organisms that are more similar "make sense," do I mean only that they make sense to me or that they should make sense to you as well? I believe they should make sense to you. Here is why. These hypotheses employ a principle which you *already accept* and apply in other instances. For you already accept the idea that folks who are more closely related look more alike and are alike in other ways. You already accept the idea that we can test for paternity by investigating whether the baby's DNA sequences are more similar to those of one possible father than to those of another. So the hypotheses of common ancestry and of more recent common ancestry for organisms that are more similar is just employing a principle that you already accept. Admittedly, these hypotheses apply that principle to longer periods of time—tens of thousands, hundreds of thousands, millions, and even billions of years—and that these time spans boggle our minds. And they apply that common sense principle to data—people's DNA—that is not accessible to most of us. But the principle is a common sense principle that you accept. So I believe that using the idea of common ancestry to explain similarities and of more recent common ancestry to explain greater similarities should make sense to you.

So we seem to have a way of making sense of the things we can observe and know, a way that involves hypotheses about relatedness in the distant past. And we don't seem to have another way of understanding why organisms are similar and dissimilar that makes sense. Should we believe it true that we are related to other life? I suggest that we should believe it in the following spirit: "I will accept my relatedness to other life as fact because it makes sense of what I can observe; it is worth believing until I have a better way of making sense of it." Shortly I will suggest that the case for relatedness may be stronger than that.

So far in this paper I have tried to explain some central ideas in evolutionary thought (notably I have not tried to explain natural selection), why I thought they made sense to me, and why, therefore, they seem worthy of being believed to be true. In the rest of the paper I will answer some objections I have heard from students. In answering these objections, the idea of evolution should become clearer.

OBJECTION: EVOLUTION IS JUST A THEORY

Evolution, at the very general level at which I have described it, is certainly a theory. Let us say that a theory is a conceptual structure that organizes and makes sense of disparate phenomena. To say that something is *just* a theory is to say that it does not do this very well and therefore we are free to either believe it or not believe it. I would not say that the theory of evolution is *just* a theory.

The periodic table of the elements is also a theory. That theory hypothesizes deep structures of the various elements: a hydrogen atom consists of a nucleus with one proton and, outside the nucleus, one electron in an energy state; the other elements are hypothesized to have different deep structures. Why suppose that they really do have the hypothesized deep structures? Those models of their atomic structures enable us to understand why elements interact with other elements as they do and sometimes form stable compounds. Without the periodic table of the elements as an organizing theory no chemical interactions or compound formations would make any sense. We would have no understanding of *why* interactions occur as they do.

I believe the case is the same with evolution. Evolution is an organizing theory, like the periodic table of the elements. Without the evolutionary hypothesis, *none of the phenomena would make any sense.* (For those of you who, like me, found high school biology taught without the theory of evolution to be incredibly boring, now you know why. You were deprived of the theory that would allow you to make sense of and give organization to the phenomena you were studying.) So you have the same reason to believe that evolution occurred as you have to believe that matter indeed has the deep structure hypothesized in the periodic table: it allows you to make sense of the world you can observe.

Of course, there are differences. The periodic table explains and makes connections through hypotheses of deep structure; evolution makes sense of things through hypotheses about *history*.[14] There are other differences as well. The hypothesized deep structures lend relatively great precision to explanations in chemistry. The hypotheses about relatedness are often stated with a great deal more tentativeness; it is difficult to reconstruct the distant past with precision. Nevertheless, as an organizing theory, only hypotheses about how living things are related allow us to understand why biological phenomena are organized as they are.

OBJECTION: I AM NOT DESCENDED FROM A MONKEY

Well, no one said you were. The hypothesis, based on such similarities as that monkeys have hands, is that we share more recent common ancestry with monkeys than we share with mammals which are not primates. If humans and monkeys shared common ancestry, then contemporary monkeys are just as removed in time from the common ancestor as humans are. And the same goes for the more recent common ancestor between humans and chimpanzees. "But," you might say, "that common ancestor looked and acted a lot more like a chimpanzee than it did like a human." According to the evidence we have, that may be true, and even the earliest bipedal (upright walking) hominids were probably, in many behaviors, more like chimpanzees than they were like modern humans. It is the line that led to *modern* humanity which has undergone the most profound changes, not just

---

14   Elliott Sober reminded me of this disanalogy.

bipedalism, but changes in sexuality, development of complex social structures based on bringing food to a central place to share, and eventually the development of articulate speech.

OBJECTION: IF WE ARE GENETICALLY SIMILAR TO CHIMPANZEES, WHY ARE WE SO DIFFERENT?

This is not an objection but a great question, an important puzzle. If it is raised as an *objection*, then the person who raises it must think that unless a theory explains everything, it is not worthy of being believed. But this is to misunderstand the nature of inquiry. The same person who insists on complete understanding of every question when considering evolution, would take a different approach in understanding the behavior of, for example, a teenage child with whom she was having difficulty. She may come to realize that her child is being drawn to a group at school whose values are very different from those of the child's home. Knowing that would explain a lot about the child's behavior. But it leads to further questions: why is she drawn to that group? What needs does this group meet for her? The fact that this explanation leads to further questions is not a reason to reject it. That also should not be a problem in evolution or any other science. It is true everywhere that with every answer there are new questions. That is just the nature of inquiry and of our way of gaining greater understanding.

However, it is a good question why, with only a small difference in genes, there is such a great difference in appearance and behavior between humans and chimpanzees. This is a cutting edge problem in genetics. It is now widely believed that some genes control the operation of other genes; these are sometimes called "control genes." Much current research concerns how they work. In understanding those genes we may come to understand more about how humans may have evolved from non-human ancestors and how later species of humans may have evolved from earlier species.

OBJECTION: WHAT WILL WE EVOLVE INTO?

This objection involves another misunderstanding of what the theory of evolution is about. It is about the past, not the future. Suppose we had an adequate theory of the evolution of many living things. Would that theory then enable us to predict future biological change? There is no reason why it should. Our understanding of the past and of all the factors that went into past biological change is bound to be incomplete. So the theory will have nothing to say about the future—or very little.

Here is another way of seeing why the theory cannot explain the future: does the theory of evolution imply that, within the next five years, there will not be an extraterrestrial impact so great as to wipe out all complex animal life? It couldn't possibly have that implication. Therefore, it cannot possibly predict the future. There are too many contingencies which it is impossible for us to know, and extraterrestrial impact is only one obvious possibility.

CONCLUSION

In this brief paper I have tried to introduce you to the theory of evolution and give some reason to believe that we are related to other living things. Some of you may not be persuaded that this theory is true. If, however, the paper has stimulated you to think about the issues more and inquire further, it will have achieved its purpose.

From "The Perplexing Case of the Female Orgasm"[15]
Elisabeth Lloyd with Natasha Mitchell

NATASHA MITCHELL: It seems pretty clear to science why the male orgasm came to be. But evolutionary biologists, even women among their ranks, have struggled to explain the biological purpose of the female orgasm, and one of them has just thrown a spanner in the works. She's rigorously reviewed 21 of the major theories in her new book *The Case of the Female Orgasm: Bias in Evolutionary Science.*

A collaborator with the late great Stephen Jay Gould, Professor Elisabeth Lloyd is a well-respected evolutionary theorist. She holds the Arnold and Maxine Tanis Chair of History and Philosophy of Science at the University of Indiana, where she's also Professor of Biology.

And she's reignited one hell of a fiery debate. Could the female orgasm be like the male nipple—a mere byproduct without an evolutionary purpose?

---

15   This interview is an extract from *All in the Mind*, "The Perplexing Case of the Female Orgasm," first published by ABC Online, 24 December 2005, and is reproduced by permission of the Australian Broadcasting Corporation and ABC Online. Copyright 2005 ABC. All rights reserved. In editing the show's transcript I left out an interview with someone who disagreed with Lloyd.

Professor Elisabeth Lloyd, thanks for joining me on the program this week.

ELISABETH LLOYD: Thank you very much. Women come in all these different flavors of whether they're very orgasmic or whether they're not orgasmic at all. That kind of variation, that range of variation is just what you would expect if the trait of orgasm were not serving an evolutionary function, because if female orgasm were under the pressure of selection, then those women with orgasm would have relatively more children and over many generations, the population would consist of more and more women being orgasmic...

NATASHA MITCHELL: Having more and more orgasms...

ELISABETH LLOYD: Yes, and women who did not have orgasm and women who rarely did would become extinct, but that's not what we find.

NATASHA MITCHELL: I guess it's perplexed people partly, too, because women don't need an orgasm to become pregnant, and so the question is: well, what's its purpose? Well, is its purpose to give us pleasure so that we have sex, so that we can become pregnant, according to the classic evolutionary theories?

ELISABETH LLOYD: The problem is even worse than it appears at first because not only is orgasm not necessary on the female side to become pregnant, there isn't even any evidence that orgasm makes any difference at all to fertility, or pregnancy rate, or reproductive success. It seems intuitive that a female orgasm would motivate females to engage in intercourse which would naturally lead to more pregnancies or help with bonding or something like that, but the evidence simply doesn't back that up.

NATASHA MITCHELL: Now just a reminder here of what it means for a trait to be an adaptation or to be *selected for* over evolutionary time.

It's all about optimizing our reproductive success. So take the anteater for example. Its long tongue is described as an "adaptation." Their distant ancestors were rather like armadillos with short tongues. But anteaters with longer tongues found more ants and so were able to better survive to have more, and healthier, offspring. So, more of their genes successfully made it into the next generations and, over thousands of years, the long tongue was selected for.

ELISABETH LLOYD: So we carry that over to the female orgasm case. The claim is that females who experienced orgasm had more children than those women who didn't experience orgasm, and that over evolutionary time, those women who had orgasm became more common in the population than those women who didn't have orgasm. Or, in some of the more subtle explanations, women who sometimes did and sometimes didn't have orgasm, depending on the quality of the male, would become prevalent in the population and that orgasm evolved in order to do that, sort of a signaling device for the quality of the male—and that's why orgasm exists in the human [female] population.

NATASHA MITCHELL: Look, on the other hand there seems to be very little debate about the evolutionary explanation for why men have an orgasm.

ELISABETH LLOYD: You know, perhaps there should be more debate about this. I give this completely short shrift in my book, but the basic understanding about male orgasm is that male orgasm is tied to male ejaculation, and a male orgasm is the pleasurable response to male ejaculation, which motivates the man to impregnate females, which obviously gets his genes into the next generation—and therefore it would be strongly selected for in males.

NATASHA MITCHELL: Some women would say, "well why should I really care about what evolutionary science has to tell me about my orgasm, thank you very much?" But I guess the female orgasm is really a crucial subject because we all have an investment in it. But your suggestion, too, is that explanations rooted in evolutionary science have a very palpable impact on contemporary women's lives.

ELISABETH LLOYD: And if you take Desmond Morris and *The Naked Ape*, you can see the widespread influence of this kind of account. We hear stories of our evolutionary past and we think about them and we think, "ah, that's how human beings are meant to be, that's how human beings are naturally." And we sort of layer on our civilization on top of that. Women hear stories about what a natural female orgasm is like. Nearly all of those stories include an account of how it's, for example, natural for her to have orgasm during intercourse. Now, this is very odd, because it's been known for 70 years in sex research that the percentage of women who reliably have orgasm with intercourse is around 25 per cent.

NATASHA MITCHELL: You've really unpicked the data there too, haven't you, to test the logic of the various evolutionary theories for the female orgasm.

ELISABETH LLOYD: One of the things that leaps out at you about these findings on orgasm with intercourse is that really only about 25 per cent of women reliably have orgasm with intercourse, and that even includes the women who self-stimulate their clitorises during intercourse or have their partners do it. About a third, a full third rarely or never have orgasm during intercourse. That's a lot of women. The rest of the women sometimes do and sometimes don't, and so these evolutionary accounts time after time after time tell the story that when the female has intercourse, then she has an orgasm and that's how it should go and that's what she evolved to do. That's three out of four women who are then painted as being abnormal, unnatural, and dysfunctional.

NATASHA MITCHELL: But some scientists have pointed to, to get around this they've said perhaps in our ancestral environment women had more frequent and reliable orgasms, it's just today that we're not, you know, having as many orgasms in intercourse. Others have suggested that the orgasm is a relatively recent adaptation. It's not fully sculpted yet and so that's why we don't sort of see it in its fully fledged operation all the time across the whole population—but we might one day.

ELISABETH LLOYD: I think that the recent adaptation argument can work, except that unfortunately, again, there's no association between orgasm and fertility—so any adaptive argument has got to overcome that. The old, you know, "back in the olden days we used to be more orgasmic" story is a bit kinky. I mean, what was it, were the Paleolithic men better lovers or...? I actually had a guy one time when I was speaking stand up and say, "back then women weren't so neurotic and professional." I mean this is very funny. But two of the authors that I consider in the book actually did propose that.

NATASHA MITCHELL: The first theory, I gather, for an evolutionary model of the female orgasm arrived on the scene in the mid-60s; that was Desmond Morris. He came up with some fairly curious conclusions, didn't he?

ELISABETH LLOYD: Yes, well, I think Desmond Morris may be most famous for his, what I dubbed his "anti-gravity" theory. This theory says that women are orgasmic so that they're satiated after orgasm and they'll be so tired after orgasm with intercourse that they'll keep lying down on their backs so that the sperm don't leak out. You can count the assumptions in that theory just for fun, but the problem is that—one is that it's men who are most likely to fall asleep after orgasm, as we all kind of know; another problem is that it's established that women are more likely to have orgasm with intercourse when they're on top of the man, which seems to go directly against the anti-gravity theory.

NATASHA MITCHELL: He also points, though, to the orgasm also being a pleasurable motivation for sex, and this sort of gave way to a whole group of theories called the "pair-bond account" of the female orgasm, didn't it?

ELISABETH LLOYD: Oh yes, in fact 11 of the theories that I looked at were variations of the pair-bond account and basically all of them said orgasm was a reward for the female to engage in intercourse, because if she engaged in intercourse, the orgasm would reward her and engaging in intercourse helps cement the pair-bond and the pair-bond was good for all sorts of reasons. Like, it helped with the rearing of the offspring and it kept men from competing with each other because they had to cooperate on the hunt, and there were lots of reasons that the pair-bond was seen as adaptive.

NATASHA MITCHELL: And that is certainly widely accepted by men and women scientists across the board.

ELISABETH LLOYD: It may well turn out that there's some aspect of pair-bonding which is adaptive and that orgasm is related to it. Some of these oxytocin studies about bonding—oxytocin is a hormone and it's known to be released with female orgasm, although the level of its release varies very widely. In other animals, oxytocin has been implicated in bonding. It isn't established in humans.

The big problem with it is that nearly all of the pair-bond accounts explicitly equate the occurrence of intercourse with the occurrence of orgasm—and again we're back to that set of statistics about the infrequency of female orgasm with intercourse. You know, you can't say that female orgasm evolved because it was the female reward for intercourse.

NATASHA MITCHELL: What is the evolutionary purpose of the female orgasm? Well the most popular contemporary explanation for the female orgasm goes by the name of the *sperm up-suck theory*, yes indeed. The suggestion here is that the uterus sucks semen up through the cervix and this helps women unconsciously select, via orgasm, which male fertilizes them.

There's been some extraordinary studies to probe this, the most famous by Robin Baker and Mark Bellis, but Elisabeth Lloyd has closely scrutinized these too, and isn't convinced by their scientific rigor. Sexual dysfunction aside, this is dysfunctional science, she says.

ELISABETH LLOYD: The problem with the Baker and Bellis study, and it's fatal, is that the statistics are hopeless. Three-quarters of the data used to support some of the conclusions came from one woman.

NATASHA MITCHELL: Elisabeth Lloyd, you've looked at 21 theories or so all up of evolutionary explanations of the female orgasm, and you remain unconvinced by all of them but one possible option—and that is that the female orgasm has no evolutionary purpose at all. You're convinced by one particular person's study. You reckon that it's a bit like the male nipple, a mere by-product.

ELISABETH LLOYD: Donald Symons proposed long ago, in 1979, the female orgasm is basically a developmental by-product of selection on the male orgasm.

Male and female embryos share the same basic female body plan during the first two months of life in the uterus, and during that period the nerve and tissue pathways for orgasm get laid down—basically because the males need orgasm in order to impregnate the female and reproduce successfully and to reward them for doing so. But because the females share the basic body plan, they get the same nerve pathways and so they can have orgasms too, but there's no relation to reproductive success that has been established. So they seem to be just for free.

It is just like the male nipple. Females need nipples in order to reproduce successfully and because the females are laid down, again, in the same basic body plan for the first two months of life, the males get them even though they're not necessary for male reproduction. So the parallel is exact—males get nipples because females need them and females get orgasms because males need them.

NATASHA MITCHELL: What's the evidence that convinces you of this theory, or is it just the case that there's no evidence for all the other theories that convinces you enough?

ELISABETH LLOYD: No, no. This is often the accusation, actually, by the adaptationists, that believing in this theory is like giving up on adaptation. But that's not it at all. I mean, take the masturbation data, for example. I mean virtually no, basically one per cent, possibly, of females masturbate by imitating the act of intercourse. Everybody else masturbates by stimulating the clitoris either directly or indirectly. Now if female sexuality were oriented around reproductive sex, you'd expect females to masturbate imitating reproductive sex but they just don't. Symons' by-product view actually explained the things about female sexuality that are really quite mysterious on all of the adaptive views.

NATASHA MITCHELL: So the idea really is that the orgasm is there to give us pleasure and little more than that. I guess the concern is that if the female orgasm isn't an adaptation, then some people have said that, okay, it doesn't have an evolutionary purpose, then why does nature bother with it at all? There's a risk that it could be phased out altogether over time through natural selection because of this.

ELISABETH LLOYD: Under this view there is no danger at all of losing female orgasm.

NATASHA MITCHELL: But it doesn't have a purpose.

ELISABETH LLOYD: Yes, but under the by-product view, male orgasm is very strongly selected, and when male orgasm is selected, the nerve pathways are ensured and when the nerve pathways are ensured in the male, they're also ensured in the female, because we share their basic body plan. We're not going to lose them, we're guaranteed to have them because the males are so strongly selected to have them.

NATASHA MITCHELL: You talk about male bias in evolutionary science but other feminist thinkers and scientists haven't been especially taken by your conclusion that the female orgasm is simply a by-product of the male orgasm, because your argument effectively suggests that the female orgasm is in a sense a useless anomaly in our evolutionary history, that it really just exists because the male orgasm exists, but it's the male orgasm that's really important for the continuation of our species.

ELISABETH LLOYD: Yes.

NATASHA MITCHELL: And then some have pointed to the fact that this is a denial of the significance of female pleasure.

ELISABETH LLOYD: My response to that is that it's a big mistake to think that cultural significance depends on evolution. Our culture and society decide what's important and that's the way it should be. Take reading, for example, or operating a computer, these are of paramount importance in our culture and they're certainly not products of selection or adaptation. Evolution doesn't tell us what's important in our culture and I don't think it should.

NATASHA MITCHELL: You point to the fact that these theories have an impact on women's lives today in very real ways. And one example that you give, the use of the *sperm up-suck theory*, that orgasm helps women suck sperm, so to speak, and you report that some fertility clinics routinely encourage women to masturbate to orgasm after artificial insemination. Is that true?

ELISABETH LLOYD: Yes. I have every reason to think that's true. In fact the by-product view of female orgasm could be seen as quite a positive view for women. This view might be used to help argue that, well, women's sexuality really shouldn't be defined purely in terms of reproduction. Female sexuality is not just for reproductive purposes. This aspect of women's sexuality doesn't seem to be tied so closely to reproduction at all.

"The Health of Black Folk: Disease, Class, and Ideology in Science"[16]

Nancy Krieger and Mary Bassett

Since the first crude tabulations of vital statistics in colonial America, one stark fact has stood out: black Americans are sicker and die younger than whites. As the epidemic infectious diseases of the nineteenth century were vanquished, the black burden of ill health shifted to the modern killers: heart disease, stroke, and cancer. Today black men under age 45 are ten times more likely to die from the effects of high blood pressure than white men. Black women suffer twice as many heart attacks as white women. A variety of common cancers are more frequent among blacks—and of cancer victims, blacks succumb sooner after diagnosis than whites. Black infant mortality is twice that of whites. All told, if the mortality rates for blacks and other minorities today were the same in the United States as for whites, more than 60,000 deaths in minority communities could be avoided each year.

What is it about being black that causes such miserable odds? One answer is the patently racist view that blacks are inherently more susceptible to disease—the genetic model. In contrast, environmental models depict blacks as victims of factors ranging from poor nutrition and germs to lack of education and crowded housing. Initially formulated as an alternative to the genetic model by liberals and much of the Left, the environmental view has now gained new support from the Right and becomes a major prop for Reagan administration health policies: instead of blaming the victims' genes, these conservatives blame black lifestyle choices as the source of the racial gap in health.

We will argue that these analytic models are seriously flawed, in essence as well as application. They are not the product of a racist use of allegedly "neutral" science, but reflect the ways in which ideology and politics penetrate scientific theory and research. Typically, they deny or obscure that the primary source of black/white health disparities is the social production of disease under conditions of capitalism and racial oppression. The "facts of being black" are not, as these models suggest, a genetically determined shade of skin color, or individual deprived living conditions, or ill-informed lifestyle choices. The facts of being black derive from the joint social relations of race and class: racism

16   This article was originally published in *Monthly Review* (July-August 1986).. Reproduced by permission of *Monthly Review*.

disproportionately concentrates blacks into the lower strata of the working class and further causes blacks in all class strata to be racially oppressed. It is the Left's challenge to incorporate this political reality into how we approach racial differences in health.

Despite overwhelming evidence to the contrary, the theory that "race" is primarily a biological category and that black-white differences in health are genetically determined continues to exert profound influence on both medical thinking and popular ideology. For example, an editorial on racial differences in birth weight (an important determinant of infant mortality) in the January 1986 *Journal of the American Medical Association* concluded: "Finally, what are the biologic or genetic differences among racial or ethnic groups? Should we shrink from the possibility of a biologic/genetic influence?" Similarly, a 1983 handbook prepared by the International Epidemiologic Association defined "race" as "persons who are relatively homogeneous with respect to biological inheritance." Public health texts continue to enshrine "race" in the demographic triad of "age, race, and sex," implying that "race" is as biologically fundamental a predictor of health as aging or sex, while the medical literature remains replete with studies that examine racial differences in health without regard to class.

The genetic model rests on three basic assumptions, all of which are flawed: that "race" is a valid biological category; that the genes which determine "race" are linked to the genes which affect health; and that the health of any community is mainly the consequence of the genetic constitutions of the individuals of which it is composed. In contrast, we will argue that the health of the black community is not simply the sum of the health of individuals who are "genetically black" but instead chiefly reflects the social forces which create racially oppressed communities in the first place.

It is of course true that skin color, hair texture, and other visible features used to identify "race" are genetically encoded—there is a biologic aspect to "race." The importance of these particular physical traits in the spectrum of human variation, however, has been determined historically and politically. People also differ in terms of stature and eye color, but these attributes are rarely accorded significance. Categories based primarily on skin color correlate with health because race is a powerful determinant of the location and life-destinies of individuals within the class structure of U.S. society. Ever since plantation owners realized that differences in skin color could serve as a readily identifiable and permanent marker for socially determined divisions of labor (black runaway slaves were easier to identify than escaped white indentured servants and convicts, the initial workforce of colonial America), race and class have been inextricably intertwined. "Race" is not a natural descriptive category, but a social category born of the antagonistic relation of white supremacy and black oppression. The basis of the relative health advantage of whites is not to be found in their genes but in the relative material advantage whites enjoy as a consequence of political prerogative and state power. As Richard Lewontin has pointed out, "If, after a great cataclysm, only Africans were left alive, the human species would have retained 93 percent of its total genetic variation, although the species as a whole would be darker skinned." The fact that we all know which race we belong to says more about our society than about our biology.

Nevertheless, the paradigm of a genetic basis for black ill health remains strong. In its defense, researchers repeatedly trot out the few diseases for which a clear-cut link of race is established: sickle cell anemia, G&PD deficiency, and lactose intolerance. These diseases, however, have a tiny impact on the health of the black population as a whole—if anything, even less than those few diseases linked to "whiteness," such as some forms of skin cancer. Richard Cooper has shown that of the tens of thousands of excess black deaths in 1977, only 277 (0.3 percent) could be attributed to diseases such as sickle cell anemia. Such uncommon genetic maladies have become important strictly because of their metaphoric value: they are used to support genetic explanations of racial differences in the "big diseases" of the twentieth century—heart disease, stroke, and cancer. Yet no current evidence exists to justify such an extrapolation.

Determined nonetheless to demonstrate the genetic basis of racial health differences, investigators today—like their peers in the past—use the latest techniques. Where once physicians compared cranial capacity to explain black/white inequalities, now they scrutinize surface markers of cells. The case of hypertension is particularly illustrative. High blood pressure is an important cause of strokes and heart attacks, contributing to about 30 percent of all deaths in the United States. At present, the black rate of hypertension in the United States is about twice that of whites. Of over five hundred recent medical journal articles on the topic, fewer than a dozen studies explored social factors. The rest instead unsuccessfully sought biochemical/genetic explanations—and of these, virtually none even attempted to "define" genetically who was "white" and who was "black," despite the alleged genetic nature of their enquiry. As a consequence of the wrong questions being asked, the causes of hypertension remain unknown. Nonetheless, numerous clues point to social factors. Hypertension does not exist in several undisrupted hunter/gatherer tribes of different "races" but rapidly emerges in these tribes after contact with industrial society; in the United States, lower social class begets higher blood pressure.

Turning to cancer, the authors of a recent major government report surmised that blacks have poorer survival rates than whites because they do not "exhibit the same immunologic reactions to cancerous processes." It is noteworthy, however, that the comparably poor survival rates of British breast cancer patients have never elicited such speculation. In our own work on breast cancer in Washington state, we found that the striking "racial" difference in survival evaporated when we took class into account: working-class women, whether black or white, die sooner than women of higher social class standing.

To account for the persistence of the genetic model, we must look to its political significance rather than its scientific content. First used to buttress biblical arguments for slavery in a period when science was beginning to replace religion as sanction for the status quo, the genetic model of racial differences in health emerged toward the end of the eighteenth century, long before any precise theory of heredity existed. In well-respected medical journals, doctors debated whether blacks and whites were even the same species (let alone race), and proclaimed that blacks were intrinsically suited to slavery, thrived in hot climates, succumbed less to the epidemic fevers which ravaged the South, and suffered extraordinary rates of insanity if allowed to live free. After the Civil War effectively settled the argument about whether blacks belonged to the human species, physicians and scientists began elaborating hereditarian theories to explain the disparate health profiles not only of blacks and whites, but of the different white "races"— as defined by national origin and immigrant status. Virtually every scourge, from TB to rickets, was postulated to be inherited. Rheumatic fever, now known to be due to strep bacteria combined with the poverty which permits its expression in immunocompromised[17] malnourished people, was long believed to be linked with the red hair and pale

---

17   [Meaning that the immune system is not working as it should. PG]

complexions of its Irish working-class victims. Overall, genetic explanations of differences in disease rates have politically served to justify existing class relations and excuse socially created afflictions as a result of immutable biology.

Nowadays the genetic model—newly dressed in the language of molecular genetics—continues to divert attention from the class origin of disease. Genetic explanations absolve the state of responsibility for the health profile of black America by declaring racial disparities (regrettably) inevitable and normal. Intervention efforts based on this model founder for obvious reasons: short of recombinant DNA therapies, genetic screening and selective reproduction stand as supposed tools to reduce the racial gap in health.

Unfortunately, the genetic model wields influence even within the progressive health movement, as illustrated by the surge of interest in sickle cell anemia in the early 1970s. For decades after its initial description in 1925, sickle cell anemia was relegated to clinical obscurity. It occurs as often in blacks as does cystic fibrosis in whites. By linking genetic uniqueness to racial pride, such groups as the Black Panther Party championed sickle cell anemia as the number one health issue among blacks, despite the fact that other health problems—such as infant mortality—took a much greater toll. Because the sickle cell gene provides some protection against malaria, sickle cell seemed to link blacks to their African past, now three centuries removed. It raised the issue of racist neglect of black health in a setting where the victims were truly blameless: the fault lay in their genes. From the point of view of the federal government, sickle cell anemia was a uniquely black disease which did not raise the troubling issues of the ongoing oppression of the black population. In a period of political turmoil, what more could the government ask for? Small wonder that President Nixon jumped on the bandwagon and called for a national crusade.

THE ENVIRONMENTAL MODEL

The genetic model's long history and foundations in the joint race and class divisions of our society assure its continued prominence in discussions on the racial gap in health. To rebut this model, many liberals and progressives have relied upon environmental models of disease causation—only to encounter the Right on this turf as well.

Whereas the rise of slavery called forth genetic models of diseases, environmental models were born of the antagonistic social relations of industrial capitalism. In the appalling filth of nineteenth-century cities, tuberculosis, typhus, and infant diarrhea were endemic in the newly forming working class; periodically, epidemics of yellow fever and cholera would attack the entire populace. A sanitary reform movement arose, advocating cleaner cities (with sewer systems and pure water) to protect the wellbeing of the wealthy as well as the poor, and also to engender a healthier, more productive workforce.

In the United States, most of the reformers were highly moralistic and staunchly procapitalist, seeing poverty and squalor as consequences of individual intemperance and ignorance rather than as necessary correlates of capital accumulation. In Europe, where the working-class movement was stronger, a class-conscious wing of the sanitary reform movement emerged. Radicals such as Frederick Engels and Rudolph Virchow (later the founder of modern pathology) argued that poverty and ill health could only be eliminated by resolving the antagonistic class relations of capitalism.

The early sanitary reform movement in the United States rarely addressed the question of racial differences in health per se. In fact, environmental models to explain black/white disparities emerged only during the mid-twentieth century, a consequence of the urban migration of blacks from the rural South to the industrial North and the rise of the civil-rights movement.

Today's liberal version of the environmental model blames poverty for black ill health. The noxious features of the "poverty environment" are catalogued and decried—lead paint from tenement walls, toxins from work, even social features like discrimination. But as in most liberal analyses, the unifying cause of this litany of woes remains unstated. We are left with an apparently unconnected laundry list of problems and no explanation of why blacks as a group encounter similar sickening conditions.

The liberal view fetishizes the environment: individuals are harmed by inanimate objects, physical forces, or unfortunate social conditions (like poverty)—by things rather than by people. That these objects or social circumstances are the creations of society is hidden by the veil of "natural science." Consequently, the "environment" is viewed as a natural and neutral category, defined as all that is external to individuals. What is not seen is the ways in which the underlying structure of racial oppression and class exploitation—which are relationships among people, not between people and things—shape the "environments" of the groups created by these relations.

The debilitating disease pellagra serves as a concrete example. Once a major health problem of poor southern farm and mill laborers in the United States, pellagra was believed to be a genetic disease. By the early 1920s, however, Joseph Goldberger had proved that the disease stemmed from a dietary deficiency in niacin and had also demonstrated that pellagra's familial nature existed because of the inheritance of nutritional options, not genes. Beyond this, Goldberger argued that pellagra, in essence, was a social disease caused by the single cash-crop economy of the South: reliance on cotton ensured seasonal starvation as food ran out between harvests, as well as periodic epidemics when the cotton market collapsed. Southern workers contracted pellagra because they had limited diets—and they had limited diets because they were southern workers. Yet governmental response was simply to supplement food with niacin: according to this view, vitamin deficiency—not socially determined malnutrition—was the chief cause of pellagra.

The liberal version of the environmental model also fails to see the causes of disease and the environment in which they exist as a historical product, a nature filtered through, even constructed by, society. What organisms and chemicals people are exposed to is determined by both the social relations and types of production which characterize their society. The same virus may cause pneumonia in blacks and whites alike, just as lead may cause the same physiologic damage—but *why* the death rate for flu and pneumonia and *why* blood lead levels are consistently higher in black as compared to white communities is not addressed. While the liberal conception of the environment can generate an exhaustive list of its components, it cannot *comprehend* the all-important assemblage of features of black life. What explains why a greater proportion of black mothers are single, young, malnourished, high-school dropouts, and so on?

Here the Right is ready with a "lifestyle" response as a unifying theme: blacks, not racism, are the source of their own health woes. Currently, the Reagan administration is the chief promoter of this view—as made evident by the 1985 publication of the Report of the Secretary's Task Force on Black and Minority Health. Just one weapon among many in the government's vicious ideological war to justify its savage gutting of health and social service programs, the report shifts responsibility for the burden of disease to the minority communities themselves. Promoting "health education" as a panacea, the government hopes to counsel minorities to eat better, exercise more, smoke and drink less, be less violent, seek health care earlier for symptoms, and in general be

better health-care consumers. This "lifestyle" version of the environmental model accordingly is fully compatible with the genetic model
(i.e., genetic disadvantage can be exaggerated by lifestyle choices) and
echoes its ideological messages that individual shortcomings are at the
root of ill health.

In focusing on individual health habits, the task force report ironi-
cally echoes the language of many "health radicals," ranging from
iconoclasts such as Ivan Illich to counterculture advocates of individually oriented self-help strategies. United in practice, if not in spirit,
these apparently disparate camps all take a "holistic" view, arguing
that disease comes not just from germs or chemicals but from lifestyle
choices about food, exercise, smoking, and stress. Their conflation of
lifestyle choices and life circumstance can reach absurd proportions.
Editorializing on the task force report, the *New York Times* agreed that:
"Disparities may be due to cultural or lifestyle differences. For example,
a higher proportion of blacks and hispanics live in cities, with greater
exposure to hazards like pollution, poor housing, and crime." But what
kind of "lifestyle" causes pollution, and who chooses to live in high-
crime neighborhoods? Both the conservative and alternative "lifestyle"
versions of the environmental model deliberately ignore or distort the
fact that economic coercion and political disenfranchisement, not free
choice, locate minority communities in the most hazardous regions of
cities. What qualitatively constrains the option of blacks to "live right"
is the reality of being black and poor in the United States.

But liberals have had little response when the Right points out that
even the most oppressed and impoverished people make choices affecting their health: it may be hard to eat right if the neighborhood grocer
doesn't sell fresh vegetables, but teenage girls do not have to become
pregnant. For liberals, it has been easier to portray blacks as passive,
blameless victims and in this way avoid the highly charged issue of
health behaviors altogether. The end result is usually just proposals
for more health services *for* blacks, Band-Aids for the gaping wounds
of oppression. Yet while adequate health services certainly are needed,
they can do little to stem the social forces which cause disease.

Too often the Left has been content merely to trail behind the liberals in campaigns for health services, or to call only for social control of
environmental and occupational exposures. The Right, however, has
shifted the terrain of battle to the issue of individual behavior, and we
must respond. It is for the Left to point out that society does not consist of abstract individuals, but rather of people whose life options are

shaped by their intrinsic membership in groups defined by the social relations of their society. Race and class broadly determined not only the conditions under which blacks and whites live, but also the ways in which they can respond to these conditions and the political power they have to alter them. The material limits produced by oppression create and constrain not only the type of housing you live in, but even the most intimate choices about what you do inside your home. Oppression and exploitation beget the reality and also the belief that bad health and personal failure are ineluctable facts of life.

Frantz Fanon wrote eloquently of the fatalistic hopelessness engendered by oppression in colonial Algeria. Eliminating self-destructive behaviors, like drug addiction or living in a battering relationship, requires that they be acknowledged as the subjective reflection of objective powerlessness. As Bylle Avery, director of the National Black Women's Health Project, has said, wellness and empowerment are linked. School-based birth control clinics, however necessary as part of the strategy to reduce teen pregnancy, will be ineffective as long as the social motivation for young black women to get pregnant remains unaddressed; for black women to improve their health, they must individually choose to act collectively in order to transform the social conditions which frame, constrain, and devalue their lives as black women.

TOWARD A MARXIST CONCEPTION

The ideological content of science is transparent in disease models now rejected as archaic or indisputably biased. The feudal view of disease as retribution of God and the eugenist science[18] underlying Nazi racial hygiene clearly resonated well with the dominant politics and ideology of their respective societies. But it is far more difficult to discern the ideological content of scientific theory in one's own time and place.

Criticism of the ideology underlying existing paradigms is an important tool in undermining reactionary science. It can help us sort out the apparent riddle of the Reagan administration's embrace of "holistic" health. Such criticism also points the way toward alternative conceptions. To construct a new paradigm, however, requires painstaking work. Moreover, the goal is not a "neutral" science, but one which openly

---

18   [Eugenics called for the improvement of the human species by sterilization of the unfit or other discouragement of their reproduction. It was popular in the United States particularly in the late nineteenth and early twentieth centuries and later was the foundation of Nazi "race science." PG]

acknowledges the ways in which ideology inevitably is incorporated into scientific concepts and theories. Accurate elucidation and prevention of the material and ideological components of disease processes necessitates the explicit adoption of an anti-racist and class-conscious standpoint.

We have only a hint of how a Marxist analysis of the social relations of race and class can illuminate the processes involved in the social production of disease. Such an approach has already shown that many "racial" differences in disease are actually attributable to differences in class. Similarly, the finding of some Marxist researchers that an absentee landlord, rather than race, is the best predictor of lead poisoning points to what this new science can offer in the way of prevention.

But these are small, isolated observations. Too often we are constrained by assumptions built into existing techniques and methodologies. The intimidating mathematics of multiple regression which dominate public health research cannot even contemplate an effect which becomes its own cause—such as the way in which malnutrition opens the way for infections, which cause diarrhea, which causes malnutrition. Further, existing analytic techniques cannot address phenomena like class relations or racial oppression which cannot be expressed as numbers. True, we can calculate the health effect of more or less income or education, but these are pale reflections of class relations, outcomes and not essences. Similarly, we are limited by disease definitions geared toward individual etiology. Treating the problems of substance abuse, infectious disease, infant mortality, and occupational exposure in the black community as separate maladies obscures their common social antecedent. Clearly, we need basically new approaches to understand the dialectical interpenetration of racism, class relations, and health.

To unravel and eliminate black/white differences in disease, we must begin by politically exposing, not merely describing, the social roots of suffering and disease. Throughout U.S. history, the functioning of capitalism has been bound up with the exploitation and racial oppression of blacks, and the racial stratification of the working class has meant that within the context of the ill health of the working class as a whole, that of blacks has been the worst.

To improve black health, progressive health-care activists must not only fight to restore and expand urgently needed health services. We must also expose the class essence of the disease models which the federal government uses to rid itself of responsibility for social intervention to deal with the problem. In order to target the social forces which produce disease, we must begin to develop an anti-racist model of disease causation. Ultimately, to call for an anti-racist science is to demand a class-conscious science. We cannot afford to do with less.

From Against Method[19]

Paul Feyerabend

... The only principle that does not inhibit progress [in science] is: anything goes....

The development of the Copernican point of view from Galileo to the 20th century is a perfect example of the situation I want to describe. We start with a strong belief that runs counter to contemporary reason and contemporary experience. The belief spreads and finds support in other beliefs which are equally unreasonable, if not more so (law of inertia; the telescope). Research now gets deflected in new directions, new kinds of instruments are built, "evidence" is related to theories in new ways until there arises an ideology that is rich enough to provide independent arguments for any particular part of it and mobile enough to find such arguments whenever they seem to be required. We can say today that Galileo was on the right track, for his persistent pursuit of what once seemed to be a silly cosmology has by now created the material needed to defend it against all those who will accept a view only if it is told in a certain way and who will trust it only if it contains certain magical phrases, called "observational reports." And this is not an exception—it is the normal case: theories become clear and "reasonable" only *after* incoherent parts of them have been used for a long time. Such unreasonable, nonsensical, unmethodical foreplay thus turns out to be an unavoidable precondition of clarity and of empirical success....

As a concrete illustration and as a basis for further discussion, I shall now briefly describe the manner in which Galileo defused an important counter-argument against the idea of the motion of the Earth. I say "defused," and not "refuted," because we are dealing with a changing conceptual system as well as with certain attempts at concealment.

According to the argument ... observation shows that "heavy bodies ... falling down from on high, go by a straight and vertical line to the surface of the Earth. This is considered an irrefutable argument for

19   This selection is from Paul K. Feyerabend's *Against Method* (London: Verso, 1979), pp. 23, 26-27, 70-71, 74-79, 81-92. The excerpts are reprinted here with permission from Verso.

the Earth being motionless. For, if it made the diurnal rotation, a tower from whose top a rock was let fall, being carried by the whirling of the Earth, would travel many hundreds of yards to the east in the time the rock would consume in its fall, and the rock ought to strike the Earth that distance away from the base of the tower."[20]

In considering the argument, Galileo at once admits the correctness of the sensory content of the observation made, viz, that "heavy bodies ... falling from a height, go perpendicularly to the surface of the Earth.... It is, therefore, better to put aside the appearance, on which we all agree, and to use the power of reason either to confirm its reality or to reveal its fallacy." The correctness of the observation is not in question. What is in question is its "reality" or "fallacy.".…

According to Copernicus the motion of a falling stone should be "mixed straight and circular." By the "motion of the stone," is meant not just its motion relative to some visible mark in the visual field of the observer, or its observed motion, but rather its motion in the solar system or in (absolute) space, i.e., its *real motion*. The familiar facts appealed to in the [tower] argument assert a different kind of motion, a simple vertical motion. This result refutes the Copernican hypothesis only if the concept of motion that occurs in the observation statement is the same as the concept of motion that occurs in the Copernican prediction. The observation statement "the stone is falling straight down" must, therefore, refer to a movement in (absolute) space [if it is to show that Copernicus's view of motion is wrong]. It must refer to a real motion.

Now, the force of an "argument from observation" derives from the fact that the observation statements involved are firmly connected with appearances. There is no use appealing to observation if one does not know how to describe what one sees, or if one can offer one's description with hesitation only, as if one had just learned the language in which it is formulated. Producing an observation statement, then, consists of two very different psychological events: (1) a clear and unambiguous *sensation* and (2) a clear and unambiguous *connection* between this sensation and parts of a language. This is the way in which the sensation is made to speak. Do the sensations in the above argument speak the language of real motion?

---

20   [Quotations are from Galileo's *Dialogue Concerning the Two Chief World Systems*. I will not cite pages, but these can be found in Feyerabend's book. I am omitting all of Feyerabend's footnotes. PG]

They speak the language of real motion in the context of 17th-century everyday thought. At least, this is what Galileo tells us. He tells us that the everyday thinking of the time assumes the "operative" character of *all* motion, or, to use well-known philosophical terms, it assumed *a naive realism with respect to motion*:[21] except for occasional unavoidable illusions, apparent motion is identical with real (absolute) motion. Of course, this distinction is not explicitly drawn. One does not first distinguish the apparent motion from the real motion and then connect the two by a correspondence rule. One rather describes, perceives, acts towards motion as if it were already the real thing. Nor does one proceed in this manner under all circumstances. It is admitted that objects may move which are not seen to move; and it is also admitted that certain motions are illusory (cf. the example of the moon [seeming to follow one down the street as one walks]). Apparent motion and real motion are not always identified. However, there are *paradigmatic cases* in which it is psychologically very difficult, if not plainly impossible, to admit deception. It is from these paradigmatic cases, and not from the exception, that naive realism with respect to motion derives its strength. These are also the situations in which *we* first learn our kinematic vocabulary. From our very childhood we learn to react to them with concepts which have naive realism built right into them, and which inextricably connect movement and the appearance of movement. The motion of the stone in the tower argument, or the alleged motion of the Earth, is such a paradigmatic case. How could one possibly be unaware of the swift motion of a large bulk of matter such as the Earth is supposed to be! How could one possibly be unaware of the fact that the falling stone traces a vastly extended trajectory through space [if this were what really happened]! From the point of view of 17th-century thought and language, the argument is, therefore, impeccable and quite forceful. However, notice how *theories* ("operative character" of all motion; essential correctness of sense reports) which are not formulated explicitly, enter the debate in the guise of observational terms. We realize again that observational terms are Trojan horses which must be watched most carefully. How is one supposed to proceed in such a sticky situation?

---

21 [By "naive realism with respect to motion" Feyerabend means the belief that ordinary motion occurs in the context of a framework of objects (the Earth and most things on it) that do not move. In the seventeenth century common sense observations of motion assumed this (what proved to be) incorrect physical theory. See my introduction for further help in understanding what Feyerabend is asserting here. PG]

The argument from falling stones seems to refute the Copernican view. This may be due to an inherent disadvantage of Copernicanism; but it may also be due to the presence of natural interpretations which are in need of improvement. The first task, then, is to *discover* and to isolate these unexamined obstacles to progress....

There is only one way out of this circle [of testing concepts against observations when the observations include questionable conceptual elements], and it consists in using an *external measure of comparison*, including new ways of relating concepts and percepts. Removed from the domain of natural discourse and from all those principles, habits, and attitudes which constitute its form of life, such an external measure will look strange indeed. This, however, is not an argument against its use. On the contrary, such an impression of strangeness reveals that natural interpretations are at work, and it is a first step toward their discovery. Let us explain this situation with the help of the tower example.

The example is intended to show that the Copernican view is not in accordance with "the facts." Seen from the point of view of these "facts," the idea of the motion of the Earth is outlandish, absurd, and obviously false, to mention only some of the expressions which were frequently used at the time, and which are still heard whenever professional squares [that is, people who are not hip] confront a new and counter-factual theory. This makes us suspect that the Copernican view is an external measuring rod of precisely the kind described above.

We can now turn the [tower] argument around and use it as a *detecting device* that helps us to discover the natural interpretations which exclude the motion of the Earth. Turning the argument around, we *first assert* the motion of the Earth and *then inquire* what changes will remove the contradiction. Such an inquiry may take considerable time, and there is a good sense in which it is not finished even today. The contradiction, therefore, may stay with us for decades or even centuries. Still, *it must be upheld* until we have finished our examination or else the examination, the attempt to discover the antediluvian[22] components of our knowledge, cannot even start. This, we have seen, is one of the reasons one can give for *retaining*, and, perhaps, even for *inventing*, theories which are inconsistent with the facts. Ideological ingredients of our knowledge and, more especially, of our observations, are discovered

---

22   ["Antediluvian" means literally "before the flood"; here it means old and out-of-date. PG]

with the help of theories which are refuted by them. *They are discovered counterinductively.* [23]

Let me repeat what has been asserted so far. Theories are tested, and possibly refuted, by facts. Facts contain ideological components, older views which have vanished from sight or were perhaps never formulated in an explicit manner. Such components are highly suspicious. Firstly, because of their age and obscure origin: we do not know why and how they were first introduced; secondly, because their very nature protects them, and always has protected them, from critical examination. In the event of a contradiction between a new and interesting theory and a collection of firmly established facts, the best procedure, therefore, is not to abandon the theory but to use it to discover the hidden principles responsible for the contradiction. Counterinduction is an essential part of such a process of discovery....

Having *discovered* a particular natural interpretation, how can we *examine* it and *test* it? Obviously, we cannot proceed in the usual way, i.e., derive predictions and compare them with the "results of observation." These results are no longer available. The idea that the senses, employed under normal circumstances, produce correct reports of real events, for example reports of the real motion of physical bodies, has now been removed from all observational statements. (Remember that this notion was found to be an essential part of the anti-Copernican argument.) But without it our sensory reactions cease to be relevant for tests....

If *one* natural interpretation causes trouble for an attractive view, and if its *elimination* removes the view from the domain of observation, then the only acceptable procedure is to use *other* interpretations and to see what happens. The interpretation which Galileo uses restores the senses to their position as instruments of exploration, *but only with respect to the reality of relative motion.* Motion "among things which share it in common" is "non-operative," that is, "it remains insensible, imperceptible,

---

23 [In this paragraph Feyerabend describes Galileo's method in responding to the tower argument: insist on the correctness of the Copernican theory and then *reinterpret* our observations to make them consistent with that theory. In that process we show how our common sense observations are distorted by what he calls "the natural interpretations that exclude the motion of the Earth," by "ideological ingredients of our knowledge," by out-of-date theory. He calls this reinterpretation "counterinduction" because rather than making the theory fit the observations (induction), we interpret the observations to fit the theory. In philosophy "counterinduction" has come to have a slightly different meaning—to develop theories that *go against* the evidence. PG]

and without any effect whatever." Galileo's first step, in his joint examination of the Copernican doctrine and of a familiar but hidden natural interpretation, consists therefore in *replacing the latter by a different interpretation.* In other words, *he introduces a new observation language....*

Galileo replaces one natural interpretation by a very different and as yet (1630) at least partly unnatural interpretation. How does he proceed? How does he manage to introduce absurd and counterinductive assertions, such as the assertion that the Earth moves, and yet get them a just and attentive hearing? One anticipates that arguments will not suffice—an interesting and highly important limitation of rationalism—and Galileo's utterances are indeed arguments in appearance only. For Galileo uses *propaganda.* He uses *psychological tricks* in addition to whatever intellectual reasons he has to offer. These tricks are very successful: they lead him to victory. But they obscure the new attitude towards experience that is in the making, and postpone for centuries the possibility of a reasonable philosophy. They obscure the fact that the experience on which Galileo wants to base the Copernican view is nothing but the result of his own fertile imagination, that it has been *invented.* They obscure this fact by insinuating that the new results which emerge are known and conceded by all, and need only be called to our attention to appear as the most obvious expression of the truth.

Galileo "reminds" us that there are situations in which the non-operative character of shared motions is just as evident and as firmly believed as the idea of the operative character of all motion is in other circumstances. (The latter idea is, therefore, not the only natural interpretation of motion.) The situations are: events in a boat, in a smoothly moving carriage, and in other systems that contain an observer and permit him to carry out some simple operations.

SAGREDO: There has just occurred to me a certain fantasy which passed through my imagination one day while I was sailing to Aleppo, where I was going as consul for our country.... If the point of a pen had been on the ship during my whole voyage from Venice to Alexandretta and had had the property of leaving visible marks of its whole trip, what trace—what mark—would it have left? SIMPLICIO: It would have left a line extending from Venice to there; not perfectly straight—or rather not lying in the perfect arc of a circle—but more or less fluctuating according as the vessel would now and again have rocked. But this bending in some places a yard or two to the right or left, up or down, in length of many hundreds

of miles, would have made little alteration in the whole extent of
the line. These would scarcely be sensible, and, without an error of
any moment, it could be called part of a perfect arc.

SAGREDO: So that if the fluctuation of the waves were taken away
and the motion of the vessel were calm and tranquil, the true and
precise motion of that pen point would have been an arc of a perfect circle. Now if I had had the same pen continually in my hand,
and had moved only a little sometimes this way or that, what altera-
tions should have I brought into the main extent of this line?

SIMPLICIO: Less than that which would be given to a straight line a
thousand yards long which deviated from absolute straightness here
and there by a flea's eye.

SAGREDO: Then if an artist had begun drawing with that pen on a
sheet of paper when he left the port and had continued doing so
all the way to Alexandretta, he would have been able to derive from
the pen's motion a whole narrative of many figures, completely
traced and sketched in thousands of directions, with landscapes,
buildings, animals, and other things. Yet the actual real essential
movement marked by the pen point would have been only a line;
long, indeed, but very simple. But as to the artist's own actions,
these would have been conducted exactly the same as if the ship
had been standing still. The reason that of the pen's long motion
no trace would remain except the marks drawn upon the paper is
that the gross motion from Venice to Alexandretta was common to
the paper, the pen, and everything else in the ship. But the small
motions back and forth, to right and left, communicated by the
artist's fingers to the pen but not to the paper, and belonging to
the former alone, could thereby leave a trace on the paper which
remained stationary to those motions.

Or

SALVIATI: ... imagine yourself in a boat with your eyes fixed on a
point of the sail yard [a sail yard is a horizontal timber attached to
the mast from which sails are set PG]. Do you think that because
the boat is moving along briskly, you will have to move your eyes in
order to keep your vision always on that point of the sail yard and
follow its motion?

SIMPLICIO: I am sure that I should not need to make any change
at all; not just as to my vision, but if I had aimed a musket I should

never have to move it a hairsbreadth to keep it aimed, no matter
how the boat moved.

SALVIATI: And this comes about because the motion which the ship
confers upon the sail yard, it confers also upon you and upon your
eyes, so that you need not move them a bit in order to gaze at the tip
of the sail yard, which consequently appears motionless to you....

It is clear that these situations lead to a non-operative concept of
motion even within common sense.

On the other hand, common sense, and I mean 17th-century Italian-
artisan common sense, also contains the idea of the *operative* character
of all motion. This latter idea arises when a limited object that does
not contain too many parts moves in vast and stable surroundings;
for example, when a camel trots through the desert, or when a stone
descends from a tower.

Now Galileo urges us to "remember" the conditions in which we
assert the non-operative character of shared motion in this case also,
and to subsume the second case under the first.

Thus, the first of the two paradigms of non-operative motion mentioned above [about the drawing on paper aboard the boat] is followed
by the assertion that—"It is likewise true that the Earth being moved,
the motion of the stone in descending is actually a long stretch of many
yards, or even many thousand; and had it been able to mark its course
in motionless air or upon some other surface, it would have left a very
long slanting line. But that part of all this motion which is common to
the rock, the tower, and ourselves remains insensible and as if it did
not exist. There remains observable only that part in which neither the
tower nor we are participants; in a word, that with which the stone, in
falling, measures the tower."

And the second paradigm [looking at the sail yard as the boat moves]
precedes the exhortation to "transfer this argument to the whirling of
the Earth and to the rock placed on top of the tower, whose motion you
cannot discern because, in common with the rock, you possess from
the Earth that motion which is required for following the tower; you
do not need to move your eyes. Next, if you add to the rock a downward motion which is peculiar to it and not shared by you, and which
is mixed with this circular motion, the circular portion of the motion
which is common to the stone and the eye continues to be imperceptible. The straight motion alone is sensible, for to follow that you must
move your eyes downwards."

This is strong persuasion indeed.

Yielding to this persuasion, we now *quite automatically* start confounding the conditions of the two cases and become relativists. This is the essence of Galileo's trickery! As a result, the clash between Copernicus and "the conditions affecting ourselves and those in the air above us" [this quotation is from Ptolemy] dissolves into thin air, and we finally realize "that all terrestrial events from which it is ordinarily held that the Earth stands still and the sun and the fixed stars are moving would necessarily appear just the same to us if the Earth moved and the other stood still."

Let us now look at the situation from a more abstract point of view. We start with two conceptual sub-systems of "ordinary" thought (see the following table). One of them regards motion as an absolute process which always has effects, effects on our senses included. The description of this conceptual system given here may be somewhat idealized; but the arguments of Copernicus' opponents which are quoted by Galileo himself and, according to him, are "very plausible," show that there was a widespread tendency to think in its terms, and that this tendency was a serious obstacle to the discussion of alternative ideas. Occasionally, one finds even more primitive ways of thinking, where concepts such as "up" and "down" are used absolutely. Examples are: the assertion "that the Earth is too heavy to climb up over the sun and then fall headlong back down again," or the assertion that "after a short time the mountains, sinking downward with the rotation of the terrestrial globe would get into such a position that whereas a little earlier one would have had to climb steeply to their peaks, a few hours later one would have to stoop and descend in order to get there." Galileo, in his marginal notes, calls these "utterly childish reasons [which] sufficed to keep imbeciles believing in the fixity of the Earth," and he thinks it unnecessary "to bother about such men as those, *whose name is legion,* or to take notice of their fooleries." Yet it is clear that the absolute idea of motion was "well-entrenched," and that the attempt to replace it was bound to encounter strong resistance.

The second conceptual system is built around the relativity of motion, and is also well-entrenched in its own domain of application. Galileo aims at replacing the first system by the second in *all* cases, terrestrial as well as celestial. Naive realism with respect to motion is to be *completely eliminated.*

Now, we have seen that this naive realism is on occasions an essential part of our observational vocabulary. On these occasions (Paradigm I), the observation language contains the idea of the efficacy of *all* motion.

PARADIGM I: Motion of compact objects in stable surroundings of great spatial extension—deer observed by the hunter.		PARADIGM II: Motion of objects in boats, coaches and other moving systems.	
Natural interpretation: All motion is operative.		*Natural interpretation*: Only relative motion is operative.	
Falling stone	Motion of Earth	Falling stone	Motion of Earth
proves	*predicts*	*proves*	*predicts*
↓	↓	↓	↓
Earth at rest	Oblique motion of stone	No relative motion between starting point and Earth	No relative motion between starting point and stone

Or, to express it in the material mode of speech, our experience in these situations is an experience of objects which move absolutely. Taking this into consideration, it is apparent that Galileo's proposal amounts to a partial revision of our observation language or of our experience. An experience which partly *contradicts* the idea of the motion of the Earth is turned into an experience that *confirms* it, at least as far as "terrestrial things" are concerned. This is what *actually happens.* But Galileo wants to persuade us that no change has taken place, that the second conceptual system is already universally *known,* even though it is not universally *used.* Salviati, his representative in the Dialogue, his opponent Simplicio and Sagredo the intelligent layman, all connect Galileo's method of argumentation with Plato's theory of *anamnesis*[24]—a clever tactical move, typically Galilean one is inclined to say. Yet we must not allow ourselves to be deceived about the revolutionary development that is actually taking place.

The resistance against the assumption that shared motion is non-operative was equated with the resistance which forgotten ideas exhibit towards the attempt to make them known. Let us accept this *interpretation* of the resistance! But let us not forget its *existence.* We must then admit that it restricts the use of the relativistic ideas, confining them to *part* of our everyday experience. *Outside* this part, i.e., in interplanetary space, they are "forgotten" and therefore not active. But outside this part there is not complete chaos. Other concepts are used, among them

24   [*Anamnesis* the idea that learning involves recollection of what we used to know—for Plato in a previous life. PG]

those very same absolutistic concepts which derive from the first paradigm. We not only use them, but we must admit that they are entirely adequate. No difficulties arise as long as one remains within the limits of the first paradigm. "Experience," i.e., the totality of all facts from all domains, cannot force us to carry out the change which Galileo wants to introduce. The motive for a change must come from a different source.

It comes, first, from the desire to see "the whole [correspond] to its parts with wonderful simplicity," as Copernicus had already expressed himself. It comes from the "typically metaphysical urge" for unity of understanding and conceptual presentation. And the motive for a change is connected, secondly, with the intention to make room for the motion of the Earth, which Galileo accepts and is not prepared to give up. The idea of the motion of the Earth is closer to the first paradigm than to the second, or at least it was at the time of Galileo. This gave strength to the Aristotelian arguments, and made them plausible. To eliminate this plausibility, it was necessary to subsume[25] the first paradigm under the second, and to extend the relative notions to all phenomena. The idea of *anamnesis* functions here as a psychological crutch, as a lever which smooths the process of subsumption by concealing its existence. As a result we are now *ready* to apply the relative notions not only to boats, coaches, birds, but to the "solid and well-established Earth" as a whole. And we have the impression that this readiness was in us all the time, although it took some effort to make it conscious. This impression is most certainly erroneous: it is the result of Galileo's propagandistic machinations. We would do better to describe the situation in a different way, as a change of our conceptual system. Or, because we are dealing with concepts which belong to natural interpretations, and which are therefore connected with sensations in a very direct way, we should describe it as a *change of experience* that allows us to accommodate the Copernican doctrine. The change corresponds perfectly to the pattern described [later in the book]: an inadequate view, the Copernican theory, is supported by another inadequate view, the idea of the non-operative character of shared motion, and both

---

25 ["Subsume" means to "bring under." Feyerabend's point is that Galileo is insisting that, contrary to seventeenth-century common sense, we interpret the apparent non-motion of the Earth and of "stationary" objects in our environment (the first paradigm) as a *complex of objects* which *do not move relative to one another* but which *are in motion* (the second paradigm) relative to the sun and the Earth's axis. The falling stone is then interpreted as *motion relative to that complex of objects*. PG]

theories gain strength and give support to each other in the process. It is this change which underlies the transition from the Aristotelian point of view to the epistemology of modern science.

For experience now ceases to be the unchangeable fundament which it is both in common sense and in the Aristotelian philosophy. The attempt to support Copernicus makes experience "fluid" in the very same manner in which it makes the heavens fluid, "so that each star roves around in it by itself." An empiricist who starts from experience, and builds on it without ever looking back, now loses the very ground on which he stands. Neither the Earth, "the solid, well-established Earth," nor the facts on which he usually relies can be trusted any longer. It is clear that a philosophy that uses such a fluid and changing experience needs new methodological principles which do not insist on an asymmetric judgement of theories by experience. *Classical physics* intuitively adopts such principles; at least the great and independent thinkers, such as Newton, Faraday, Boltzmann proceed in this way. But its *official doctrine* still clings to the idea of a stable and unchanging basis. The clash between this doctrine and the actual procedure is concealed by a tendentious presentation of the *results* of research that hides their revolutionary origin and suggests that they arose from a stable and unchanging source. These methods of concealment start with Galileo's attempt to introduce new ideas under the cover of anamnesis, and they culminate in Newton. They must be exposed if we want to arrive at a better account of the progressive elements in science.

My discussion of the anti-Copernican argument is not yet complete. So far, I have tried to discover what assumption will make a stone *that moves alongside a moving tower* appear to fall "straight down," instead of being seen to move in an arc. The assumption, which I shall call the *relativity principle*, that our senses notice only relative motion and are completely insensitive to a motion which objects have in common, was seen to do the trick. What remains to be explained is *why the stone stays with the tower* and is not left behind. In order to save the Copernican view, one must explain not only why a motion that preserves the relation among visible objects remains unnoticed, but also, why a common motion of various objects does not affect their relation. That is, one must explain why such a motion is not a *causal agent.* Turning the question around in the manner explained [earlier], it is now apparent that the anti-Copernican argument described there rests on *two* natural interpretations: viz., the *epistemological assumption* that absolute motion is always *noticed,* and the *dynamical principle* that objects (such as the falling stone) which are not interfered with assume their natural motion. The present problem is to supplement the relativity principle with the new law of inertia in such a fashion that the motion of the Earth can still be asserted. One sees at once that the following law, *the principle of circular inertia* as I shall call it, provides the required solution: an object that moves with a given angular velocity on a frictionless sphere around the centre of the Earth will continue moving with the same angular velocity forever. Combining the appearance of the falling stone with the relativity principle, the principle of circular inertia and with some simple assumptions concerning the composition of velocities, we obtain an argument which no longer endangers Copernicus' view, but can be used to give it partial support.

The relativity principle was defended in two ways. The first was by showing how it helps Copernicus: this defense is truly *ad hoc*. The second was by pointing to its function in common sense, and by surreptitiously generalizing that function (see above). No independent argument was given for its validity. Galileo's support of the principle of circular inertia is of exactly the same kind. He introduces the principle, again not by reference to experiment or to independent observation, but by reference to what everyone is already supposed to know.

> SIMPLICIO: So you have not made a hundred tests, or even one? And yet you so freely declare it to be certain? ...
> SALVIATI: Without experiment, I am sure that the effect will happen as I tell you, because it must happen that way; and I might add that you yourself also know that it cannot happen otherwise, no matter how you may pretend not to know it.... But I am so handy at picking people's brains that I shall make you confess this in spite of yourself.

Step by step, Simplicio is forced to admit that a body that moves, without friction, on a sphere concentric with the centre of the Earth will carry out a "boundless," a "perpetual" motion. We know, of course, especially after the analysis we have just completed of the non-operative character of shared motion, that what Simplicio accepts is based neither on experiment nor on corroborated theory. It is a daring new suggestion involving a tremendous leap of the imagination....

SECTION III

WHY DO WE BELIEVE OTHERS?

INTRODUCTION

WHEN STEPHEN GOULD WROTE THAT THE ALVAREZES "PROPOSED THEIR
hypothesis [that extraterrestrial impact caused dinosaur extinction] after
laborious geochemical studies with Frank Asaro and Helen Michael had
revealed a massive increase of iridium in rocks deposited right at the
time of extinction" and that other investigators "found abnormally high
amounts of iridium everywhere—from continental rocks of the western United States to deep sea cores from the South Atlantic," Gould
was taking other scientists at their word. He did not go out himself to
test for iridium. While scientists sometimes seek to replicate surprising results, generally they rely on other scientists' reports; they believe
they are telling the truth. In this sense, science is a socially cooperative process. At the same time, scientists criticize the work of others,
as Gould's essay also illustrates. So scientific investigation is a social
enterprise where people criticize and confirm ideas in a cooperative

and conflictual process. At the root of this social cooperation is the fact that scientists trust and believe one another, at least to some degree. But believing a person—believing God in particular—is central to some religious thought as well. In this section we investigate why we believe others. Thus this section connects the discussion of scientific method and practice in the previous section with the discussion of religious belief in the section to follow.

Generally two sorts of answers are given to the question of believing others. On one view, that advanced by David Hume and William Clifford, we should believe others when and only when the preponderance of evidence would indicate that what they say is true. Thus, in Hume's and Clifford's view, belief in what others tell us has to be *justified* in the context of all the evidence we have about what is true. The alternative view, advanced by Thomas Reid (as explicated by Nicholas Wolterstorff), Elizabeth Anscombe, and me, is that believing others, in many contexts, does not need justification. Believing others, like trusting our senses and memory, is something we can take for granted unless we have reason to be suspicious of what they say (which we sometimes, perhaps even often, do).

Hume's discussion of miracles is concerned with how we decide to believe what another has told us; when can we justifiably regard someone's testimony that something is the case as evidence or proof that it is the case? Hume argues that the justification of belief based on testimony is a form of causal reasoning from experience. Where our experience supports believing the testimony of others, belief is justified; where it does not, belief is not justified. Hume argues that belief in miracles can never be justified. But note what he means by a miracle and whether it is the same as what I meant by a miracle in my essay in the previous section.

("A wise man," Hume writes, "proportions his belief to the evidence." While Hume discusses the case of *testimony* that a miracle has occurred, wouldn't his general point apply to believing our senses or memory as well? So we might conclude that an apparent "miracle" was a trick or illusion, based on the totality of the evidence.)

Clifford develops a Humean account of belief based on authority. He writes that there are three conditions that must be met if we are to believe what another says. First, we must have reason to believe that he is telling us the truth as he understands it. Second, we must have reason to think he has some way of knowing the truth of the matter of which he speaks. Third, we must have reason to think he has exercised good judgment in coming to his belief from the evidence he has. He then applies this account to argue that we should not believe testimony of miracles such as Mohammed's report of the angel Gabriel speaking to him. Generally Clifford is clearly skeptical that religious beliefs can be based on sufficient evidence. In a tactical move, he attacks Islam to his predominately Christian audience, but he is assuming that his audience will see that, objectively, their Christianity is just as suspect as the Islam he explicitly attacks.

Clifford also appeals to the fact that not everyone shares the same religious authority: some look to the Koran and to Mohammed's words and others to Buddha (and yet others to Christian scriptures or the Pope, we might add). What should we believe when authorities disagree?

Nicholas Wolterstorff develops two points from Thomas Reid's epistemology of testimony the importance of which Hume appears to underestimate: that we are naturally social beings who naturally trust and believe one another; that we naturally recognize the feelings and attitudes of others—this recognition is also part of our social nature. He then applies these principles to our believing the words of others. Our tendency to speak the truth (as we understand it) and to believe what others tell us allow that, as we gain more experience, we can become more skeptical, recognizing when we need to be more distrustful of what we are told. So Reid views believing others as essential to human experience, but he also acknowledges that not *all* others are worthy of belief.

Elizabeth Anscombe, like Wolterstorff, has vigorously defended her Christianity. She is specifically concerned with understanding what is involved in believing another, including believing God, and believing that what someone tells us is true because we believe the person.

Anscombe thinks the issue of believing others is important not only for philosophy of religion but for epistemology—the philosophy of knowledge—more generally. Of Hume's view that believing testimony is justified because we have discovered from experience that what others say is true, she writes this view "was always absurd, and the mystery is how Hume could ever have entertained it." So she wants to advance our understanding of knowledge in general by pointing out that our belief in testimony must have another source than causal reasoning. She also points out how central testimony is to all of our beliefs: "We must acknowledge testimony as giving us our larger world in no small degree, or even in a greater degree, than the relation of cause and effect; and believing it is quite dissimilar in structure from belief in causes and effects." She then compares the way that testimony is linked to our perceptual knowledge to the way the fat in a steak is marbled throughout the meat. Do you think she is right? Is there anything you believe (for example, based on what you have directly observed) that does not in some way also depend on the beliefs we have acquired from others? Look at the examples she gives to try to persuade us of the marbled fat metaphor.

Anscombe then develops a subtle and sophisticated account of what is involved in taking it that something is true on someone else's say-so. She gives many cases, and sometimes the reader has to think hard about each case just to understand what she is saying about it. This can make her writing difficult to understand. Still, thinking about a particular example she gives—particularly if you can develop and explain the example in a way meaningful to you—allows you to see the point she is making, at least where the point is clear and correct (as, I believe it often is). She considers many cases of believing someone who is not present to us, even cases of believing someone who may not exist. This last point is meant to bring our thinking back to the issue of believing God. Anscombe's (unstated) conclusion may be this: because believing others is essential to all of us, in order to have any knowledge whatsoever, then believing God, as one instance of believing others, makes sense as well. Anscombe concludes that "believing someone ... is trusting him for the truth."

In my essay on trust and modesty I argue that two virtues are necessary to critical belief. The first is trusting what we are told, for without trusting others we could not know anything (here I side with Reid and Anscombe against Hume). But if everyone trusts what they have been told and their trust is unchecked by a sense that what we have been told could be wrong, people will have contradictory beliefs that cannot all be true. Thus trust must be supplemented by epistemic modesty (or skepticism) and some method of dealing with conflicting beliefs. Social knowledge—science is paradigmatic of this—depends on our epistemic modesty checking our trust. In this paper I (like Reid) try to reconcile Hume's (and Clifford's) point that we must critically evaluate what others tell us with the need for trust. But religious believers may belong to different communities of trust from non-believers. The separateness of these communities can mean that we will be unable to come to agreement in our beliefs. Yet we can ask a further question, provided that we can step back from our communities of trust: does a community of trust to which I belong practice a proper safeguarding of reasons for belief that would make the community *worthy* of trust?

From "Of Miracles"[1]
David Hume

I have discovered an argument ..., which, if just, will, with the wise and learned, be an everlasting check to all kinds of superstitious delusion, and consequently, will be useful as long as the world endures. For so long, I presume, will the accounts of miracles and prodigies be found in all history, sacred and profane.

Though experience be our only guide in reasoning concerning matters of fact; it must be acknowledged, that this guide is not altogether infallible, but in some cases is apt to lead us into errors. One, who in our climate, should expect better weather in any week of June than in one of December, would reason justly, and conformably to experience; but it is certain, that he may happen, in the event, to find himself mistaken. However, we may observe, that, in such a case, he would have no cause to complain of experience; because it commonly informs us beforehand of the uncertainty, by that contrariety of events, which we may learn from a diligent observation. All effects follow not with like certainty from their supposed causes. Some events are found, in all countries and all ages, to have been constantly conjoined together: Others are found to have been more variable, and sometimes to disappoint our expectations; so that, in our reasonings concerning matter of fact, there are all imaginable degrees of assurance, from the highest certainty to the lowest species of moral evidence.

A wise man, therefore, proportions his belief to the evidence. In such conclusions as are founded on an infallible experience, he expects the event with the last degree of assurance, and regards his past experience as a full proof of the future existence of that event. In other cases, he proceeds with more caution: He weighs the opposite experiments: He considers which side is supported by the greater number of experiments: to that side he inclines, with doubt and hesitation; and when at last he fixes his judgement, the evidence exceeds not what we properly call probability. All probability, then, supposes an opposition of experiments and observations, where the one side is found to overbalance the other, and to produce a degree of evidence, proportioned to the superiority. A hundred instances or experiments on one side, and fifty on

1   This is an excerpt from Section x of Hume's *An Enquiry concerning Human Understanding*, the 1777 "new edition," which is generally considered the final version authorized by Hume.

another, afford a doubtful expectation of any event; though a hundred
uniform experiments, with only one that is contradictory, reasonably
beget a pretty strong degree of assurance. In all cases, we must balance the opposite experiments, where they are opposite, and deduct
the smaller number from the greater, in order to know the exact force
of the superior evidence.

To apply these principles to a particular instance; we may observe
that there is no species of reasoning more common, more useful, and
even necessary to human life, than that which is derived from the testimony of men, and the reports of eye-witnesses and spectators. This
species of reasoning, perhaps, one may deny to be founded on the
relation of cause and effect. I shall not dispute about a word. It will be
sufficient to observe that our assurance in any argument of this kind
is derived from no other principle than our observation of the veracity of human testimony, and of the usual conformity of facts to the
reports of witnesses. It being a general maxim, that no objects have any
discoverable connexion together, and that all the inferences, which we
can draw from one to another, are founded merely on our experience
of their constant and regular conjunction; it is evident that we ought
not to make an exception to this maxim in favour of human testimony,
whose connexion with any event seems, in itself, as little necessary as
any other. Were not the memory tenacious to a certain degree; had
not men commonly an inclination to truth and a principle of probity;
were they not sensible to shame, when detected in a falsehood: Were
not these, I say, discovered by experience to be qualities, inherent in
human nature, we should never repose the least confidence in human
testimony. A man delirious, or noted for falsehood and villany, has no
manner of authority with us.

And as the evidence, derived from witnesses and human testimony,
is founded on past experience, so it varies with the experience, and is
regarded either as a proof or a probability, according as the conjunction between any particular kind of report and any kind of object has
been found to be constant or variable. There are a number of circumstances to be taken into consideration in all judgements of this kind;
and the ultimate standard, by which we determine all disputes, that may
arise concerning them, is always derived from experience and observation. Where this experience is not entirely uniform on any side, it is
attended with an unavoidable contrariety in our judgements, and with
the same opposition and mutual destruction of argument as in every
other kind of evidence. We frequently hesitate concerning the reports

of others. We balance the opposite circumstances, which cause any doubt or uncertainty; and when we discover a superiority on any side, we incline to it; but still with a diminution of assurance, in proportion to the force of its antagonist.

This contrariety of evidence, in the present case, may be derived from several different causes; from the opposition of contrary testimony; from the character or number of the witnesses; from the manner of their delivering their testimony; or from the union of all these circumstances. We entertain a suspicion concerning any matter of fact, when the witnesses contradict each other; when they are but few, or of a doubtful character; when they have an interest in what they affirm; when they deliver their testimony with hesitation, or on the contrary, with too violent asseverations. There are many other particulars of the same kind, which may diminish or destroy the force of any argument, derived from human testimony.

Suppose, for instance, that the fact, which the testimony endeavours to establish, partakes of the extraordinary and the marvellous;[2] in that case, the evidence, resulting from the testimony, admits of a diminution, greater or less, in proportion as the fact is more or less unusual. The reason why we place any credit in witnesses and historians, is not derived from any connexion, which we perceive a priori, between testimony and reality, but because we are accustomed to find a conformity between them. But when the fact attested is such a one as has seldom fallen under our observation, here is a contest of two opposite experiences; of which the one destroys the other, as far as its force goes, and the superior can only operate on the mind by the force, which remains. The very same principle of experience, which gives us a certain degree of assurance in the testimony of witnesses, gives us also, in this case, another degree of assurance against the fact, which they endeavour to establish; from which contradiction there necessarily arises a counterpoise, and mutual destruction of belief and authority....

But in order to encrease the probability against the testimony of witnesses, let us suppose, that the fact, which they affirm, instead of being only marvellous, is really miraculous; and suppose also, that the testimony considered apart and in itself, amounts to an entire proof; in that case, there is proof against proof, of which the strongest must prevail, but still with a diminution of its force, in proportion to that of its antagonist.

---

2   [Here Hume means astonishing or surprising. PG]

A miracle is a violation of the laws of nature; and as a firm and unalterable experience has established these laws, the proof against a miracle, from the very nature of the fact, is as entire as any argument from experience can possibly be imagined. Why is it more than probable, that all men must die; that lead cannot, of itself, remain suspended in the air; that fire consumes wood, and is extinguished by water; unless it be, that these events are found agreeable to the laws of nature, and there is required a violation of these laws, or in other words, a miracle to prevent them? Nothing is esteemed a miracle, if it ever happen in the common course of nature. It is no miracle that a man, seemingly in good health, should die on a sudden: because such a kind of death, though more unusual than any other, has yet been frequently observed to happen. But it is a miracle, that a dead man should come to life; because that has never been observed in any age or country. There must, therefore, be a uniform experience against every miraculous event, otherwise the event would not merit that appellation. And as a uniform experience amounts to a proof, there is here a direct and full proof, from the nature of the fact, against the existence of any miracle; nor can such a proof be destroyed, or the miracle rendered credible, but by an opposite proof, which is superior.[3]

The plain consequence is (and it is a general maxim worthy of our attention), "That no testimony is sufficient to establish a miracle, unless the testimony be of such a kind, that its falsehood would be more miraculous, than the fact, which it endeavours to establish; and even in that case there is a mutual destruction of arguments, and the superior only

---

3   Sometimes an event may not, *in itself*, seem to be contrary to the laws of nature, and yet, if it were real, it might, by reason of some circumstances, be denominated a miracle; because, in *fact*, it is contrary to these laws. Thus if a person, claiming a divine authority, should command a sick person to be well, a healthful man to fall down dead, the clouds to pour rain, the winds to blow, in short, should order many natural events, which immediately follow upon his command; these might justly be esteemed miracles, because they are really, in this case, contrary to the laws of nature. For if any suspicion remain, that the event and command concurred by accident, there is no miracle and no transgression of the laws of nature. If this suspicion be removed, there is evidently a miracle, and a transgression of these laws; because nothing can be more contrary to nature than that the voice or command of a man should have such an influence. A miracle may be accurately defined, *a transgression of a law of nature by a particular volition of the Deity, or by the interposition of some invisible agent.* A miracle may either be discoverable by men or not. This alters not its nature and essence. The raising of a house or ship into the air is a visible miracle. The raising of a feather, when the wind wants ever so little of a force requisite for that purpose, is as real a miracle, though not so sensible with regard to us.

gives us an assurance suitable to that degree of force, which remains, after deducting the inferior." When anyone tells me, that he saw a dead man restored to life, I immediately consider with myself, whether it be more probable, that this person should either deceive or be deceived, or that the fact, which he relates, should really have happened. I weigh the one miracle against the other; and according to the superiority, which I discover, I pronounce my decision, and always reject the greater miracle. If the falsehood of his testimony would be more miraculous, than the event which he relates; then, and not till then, can he pretend to command my belief or opinion....

Upon the whole, then, it appears, that no testimony for any kind of miracle has ever amounted to a probability, much less to a proof; and that, even supposing it amounted to a proof, it would be opposed by another proof, derived from the very nature of the fact, which it would endeavour to establish. It is experience only, which gives authority to human testimony; and it is the same experience, which assures us of the laws of nature. When, therefore, these two kinds of experience are contrary, we have nothing to do but subtract the one from the other, and embrace an opinion, either on one side or the other, with that assurance which arises from the remainder. But according to the principle here explained, this subtraction, with regard to all popular religions, amounts to an entire annihilation; and therefore we may establish it as a maxim, that no human testimony can have such force as to prove a miracle, and make it a just foundation for any such system of religion.

From "The Ethics of Belief"[4]
William K. Clifford

THE WEIGHT OF AUTHORITY

Are we then to become universal sceptics, doubting everything, afraid always to put one foot before the other until we have personally tested the firmness of the road? Are we to deprive ourselves of the help and guidance of that vast body of knowledge which is daily growing upon the world, because neither we nor any other one person can possibly test a hundredth part of it by immediate experiment or observation,

---

4   This essay was originally published in *Contemporary Review*, 1877. It was reprinted in *Lectures and Essays* (1879) and is presently in print in *The Ethics of Belief and Other Essays* (Amherst, NY: Prometheus Books, 1999).

and because it would not be completely proved if we did? Shall we steal and tell lies because we have had no personal experience wide enough to justify the belief that it is wrong to do so?

There is no practical danger that such consequences will ever follow from scrupulous care and self-control in the matter of belief. Those men who have most nearly done their duty in this respect have found that certain great principles, and these most fitted for the guidance of life, have stood out more and more clearly in proportion to the care and honesty with which they were tested, and have acquired in this way a practical certainty. The beliefs about right and wrong which guide our actions in dealing with men in society, and the beliefs about physical nature which guide our actions in dealing with animate and inanimate bodies, these never suffer from investigation; they can take care of themselves, without being propped up by "acts of faith," the clamour of paid advocates, or the suppression of contrary evidence. Moreover there are many cases in which it is our duty to act upon probabilities, although the evidence is not such as to justify present belief; because it is precisely by such action, and by observation of its fruits, that evidence is got which may justify future belief. So that we have no reason to fear lest a habit of conscientious inquiry should paralyse the actions of our daily life.

But because it is not enough to say, "It is wrong to believe on unworthy evidence," without saying also what evidence is worthy, we shall now go on to inquire under what circumstances it is lawful to believe on the testimony of others; and then, further, we shall inquire more generally when and why we may believe that which goes beyond our own experience, or even beyond the experience of mankind.

In what cases, then, let us ask in the first place, is the testimony of a man unworthy of belief? He may say that which is untrue either knowingly or unknowingly. In the first case he is lying, and his moral character is to blame; in the second case he is ignorant or mistaken, and it is only his knowledge or his judgment which is in fault. In order that we may have the right to accept his testimony as ground for believing what he says, we must have reasonable grounds for trusting his veracity, that he is really trying to speak the truth so far as he knows it; his knowledge, that he has had opportunities of knowing the truth about this matter; and his judgment, that he has made proper use of those opportunities in coming to the conclusion which he affirms.

However plain and obvious these reasons may be, so that no man of ordinary intelligence, reflecting upon the matter, could fail to arrive at them, it is nevertheless true that a great many persons do habitually disregard them in weighing testimony. Of the two questions, equally important to the trustworthiness of a witness, "Is he dishonest?" and "May he be mistaken?" the majority of mankind are perfectly satisfied if one can, with some show of probability, be answered in the negative. The excellent moral character of a man is alleged as ground for accepting his statements about things which he cannot possibly have known. A Mussulman, for example, will tell us that the character of his Prophet was so noble and majestic that it commands the reverence even of those who do not believe in his mission. So admirable was his moral teaching, so wisely put together the great social machine which he created, that his precepts have not only been accepted by a great portion of mankind, but have actually been obeyed. His institutions have on the one hand rescued the negro from savagery, and on the other hand have taught civilization to the advancing West; and although the races which held the highest forms of his faith, and most fully embodied his mind and thought, have all been conquered and swept away by barbaric tribes, yet the history of their marvellous attainments remains as an imperishable glory to Islam. Are we to doubt the word of a man so great and so good? Can we suppose that this magnificent genius, this splendid moral hero, has lied to us about the most solemn and sacred matters? The testimony of Mohammed is clear, that there is but one God, and that he, Mohammed, is his Prophet; that if we believe in him we shall enjoy everlasting felicity, but that if we do not we shall be damned. This testimony rests on the most awful of foundations, the revelation of heaven itself; for was he not visited by the angel Gabriel, as he fasted and prayed in his desert cave, and allowed to enter into the blessed fields of Paradise? Surely God is God and Mohammed is the Prophet of God.

What should we answer to this Mussulman? First, no doubt, we should be tempted to take exception against his view of the character of the Prophet and the uniformly beneficial influence of Islam: before we could go with him altogether in these matters it might seem that we should have to forget many terrible things of which we have heard or read. But if we chose to grant him all these assumptions, for the sake of argument, and because it is difficult both for the faithful and for infidels to discuss them fairly and without passion, still we should have something to say which takes away the ground of his belief, and therefore shows that it is wrong to entertain it. Namely this: the character of Mohammed is excellent evidence that he was honest and spoke the truth so far as he knew it; but it is no evidence at all that he knew what the truth was. What means could he have of knowing that the form which appeared to him to be the angel Gabriel was not a hallucination, and that his apparent visit to Paradise was not a dream? Grant that he himself was fully persuaded and honestly believed that he had the guidance of heaven, and was the vehicle of a supernatural revelation, how could he know that this strong conviction was not a mistake? Let us put ourselves in his place; we shall find that the more completely we endeavour to realise what passed through his mind, the more clearly we shall perceive that the Prophet could have had no adequate ground for the belief in his own inspiration. It is most probable that he himself never doubted of the matter, or thought of asking the question; but we are in the position of those to whom the question has been asked, and who are bound to answer it. It is known to medical observers that solitude and want of food are powerful means of producing delusion and of fostering a tendency to mental disease. Let us suppose, then, that I, like Mohammed, go into desert places to fast and pray; what things can happen to me which will give me the right to believe that I am divinely inspired? Suppose that I get information, apparently from a celestial visitor, which upon being tested is found to be correct. I cannot be sure, in the first place, that the celestial visitor is not a figment of my own mind, and that the information did not come to me, unknown at the time to my consciousness, through some subtle channel of sense. But if my visitor were a real visitor, and for a long time gave me information which was found to be trustworthy, this would indeed be good ground for trusting him in the future as to such matters as fall within human powers of verification; but it would not be ground for trusting his testimony as to any other matters. For although his tested character would justify me in believing that he spoke the truth so far as he knew, yet the same question would present itself—what ground is there for supposing that he knows?

Even if my supposed visitor had given me such information, subsequently verified by me, as proved him to have means of knowledge about verifiable matters far exceeding my own; this would not justify me in believing what he said about matters that are not at present capable of verification by man. It would be ground for interesting conjecture, and for the hope that, as the fruit of our patient inquiry, we might by and by attain to such a means of verification as should rightly turn conjecture into belief. For belief belongs to man, and to the guidance of human affairs: no belief is real unless it guide our actions, and those very actions supply a test of its truth.

But, it may be replied, the acceptance of Islam as a system is just that action which is prompted by belief in the mission of the Prophet, and which will serve for a test of its truth. Is it possible to believe that a system which has succeeded so well is really founded upon a delusion? Not only have individual saints found joy and peace in believing, and verified those spiritual experiences which are promised to the faithful, but nations also have been raised from savagery or barbarism to a higher social state. Surely we are at liberty to say that the belief has been acted upon, and that it has been verified.

It requires, however, but little consideration to show that what has really been verified is not at all the supernal character of the Prophet's mission, or the trustworthiness of his authority in matters which we ourselves cannot test, but only his practical wisdom in certain very mundane things. The fact that believers have found joy and peace in believing gives us the right to say that the doctrine is a comfortable doctrine, and pleasant to the soul; but it does not give us the right to say that it is true. And the question which our conscience is always asking about that which we are tempted to believe is not, "Is it comfortable and pleasant?" but, "Is it true?" That the Prophet preached certain doctrines, and predicted that spiritual comfort would be found in them, proves only his sympathy with human nature and his knowledge of it; but it does not prove his superhuman knowledge of theology.

And if we admit for the sake of argument (for it seems that we cannot do more) that the progress made by Moslem nations in certain cases was really due to the system formed and sent forth into the world by Mohammed, we are not at liberty to conclude from this that he was inspired to declare the truth about things which we cannot verify. We are only at liberty to infer the excellence of his moral precepts, or of the means which he devised for so working upon men as to get them obeyed, or of the social and political machinery which he set up. And it would require a great amount of careful examination into the history of those nations to determine which of these things had the greater share in the result. So that here again it is the Prophet's knowledge of human nature, and his sympathy with it, that are verified; not his divine inspiration or his knowledge of theology.

If there were only one Prophet, indeed, it might well seem a difficult and even an ungracious task to decide upon what points we would trust him, and on what we would doubt his authority; seeing what help and furtherance all men have gained in all ages from those who saw more clearly, who felt more strongly, and who sought the truth with

more single heart than their weaker brethren. But there is not only
one Prophet; and while the consent of many upon that which, as men,
they had real means of knowing and did know, has endured to the end,
and been honourably built into the great fabric of human knowledge,
the diverse witness of some about that which they did not and could
not know remains as a warning to us that to exaggerate the prophetic
authority is to misuse it, and to dishonour those who have sought only
to help and further us after their power. It is hardly in human nature
that a man should quite accurately gauge the limits of his own insight;
but it is the duty of those who profit by his work to consider carefully
where he may have been carried beyond it. If we must needs embalm his
possible errors along with his solid achievements, and use his authority
as an excuse for believing what he cannot have known, we make of his
goodness an occasion to sin.

To consider only one other such witness: the followers of the Buddha
have at least as much right to appeal to individual and social experience
in support of the authority of the Eastern saviour. The special mark
of his religion, it is said, that in which it has never been surpassed, is
the comfort and consolation which it gives to the sick and sorrowful,
the tender sympathy with which it soothes and assuages all the natural
griefs of men. And surely no triumph of social morality can be greater
or nobler than that which has kept nearly half the human race from
persecuting in the name of religion. If we are to trust the accounts of
his early followers, he believed himself to have come upon Earth with
a divine and cosmic mission to set rolling the wheel of the law. Being a
prince, he divested himself of his kingdom, and of his free will became
acquainted with misery, that he might learn how to meet and subdue
it. Could such a man speak falsely about solemn things? And as for his
knowledge, was he not a man miraculous with powers more than man's?
He was born of woman without the help of man; he rose into the air
and was transfigured before his kinsmen; at last he went up bodily into
heaven from the top of Adam's Peak. Is not his word to be believed in
when he testifies of heavenly things?

If there were only he, and no other, with such claims! But there is
Mohammed with his testimony; we cannot choose but listen to them
both. The Prophet tells us that there is one God, and that we shall live
for ever in joy or misery, according as we believe in the Prophet or not.
The Buddha says that there is no God, and that we shall be annihilated
by and by if we are good enough. Both cannot be infallibly inspired;

one or other must have been the victim of a delusion, and thought he knew that which he really did not know. Who shall dare to say which? and how can we justify ourselves in believing that the other was not also deluded?

We are led, then, to these judgments following. The goodness and greatness of a man do not justify us in accepting a belief upon the warrant of his authority, unless there are reasonable grounds for supposing that he knew the truth of what he was saying. And there can be no grounds for supposing that a man knows that which we, without ceasing to be men, could not be supposed to verify....

A question rightly asked is already half answered, said Jacobi; we may add that the method of solution is the other half of the answer, and that the actual result counts for nothing by the side of these two. For an example let us go to the telegraph, where theory and practice, grown each to years of discretion, are marvellously wedded for the fruitful service of men. Ohm found that the strength of an electric current is directly proportional to the strength of the battery which produces it, and inversely as the length of the wire along which it has to travel. This is called Ohm's law; but the result, regarded as a statement to be believed, is not the valuable part of it. The first half of the question: what relation holds good between these quantities? So put, the question involves already the conception of strength of current, and of strength of battery, as quantities to be measured and compared; it hints clearly that these are the things to be attended to in the study of electric currents. The second half is the method of investigation; how to measure these quantities, what instruments are required for the experiment, and how are they to be used? The student who begins to learn about electricity is not asked to believe in Ohm's law: he is made to understand the question, he is placed before the apparatus, and he is taught to verify it. He learns to do things, not to think he knows things; to use instruments and to ask questions, not to accept a traditional statement. The question which required a genius to ask it rightly is answered by a tiro.[5] If Ohm's law were suddenly lost and forgotten by all men, while the question and the method of solution remained, the result could be rediscovered in an hour. But the result by itself, if known to a people who could not comprehend the value of the question or the means of

---

5 [A tiro (now spelled "tyro") is a beginner. PG]

solving it, would be like a watch in the hands of a savage who could not wind it up, or an iron steamship worked by Spanish engineers.

In regard, then, to the sacred tradition of humanity, we learn that it consists, not in propositions or statements which are to be accepted and believed on the authority of the tradition, but in questions rightly asked, in conceptions which enable us to ask further questions, and in methods of answering questions. The value of all these things depends on their being tested day by day. The very sacredness of the precious deposit imposes upon us the duty and the responsibility of testing it, of purifying and enlarging it to the utmost of our power. He who makes use of its results to stifle his own doubts, or to hamper the inquiry of others, is guilty of a sacrilege which centuries shall never be able to blot out. When the labours and questionings of honest and brave men shall have built up the fabric of known truth to a glory which we in this generation can neither hope for nor imagine, in that pure and holy temple he shall have no part nor lot, but his name and his works shall be cast out into the darkness of oblivion for ever....

To sum up:—

We may believe what goes beyond our experience, only when it is inferred from that experience by the assumption that what we do not know is like what we know.

We may believe the statement of another person, when there is reasonable ground for supposing that he knows the matter of which he speaks, and that he is speaking the truth so far as he knows it.

It is wrong in all cases to believe on insufficient evidence; and where it is presumption to doubt and to investigate, there it is worse than presumption to believe.

From "The Epistemology of Testimony"[6]
Nicholas Wolterstorff

"The wise and beneficent Author of nature ... intended," says Reid, "that we should be social creatures, and that we should receive the greatest and most important part of our knowledge by the information of others." That is by no means a stray, decorative comment on Reid's part.

---

6   This selection consists of parts of chapter VII of Wolterstorff's *Thomas Reid and the Story of Epistemology* (Cambridge: Cambridge University Press, 2001). It is reprinted here with permission from Cambridge University Press.

It points to an important and fascinating component of his thought; namely, his development of an epistemology of testimony.

THE SIGNIFICANCE OF REID'S DISCUSSION OF TESTIMONY

Before we set out on an exploration of Reid's account of testimony let's reflect for a moment on the significance of the fact that he gives such an account. In chapter viii of Essay I of his *Essays on the Intellectual Powers of Man*, Reid, after distinguishing between the "social" operations of our mind and the "solitary," asks: "Why have speculative men laboured so anxiously to analyze our solitary operations, and given so little attention to the social?" I judge the situation not to have changed significantly since Reid's day.

By "social operations" he understands, says Reid, "such operations as necessarily suppose an intercourse with some other intelligent being." When a person "asks information, or receives it; when he bears testimony, or receives the testimony of another; when he asks a favour, or accepts one; when he gives a command to his servant, or receives one from a superior; when he plights his faith in a promise or contract: these are acts of social intercourse between intelligent beings, and can have no place in solitude."

It seems obvious, says Reid, that "the Author of our being intended us to be social beings, and has, for that end, given us social intellectual powers, as well as social affections. Both are original parts of our constitution, and the exertions of both no less natural than the exertions of those powers that are solitary and selfish." ...

WHY DO WE BELIEVE TESTIMONY

... [When someone asserts that P, the listener has a propensity to believe that P.] The main question that draws Reid's attentions is: Why does that happen? Why is it that, upon interpreting someone as telling me that P, I immediately believe that P? ...

The question divides into two: What accounts for the fact that the assertions people make are signs of what they believe—that my asserting P is a sign of my believing P? And what accounts for the fact that hearers tend to *believe* what they take speakers to be asserting—and readers, what they take authors to be asserting? As one would expect, prominent in Reid's treatment of the latter question will be his persistent question: Are we dealing here with "original" principles or with "acquired" ones?

Begin with the first question. Reid's thesis is that our assertions are
signs of our beliefs because God has "implanted in our natures" what
may be called "the principle of veracity"—that is, the "propensity to
speak truth, and to use the signs of language, so as to convey our real
sentiments." Of course, we are, on Reid's view, free agents. So this propensity to speak truth is just that: a propensity, not a causal necessity. It
can be resisted; rather often it *is* resisted. We are not dealing here with
causal laws. Nonetheless, there is the propensity. "Truth ... is the natural issue of the mind. It requires no art or training, no inducement or
temptation, but only that we yield to a natural impulse. Lying, on the
contrary, is doing violence to our nature; and is never practised, even
by the worst of men, without some temptation."

Thus, an asymmetry. We speak truth out of an innate disposition to
do so; "speaking truth is like using our natural food, which we do from
appetite, although it answered no end." We tell lies to achieve some
purpose or other; "lying is like taking physic, which is nauseous to the
taste, and which no man takes but for some end which he cannot otherwise attain."

The objection is likely to be forthcoming that though it's true that
when people lie they have some purpose in mind for doing so, the same
is true for telling the truth; they may, for example, "be influenced by
moral or political considerations" to tell the truth. Hence their speaking truth "is no proof of [an] original principle" of veracity. There is no
asymmetry. No matter whether a person speaks truth or falsehood, he
or she does so for a purpose.

Reid does not deny that we do sometimes speak the truth to achieve
some purpose. His reason for thinking that that is not the case in general, however, is twofold. In the first place,

> moral or political considerations can have no influence until we
> arrive at years of understanding and reflection; and it is certain,
> from experience, that children keep to truth invariably, before
> they are capable of being influenced by such considerations.... If
> nature had left the mind of the speaker *in equilibrio*, without any
> inclination to the side of truth more than to that of falsehood; chil-
> dren would lie as often as they speak truth, until reason was so far
> ripened, as to suggest the imprudence of lying, or conscience, as to
> suggest its immorality.
> And secondly,

when we are influenced by moral or political considerations, we must be conscious of that influence, and capable of perceiving it upon reflection. Now, when I reflect upon my actions most attentively, I am not conscious, that in speaking truth, I am influenced *on ordinary occasions* [italics added], by any motive moral or political. I find, that truth is always at the door of my lips, and goes forth spontaneously, if not held back. It requires neither good nor bad intention to bring it forth.... where there is no ... temptation [to falsehood], we speak truth by instinct.

Looking ahead a bit, it has to be said that Reid's argument here does not establish all that is required to be established if the other half of his full account of testimony is to go through—the half, that is, consisting of his account of why we *believe* what people tell us. Reid's argument thus far is for the conclusion that there is in us an innate propensity to assert something only if we believe it. One might describe it with Reid's own words as the propensity "to use the signs of language, so as to convey our real sentiments." For Reid's account of the epistemology of testimony, he needs more. In the very same sentence he indicates the "more" that's needed when he describes the propensity in question as the "propensity to speak truth." These are two quite different propensities. One might have the propensity to assert only what one believes, while not having the propensity to speak truth; there might, sad to say, be a high proportion of falsehood in what one believes. If I found you to be regularly insincere in your assertions, that would lead me to place little confidence in them in the future; but likewise, if I found you to be regularly sincere but misguided in your assertions, that would lead me to place little confidence in them in the future. Reid's full account of testimony requires that the principle of veracity be understood not just as the disposition to assert only what one believes, but as that disposition combined with some other sort of tendency to get it right. It would be better to call the explanatory principle the principle of *verisimilitude* than the principle of veracity.

What sort of tendency to get it right? Was Reid of the view, and is it an essential part of his account of testimony, that most beliefs of most people are true? If so, his account would not have much going for it. To see how he was probably thinking, it's best to move on to the other side of his account.

Corresponding to the principle of veracity, says Reid, is the *principle of credulity*; that is, the innate disposition to "confide in the veracity of others, and to believe what they tell us." "The wise and beneficent Author of nature, who intended that we should be social creatures, and that we should receive the greatest and most important part of our knowledge by the information of others, hath, for these purposes, implanted in our natures two principles that tally with each other."

"To believe what they tell us": I suggest that those words, and similar words sprinkled throughout the text, indicate that Reid did not intend his principle of credulity to apply to all cases of assertion. His examples indicate this as well, plus the fact that over and over he says that what he's speaking about is testimony. It's cases of someone *telling* me something that Reid invites me to reflect on—and cases of someone *telling you* something that he invites you to reflect on. Lots of cases of assertion are not like that. In writing his dialogues, Plato was making assertions; but he wasn't telling me anything, and probably wasn't telling anyone anything. Perhaps we ought to insert one additional qualifier: It is cases of someone *confidently* telling me something that Reid invites *me* to reflect on; hesitant testimony is a different matter. And now to return to the other side of the matter, Reid's assumption must be that when people tell others something, they by and large speak truth— that is, by and large they say what they believe and what they believe is true. This is the principle of verisimilitude that "tallies with" the principle of credulity.

Of course we often accept the say so of other persons when that say so is not a case of their *telling us* something; it's indispensable that we do so. But as we shall see, Reid is of the view that the "principle" that accounts for such belief is different from the "principle" that accounts for very much, if not most, of what we believe of what people confidently tell us. Admittedly, the concept of *someone confidently telling someone something* is not among the clearest of concepts; but it's clear enough to discern Reid's line of thought, and also clear enough, I judge, to discern the plausibility of that line of thought.

Reid's argument for the presence of a principle of credulity in us— the disposition to believe what people confidently tell us, what they testify to us—goes as follows:

If nature had left the mind of the hearer *in equilibrio*, without any inclination to the side of belief more than to that of disbelief, we should take no man's word until we had positive evidence that he spoke the truth.... It is evident, that, in the matter of testimony, the balance of human judgment is by nature inclined to the side of belief; and turns to that side of itself, when there is nothing put into the opposite scale. If it was not so, no proposition that is uttered in discourse would be believed, until it was examined and tried by reason; and most men would be unable to find reasons for believing the thousandth part of what is told them....

Children, on this supposition, would be absolutely incredulous; and therefore incapable of instruction: those who had little knowledge of human life, and of the manners and characters of men, would be in the next degree incredulous: and the most credulous of men would be those of greatest experience, and of the deepest penetration; because, in many cases they would be able to find good reasons for believing the testimony, which the weak and the ignorant could not discover.

In a word, if credulity were the effect of reasoning and experience, it must grow up and gather strength, in the same proportion as reason and experience do. But if it is the gift of nature, it will be strongest in childhood, and limited and restrained by experience; and the most superficial view of human life shows, that the last is really the case, and not the first.

Though he doesn't actually say so here, Reid's thought is that the principle of credulity is a principle of immediate belief formation.

Upon taking someone to be telling me that P, I immediately believe that P. I believe *on the basis of* her telling me that P. If someone asks me why I believe that P, meaning thereby, *what ground* do I have for believing it, my answer is that I believe it because she asserted it. The principle of credulity thus operates, in several ways, like inference— when inference is operating as principle of belief formation. (Inference need not operate that way: One can infer that Q from P without believing P, in which case the inference will not produce the belief that Q.) Inference as a principle of belief formation starts, like credulity, from belief. And I believe the conclusion on the basis of the premises—that is, on the basis of the propositional content of the belief from which the process starts.

So wherein lies the difference? Well, in the case of inference as a principle of belief formation, not only must I believe the propositions that are the premises; I must believe that those premises logically support the conclusion—that they entail the conclusion, or if not that, that they at least make the conclusion significantly more probable than not. It's that combination of beliefs that evokes my belief of the conclusion.

My acceptance of the conclusion on the basis of the premises is mediated by my belief that those premises logically support the conclusion. I might believe that the premises support the conclusion because somebody told me that they do; in the ideal case, however, I "see" that they do. That is to say: I'm aware of the fact that they do. What's different, as Reid sees it, about the working of the principle of credulity, is that there is no such mediating belief. I believe that she asserted that P; and *thereupon* I believe that P. My believing that P is not mediated by the additional belief, that the proposition that she asserted that P logically supports the proposition that P. What activates the principles of credulity in me is just the belief that she asserted that P—this belief of mine then producing in me the belief that P.

Reid noted that there's a strong temptation in philosophers to try to assimilate all cases of believing what people assert—including, then, cases of believing what they tell us—to believing for reasons. He has Hume especially in mind. The philosopher suggests that what *really* happens, when I believe what someone asserts on the basis of her asserting it, is that I believe on the basis of an argument whose premises are of this sort:

    i.   she asserted that P,
    ii. her assertion that P is an example of a type of assertion whose examples exhibit a relatively high proportion of true assertings,
    iii. so probably this example of that type is true.

The thought is, of course, that (ii) is confirmed by induction.

As we saw, Reid's argument against this analysis is that it is exceedingly implausible to suppose that children who believe what's told them have gone through, or even could go through, such a process of reasoning. But suppose they could, and that to some extent they do. The relevant question would then be how we could ever acquire the evidential basis necessary, on this analysis, for believing the bulk of what we do believe. For notice that in our determination of the truth of assertions, we are never to make use of what anybody asserts unless we have confirmed that the assertion belongs to a reliable type. In fact, of course, what any one of us believes to be true depends massively on believing what others assert. My teacher of high school chemistry based his teaching almost entirely on what others had said; they, in turn, based theirs heavily on what others had said; those, on yet others; and so forth. What would my *personal* evidential basis for the reliability of this massive and intricate body of claims even look like, if it contained nothing that I believe on say so unless I had confirmed that that say so belongs to a reliable type?

... Given these rather obvious difficulties, the question arises: Why have great philosophers been tempted to analyze believing on say so as a case of reasoning? Well, when I believe P on someone's say so, my belief is produced neither by my acquaintance with the fact that P nor by evidence that I might have for P. To believe on say so is in that way to form ungrounded beliefs. It's to trust one's fellow human beings.... [A] good many philosophers have found it difficult to acknowledge that our constitution as human beings falls this far short of their ideal of "rational animals"—and that in the nature of the case this is how it must be....

Lest the precise force of Reid's argument be misunderstood, it's important to add that he is by no means of the view that reasoning plays no role whatsoever in our believing what people assert—not even, more particularly, in our believing what people tell us. This is what he says:

It is the intention of nature, that we should be carried in arms before we are able to walk upon our legs; and it is likewise the intention of nature, that our belief should be guided by authority and reason of others, before it can be guided by our own reason. The weakness of the infant, and the natural affection of the mother, plainly indicate the former; and the natural credulity of youth and authority of age, as plainly indicate the latter. The infant, by proper nursing and care, acquires strength to walk without support. Reason hath likewise her infancy, when she must be carried in arms: then she leans entirely upon authority, by natural instinct, as if she was conscious of her own weakness; and without this support, she becomes vertiginous. When brought to maturity by proper culture, she begins to feel her own strength, and leans less upon the reason of others; she learns to suspect testimony in some cases, and to disbelieve it in others; and sets bounds to that authority to which she was at first entirely subject. But still, to the end of life, she finds a necessity of borrowing light from testimony, where she has none within herself, and of leaning in some degree upon the reason of others, where she is conscious of her own imbecility.

And as in many instances, Reason, even in her maturity, borrows aid from testimony; so in others she mutually gives aid to it, and strengthens its authority. For as we find good reason to reject testimony in some cases, so in others we find good reason to rely upon it with perfect security, in our most important concerns. The character, the number, and the disinterestedness of witnesses, the impossibility of collusion, and the incredibility of their concurring in their testimony without collusion may give an irresistible strength to testimony, compared to which, its native and intrinsic authority is very inconsiderable.

As we mature, we slowly develop a repertoire of types of testimony relevant to our interest in believing what's true and not believing what's false, with the consequence that, rather than believing pretty much what anyone tells us, we now "suspect testimony in some cases," "disbelieve it in others," and in yet others, find ourselves believing with even more firmness than otherwise we would have. Never, though, do we find ourselves in the position of no longer depending on the workings of our credulity principle.

Reid understands this process of maturation, in our believing what people tell us, as the result of the interplay of two "principles": the credulity principle and the reasoning principle. The interplay goes like this. What happens first is that now and then, after believing what someone says, we subsequently learn that it was false—or at least, come to believe that it was false. The occurrence of such learning presupposes, of course, that the proposition that we concluded to be false was believed by us with less firmness than some other proposition that we took to be in conflict with it—and also with less firmness than the proposition that the other was indeed in conflict with it. The least firmly held belief gives way. What makes it possible to learn that something one believed, on someone's telling it to one, is false, is that one's believing it because they told it to one is done with less than maximal firmness.

What happens secondly is that, beyond learning on a number of occasions that what one earlier believed on someone's testimony was in fact false, we also learn to spy cues to false speech—and more generally, to unreliable speech. For there are such cues. We learn that what is said by a certain sort of person speaking in a certain sort of situation is often false; and we learn to pick out such cases from the totality of speakings—to discriminate them from the others. Likewise we learn how to pick out speakings of extremely reliable sorts. For there are those as well, along with discernible and discriminable cues to some of them. All these learnings are stored in memory in the form of beliefs.

The proclivity to believe what someone tells one remains a component of one's constitution. But now that one is an adult, that proclivity gets inhibited for certain tellings because one sorts those into types for whose unreliability one remembers having gained evidence: one has learned that people with that sort of slick manner are not to be trusted. The belief that the case before one belongs to a relevantly unreliable type inhibits the workings of the credulity principle. It is along these lines that I take Reid to be thinking....

From "What Is It to Believe Someone?"[7]
Elizabeth Anscombe

...Believing someone is not merely a neglected topic in philosophical discussion; it seems to be unknown. I have found people experiencing difficulty in grasping it from the title—found them assuming, for example, that I must really mean "believing *in* someone." How do I mean, believing someone? If you told me you had eaten sausages for break- fast, I would believe you. The thing itself is extremely familiar. Does it deserve the attention of a philosophical enquirer? I hope to show that it does. It is of great importance in philosophy and in life, and it is itself problematic enough to need philosophical investigation.

If words always kept their old values, I might have called my subject "Faith." That short term has in the past been used in just this meaning, of believing someone. (Of course that term had also other meanings like *loyalty*, etc.) This old meaning has a vestige in such an expression as "You merely took it on faith"—i.e., you believed someone without fur- ther enquiry or consideration. This is only actually *said* as a reproach— but it is often true when it is not blameworthy.

At one time, there was the following way of speaking: faith was dis- tinguished as human and divine. Human faith was believing a mere human being; divine faith was believing God. Occurring in discussion without any qualifying adjective, the word "faith" tended to mean only or mostly 'divine faith'. But its value in this line of descent has quite altered. Nowadays it is used to mean much the same thing as 'religion' or possibly 'religious belief'. Thus belief in God would now generally be called 'faith'—belief in God at all, not belief that God will help one, for example. This is a great pity. It has a disgusting effect on thought about religion. The astounding idea that there should be such a thing

---

7   This essay first appeared in C.F. Delaney (ed.), *Rationality and Religious Belief* (Notre Dame, IN: University of Notre Dame Press, 1979). It is reprinted here with some sections removed. Reprinted by permission of Mary Gormally.

as *believing God* has been lost sight of. "Abraham believed God, and that counted as his justification." Hence he was called "the father of faith." Even in this rather well-known context where the words appear plainly, they are not attended to. The story itself has indeed remained well known even to ignorant intellectuals mainly because of the thoughts of the fictitious author Johannes de Silentio.[8] Interesting as these thoughts are, we should notice that the author gets into the territory of his interest by cunningly evading the first point of the story, that *Abraham believed God*. He knows it is there, but he does not confront it. This has had its effect; for in matters of intellectual fashion we tend to be like sheep. And so, even though the words appear plainly, they are not, it seems, reflected on. Rather, we are deluged with rubbish about 'believing in' as opposed to 'believing that'. Like the chorus of animals in Orwell, there is a *claque* chanting "believing in goo-ood, believing that ba-ad."

Naturally anyone thinking on those lines won't take an interest in belief with a personal object. For that is necessarily always also 'believing that'. It is indeed convenient, and for my purposes all but necessary, to coin the form of expression: believing *x* that *p*.

I am not interested here in any sense of 'believing in——' except that in which it means 'believe that —— exists'. This belief, with God as an argument, could not be "divine faith." This comes out quite clearly if we use my suggested form: believing *x* that *p*. It would be bizarre to say that one believed N that N existed. Let us consider the most favorable case for this being possible: an unheard-of relation, who writes to you out of the blue to apprise you of his existence and circumstances. Believing that he does indeed exist is accepting the letter as genuinely what it purports to be, and hence that the writer is who he says he is. If you do accept that, you may believe more things—as, that he has a sheep farm in New South Wales—on his say-so. That will be believing him. But the actual existence of the ostensible *he*, whose say-so this is, cannot be believed in the same manner. "He says he exists, and I suppose he knows and doesn't mean to deceive me."[9]

My topic is important not only for theology and for the philosophy of religion. It is also of huge importance for the theory of knowledge. The greater part of our knowledge of reality rests upon the belief that we repose in things we have been taught and told. Hume thought that the

---

8   *Fear and Trembling*, to be obtained from booksellers by citing the author S. Kierkegaard.

9   [Anscombe's point: this would be an absurd thing to say. PG]

idea of cause-and-effect was the bridge enabling us to reach any idea of a world beyond personal experience. He wanted to subsume belief in testimony under belief in causes and effects, or at least to class them together as examples of the same form of belief. We believe in a cause, he thought, because we perceive the effect, and cause and effect have been found always to go together. Similarly we believe in the truth of testimony because we perceive the testimony and we have (well! often have) found testimony and truth to go together! The view needs only to be stated to be promptly rejected. It was always absurd, and the mystery is how Hume could ever have entertained it. We must acknowledge testimony as giving us our larger world in no smaller degree, or even in a greater degree, than the relation of cause and effect; and believing it is quite dissimilar in structure from belief in causes and effects. Nor is what testimony gives us entirely a detachable part, like the thick fringe of fat on a chunk of steak. It is more like the flecks and streaks of fat that are often distributed through good meat; though there are lumps of pure fat as well. Examples could be multiplied indefinitely. You have received letters; how did you ever learn what a letter was and how it came to you? You will take up a book and look in a certain place and see "New York, Dodd Mead and Company, 1910." So do you know from personal observation that that book was published by that company, and then, and in New York? Well, hardly. But you do know it *purports* to have been so. How? Well, you know that is where the publisher's name is always put, and the name of the place where his office belongs. How do you know that? You were taught it. What you were taught was your tool in acquiring the new knowledge. "There was an American edition" you will say, "I've seen it." Think how much reliance on believing what you have been told lies behind being able to say that. It is irrelevant at this level to raise the question about possible forgery; without what we know by testimony, there is no such thing as what a forgery is *pretending* to be.

You may think you know that New York is in North America. What is New York, what is North America? You may say you have been in these places. But how much does that fact contribute to your knowledge? Nothing, in comparison with testimony. How did you know you were there? Even if you inhabit New York and you have simply learned its name as the name of the place you inhabit, there is the question: How extensive a region is this place you are calling "New York"? And what has New York got to do with this bit of a map? Here is a complicated network of received information.

With this as preamble, let us begin an investigation.

'Believe' with a personal object cannot be reflexive. Since one can tell oneself things, that may seem odd. We shall see why it is so later.

One might think at first blush that to believe another is simply to believe what he says, or believe that what he says is true. But that is not so, for one may already believe the thing he says. (If you tell me "Napoleon lost the battle of Waterloo" and I say "I believe you," that is a joke.[10]) Again, what someone's saying a thing may bring about, is that one forms one's *own* judgment that the thing is true. In teaching philosophy we do not hope that our pupils will *believe us,* but rather, that they will *come to see* that what we say is true—if it is.

A witness might be asked "Why did you think the man was dying?" and reply "Because the doctor told me." If asked further what his own judgment was, he may reply "I had no opinion of my own—I just believed the doctor." This brings out how believing x that p involves relying on x for it that p. And so one might think that believing someone is believing something on the strength of his saying that it is so. But even that is not right. For suppose I were convinced that B wished to deceive me, and would tell the opposite of what he believed, but that on the matter in hand B would be believing the opposite of the truth. By calculation on this, then, I believe what B says, on the strength of his saying it—but only in a comical sense can I be said to believe *him.*[11]

... We also see why one cannot "believe oneself" when one tells oneself something. To believe N one must believe that N himself believes what he is saying.

So far we have considered cases of believing people who are perceived. But often all we have is the communication without the speaker. This is so almost any time we find something out because it is told us in a book.

Of course we may be handed the book by a teacher who tells us something about the author. Then we have a communication with a perceived person communicating; and this is about another communication where the communicator is unperceived. It is interesting that when we are introduced to books as sources of information in our childhood it does not usually go like that. We are taught to consult books like oracles, and the idea of the author is not much brought to our attention

---

10   [Anscombe is assuming that the hearer already believes that Napoleon lost the battle of Waterloo. PG]

11   This case was described to me in discussion by Mary Geach.

at first. In any case, after a time we come to receive communications in books without anyone introducing them to us, and we are apt to believe—as we put it—what the book says about itself; for example that it was printed by a certain printer.

To believe a person is not necessarily to treat him as an original authority. He is *an* original authority on what he himself has done and seen and heard: I say *an* original authority because I only mean that he does himself contribute something, e.g., is in some sort a witness, as opposed to one who only transmits information received. But his account of what he is a witness to is very often, as in the example of there being an American edition, heavily affected or rather all but completely formed by what information *he* had received. I do not mean that if he says "I ate an apple this morning" he is relying on information that that was an apple; if he is in the situation usual among us, he knows what an apple is—i.e., can recognize one. So, though he was "taught the concept" in learning to use language in everyday life, I do not count that as a case of reliance on information received. But if he says he saw a picture by Leonardo da Vinci, that *is* such a case. He has necessarily depended an some tradition of information. Thus a speaker may be a total original authority for the fact that he gives, as would usually be the case if one of us said he had eaten an apple, or *an* original authority, but not a total one, as if he says he saw some of Leonardo's drawings; or he may not be an original authority at all, as if he says that Leonardo made drawings for a flying machine. In this latter case he almost certainly knows it from having been told, *even* if he's seen the drawings. (It is true that he *might* have "discovered it for himself." If so, then all the same he has relied on information received that these are Leonardo drawings; or that drawings like to these are Leonardo drawings; and he has noticed—*here* he is an original authority—that *these* drawings are drawings of a flying machine; that *Leonardo* made drawings for flying machines will then be inference on his part.)

When he knows it just from being told (as most of us do) then, as I say, he is in no way an original authority. But that does not mean that there is no such thing as believing *him*. Much information is acquired from teachers who are not original authorities, and their pupils who acquire it believe *them*. As opposed to what? As opposed to merely believing that what they say is true. Consider belief reposed in what an interpreter says—I mean the case of believing the sentences he comes out with. If you believe those communications, probably—i.e., in the normal case—you are believing his principal: your reliance on the interpreter is only belief that he has reproduced what his principal said. But *he* is not wrong if what he says is untrue, so long as it does not falsely represent what his principal said. A teacher, on the other hand, even though in no way an original authority, *is* wrong if what he says is untrue, and that hangs together with the fact that his pupils believe (or disbelieve) *him.*

These various considerations draw attention to the further beliefs that are involved in believing someone. First of all, it must be the case that you believe that something is a communication from him (or "from someone") and second, you have to believe that by it he means to be telling you *this.* It is important for us that natural noises and visual phenomena do not usually sound or look like language, that the question whether someone is speaking or whether this is a bit of written language is hardly ever a difficult one to answer. Someone who saw the markings of leaves as language and strove to decipher them as messages possibly directed to himself, would strike us as demented. And this brings out another aspect: that the communication is *addressed* to someone, even if only to "whom it may concern," or "the passer-by" or "whoever may happen in the future to read this."

We see, then, that various questions arise: (1) Suppose that someone gets hold of written communications, but that they are not addressed to him at all, not even meant to reach him. Can he be said to believe the writer if he believes what they tell the addressee? Only in a reduced or extended sense, though the matter is perhaps not of any importance. (2) Suppose someone gets a written communication which is addressed to him, but the actual writer—I mean the author—is not the ostensible communicator. For example, I write letters to someone as from a pen-friend in Oklahoma. Can the recipient be said to believe (or disbelieve) either the actual author or the ostensible communicator? Surely not the former, except in a very special case and in a roundabout way: I mean, he might himself discern that this comes from the actual writer, myself; and judge that I was trying to tell him something. But otherwise not. This case, where there is intervening judgment and speculation should alert us to the fact that in the most ordinary cases of believing someone, there is no such mediation. In order to believe NN, one "must believe" that, e.g., this is a communication from NN; but that is not believing in the sense of forming a judgment. If one learned it was not a communication from NN, one would straightway cease to say one was believing NN. Now can the recipient, if he *is* deceived, be said to believe or disbelieve the ostensible communicator? Here we have to consider two distinct cases, according as the ostensible communicator exists or not. If he does not exist, then the decision to speak of 'believing him' or 'disbelieving him' is a decision to give those verbs an "intentional" use, like the verb 'to look for'. "The child had an imaginary companion whom he call Efelin and who told him all sorts of things—he always believed Efelin." And so one might speak of someone as believing the god (Apollo, say), when he consulted the oracle of the god—without thereby implying that one believed in the existence of that god oneself. All we want is that we should know what is called the god's telling him something.

If on the other hand the ostensible communicator does exist, then a third party may be the less likely to use the verb 'believe' "intentionally," i.e., to say "So, thinking that NN said this, he believed him." But it is an intelligible way of speaking. And NN himself might say "I see, you thought I said this, and you believed me." If the recipient, however, says "Naturally I believed *you*," NN might reject this, saying "Since I didn't say it, you weren't believing me." Thus there is an *oscillation* here in the use of the notion of believing and disbelieving a person.

(3) This comes out in another way where the recipient does not believe that the communication *is* from NN. This, it seems, lets him off the hook of any reproach from NN about his not having believed him, not having done what he asked, and so on. But may not NN have a complaint at the very doubt whether a communication that *is* from him, really is so? It depends on the circumstances; but NN may well regard it as an evasion, if the recipient seizes on the possibility of treating the communication as not coming from him when it did. NN may call it a refusal to believe him.

(4) If X is to believe NN, something must be being taken as a communication, and since X must be believing something "on NN's say-so," there is also involved the belief that *this* communication says such-and-such. This may seem absurd; surely I may simply believe *your words*, and not have a different version of their meaning and say that what you said meant *that*. On the other hand I ought to be able to elaborate upon anything that I believe: to be able to say who is being referred to, or what time, or what sort of action if I am told, and believe, e.g., "John's daughter eloped at Christmas." Nor are one's beliefs tied to particular words; one reproduces the gist of what one has been told in various ways, and so there is, after all, room for the belief that *that* communication told one such-and-such. So when someone says that he believes such-and-such because he believes NN, we may say "We suspect a misunderstanding. What did you take as NN's telling you that?"

Now, therefore, instead of speaking of the "actual writer"—by whom in the case of the pen-friend I understand the author—we can speak of the immediate producer of what is taken, or makes an internal claim to be taken, as a communication from NN. Such a producer may be a messenger, anyone who "passes on" some communication, or an interpreter (translator) of it. And the recipient can at any rate *fail to believe* (as opposed to disbelieving) NN out of a variety of attitudes. He may not notice the communication at all. He may notice it but not take it as language. He may notice it and take it as language but not make anything of it. He may notice it and take it as language and make something of it but not take it as addressed to himself. Or he may notice it and take it as language and yet, whether or not he takes it as addressed to himself, he may make the wrong thing of it. And he may take it as addressed to himself and not make the wrong thing of it but not believe that it comes from NN.

Only when we have excluded all the cases—or, more probably, simply *assumed* their exclusion—do we come to the situation in which the question simply is: Does X believe NN or not? That is to say, there are many presuppositions to that question as we ordinarily understand it.

It is an insult and it may be an injury not to be believed. At least it is an insult if one is oneself made aware of the refusal, and it may be an injury if others are. Note that here the difference between disbelief and suspension of judgment is of less importance than where the object is only a proposition and not a person. And failure of some of the presuppositions allows scope for reproach. If A has not believed that something was a message from NN when it was, or has given it some false interpretation, NN may (perhaps justly) see in this a readiness on A's part not to believe him. And even if A has falsely believed that something *was* a message from NN and has disbelieved it, while NN cannot say (except in an extended sense) "You disbelieved me!" he may be able to say "You showed yourself very ready to disbelieve me." Or: "You showed yourself ready to credit me with saying something that could not be worthy of belief." For it would be a megalomaniac who complained of not being believed, when he agrees that the thing that was not believed was, anyway, not true. Falsehood lets one off all hooks. Compare the irritation of a teacher at not being believed. On the whole, such irritation is just—in matters where learners must learn by believing teachers. But if what was not believed should turn out to be false, his complaint collapses.

Let us suppose that all the presuppositions are in. A is then in the situation—a very normal one—where the question arises of believing or doubting (suspending judgment in face of) NN. Unconfused by all the questions that arise because of the presuppositions, we can see that believing someone (in the particular case) is trusting him for the truth—in the particular case.

I will end with a problem. I imagined the case where I believed what someone told me, and got the information from his telling me, but did not believe *him*. This was because I believed he would tell me what he thought was false, but also would be clean wrong in what he thought. Now I *may*—it is not the normal case, but it certainly occurs—have to reflect on whether someone is·likely to be right and truthful in a particular case when he is telling me that *p*. If I conclude that he is, I will then believe him that *p*. I think it is clear that this could not be the case for learners, at least elementary learners or young children. But someone might say: "What is the difference between the two cases, culminating in belief that *p* because NN has told one that *p*?" In both cases there is a calculation; in one, you believe what the man says as a result of a calculation that he is a liar but wrong, and in the other, you calculate that he is truthful and right. (No belief in his *general* truthfulness is involved.) The difference between the two cases is only as stated. When you say that in the first case you do not believe *the man*, only what he tells you, and in the second you believe the man, that is just a bit of terminology: you are only willing to *call* it believing the man when you believe he is right and truthful in intent.

It appears to me that there is more to be said than that about the priority of rightness and truthfulness in this matter, but I am not clear what it is.

Trust and Modesty in Belief and Knowledge
Paul Gomberg

This paper addresses the question "What should I believe?" in light of the fact that different people whom we know and have reason to trust do not all believe the same things. In fact, different people whom we have reason to trust believe things that cannot all possibly be true. These conflicts may arise about faith convictions or about conflicts between faith convictions and apparent results of scientific investigation among many other things. I argue that a normal human life and reliable knowledge of the world around us requires us to have two virtues: we must trust what others tell us; we must be modest about what we believe ourselves to know when we recognize we may be wrong. I argue that, while both are virtues, epistemic trust and modesty ("epistemic" meaning concerning what we know) are frequently *conflicting* virtues. The difficulty I will address is how to deal with these conflicts. I argue that, when there is a conflict between trust and modesty, we can have confidence in our beliefs only if modesty triumphs over trust.

PHILOSOPHICAL METHOD

In this paper I will not tell you anything. Well, I may tell you something, but mostly I will not. Let me explain. Suppose I tell you that Mary and I were married in 1965. (See? I told you something; still mostly I won't do that.) And suppose that you believe me. What does this assume?[12]

First, *ideally* I cannot tell you something you already know such as your name or your birthday.[13]

But I also can't tell you something if I don't at least represent myself as knowing it, and, again *ideally*, I do know it. It is an abuse of telling to tell people things you don't know. It misleads them. Presumably I know the year that Mary and I were married, and so I can tell you that—at least normally. On the other hand, I cannot tell you the year in which my house was built because I don't know the year. Ideally I should tell you what I know and you don't.

I would not tell you something (normally) if I thought I would not be believed. If you are to believe me you must trust me—at least to a degree. You must trust that I know what I am telling you and that I am telling you the truth as I know it. If you don't trust me—if you think either that I don't know what I represent myself as knowing or that I am misrepresenting what I believe (lying)—then you will not believe me.

So telling someone something and being believed is, in the ideal case, a matter of one person knowing something that someone else doesn't know, of the first telling that something to the second, and of the second believing the first because he trusts her to know what she represents herself as knowing and to tell the truth.

---

12   This discussion of telling and being believed is indebted to Richard Moran, "Getting Told and Being Believed," *Philosophers' Imprint* 5 (2005), available online.
13   Ideally because in using language, we assume the intent to cooperate. The purpose of telling is to inform, and you can't inform someone of something that person already knows. So telling people things they already know violates the cooperative ideal implied in telling. This is "telling" gone wrong, a common enough occurrence. In the 1960s H. Paul Grice developed a theory of conversational implications grounded in the assumption that language is used cooperatively.

Typically in philosophy no one tells anyone anything. As Elizabeth Anscombe noted in "What Is It to Believe Someone?" in philosophy, we say things in the hope that what we say will *make sense to the listener* and be believed for *that* reason. In contrast, in telling someone something, I expect the hearer to believe it *because I said it.*

Many students new to philosophy have trouble with that subject if their education has consisted largely of being told things and believing what they are told (or—worse yet—being told things and not believing what they are told, a situation that is common for the most alienated students). Philosophy (and, to an extent that is often unrecognized, science as well) is about thinking, not about being told things. Philosophers typically do not know anything that they are in a position to tell their students.[14] Nevertheless, we often know things that our students don't know. "But, wait, Paul, didn't you just say that to tell someone something the teller must know it and the one being told does not know it? Now you say that this is often the case in philosophy. So why aren't you telling your students something when you say something that you know and they don't?" All true, but I don't expect my students to believe me because I tell them.

This is what can make philosophy difficult for beginning students (and can make some science difficult as well). Nothing that I write in this paper (except that Mary and I married in 1965) will be worthy of your belief unless you think about it and, as a result, you realize that it makes sense *to you* and believe it for that reason, not because I said it. (And that is true of everything I just wrote about telling and being believed.) If it doesn't make sense to you, then that is a problem for me as a philosopher and teacher. I assume that what makes sense to me will make sense to others. So if I say something in class or write something in this paper that (I think) makes sense to me, and you, thinking about it, reply that it makes no sense to you, then I think, "Uh, oh; one of us must be wrong." I confess (and this can be my weakness as a teacher) that I often think that you have not really thought about it or have not thought about the very same thing that I am thinking about. But even if I am right about that, my task is still how to bring others to think about the things I am thinking about and, at least, understand why I think they make sense to me. And I should be open to the possibility

14   Typically but not always. If I am discussing evolution with a class I may *tell* my student about the discovery of fossil Australopithecines, something that they may not know of; I may know because I read paleoanthropology avocationally. But as a *philosopher* I tell them nothing. I only ask that they think.

that I have not thought about the matter clearly enough and that what I thought made sense really does not.

So in this paper, as I continue, I ask you to believe nothing *because I write it.* I am *not* asking you to trust me. I ask only that you think about it and believe it if it make sense to you. If it doesn't, let me know, and I will try to figure out whether I am right or not. If I think I am right, I will try to get you to see what makes sense to me and why. If you persuade me that I am wrong, then I will change what I write. That is the method I will try to follow in philosophy.

TRUST

I address here what it is like to grow up as a normal child. Children hear the language of adults and, as they begin to comprehend it, they believe what the adults closest to them—typically the child's parents—say to them. Our adult caretakers call us by our name and, as we come to understand the naming of people, we come to recognize this as our name. And so we learn, sometimes from our caretakers, more words for common things—the parts of our bodies, colors, common objects in the home, animals whose pictures we may see in books. These are common experiences of childhood. Philosophers who have taken an interest in this way of acquiring information from others have called this the problem of "testimony," as a special way of acquiring knowledge. But here I propose that this is not a *special* way of acquiring knowledge; it is, in the beginning, *how we come to know anything at all.* Humans come to know the world using language we learn from others. This shared language shapes our knowledge of the world. It tells us what things are and how things are affected: that this is my finger and that if I close the door of the refrigerator on it, it will hurt. Non-linguistic relatives such as chimpanzees may also come to know the world, but our way of knowing is inseparable from our sharing with others a language for the things around us and for ourselves.

As children, when we believe others, we are trusting them for the truth. Even if, as young children, we are not aware of this element of trust in what we are told, it surely becomes apparent to us later, when we learn that sometimes we should *not* trust some people's words. It then becomes apparent that we have been trusting the words of others all along.

Normal development and development of knowledge are impossible without trust. As children we trust our caretakers to care for us. We trust them to help us understand the world around us. To imagine otherwise is to imagine an unfortunate child, a child who cannot trust.

As we become older the trust we have in others often takes the form of consciously believing what they have told us (as we discussed in the previous section). Because we trust them, we believe them, and because we believe *them*, we believe what they say and thus learn of things we do not know personally. We learn of a larger world, not just the number of our house and the name of our street, our school, and our teacher, but the name of the city or town in which we live, the state, and the country. We learn that there is a wider world, that we live on a roughly spherical planet earth covered by immense oceans as well as land, and that there are continents far away—Europe, Africa, Asia, even Antarctica—at other places on this planet. Depending on our schooling, we may learn that the Earth is a planet in orbital motion about the Sun and in rotational motion on its axis, and that these motions account for the night and day and for the change of the seasons. We may—or may not—learn of an immense history of life and of many extinct plants and animals, for example, dinosaurs, which once lived on Earth but no longer do. This knowledge is essential to understanding who we are and how our lives may affect and be affected by the lives of other people. Without trust we could not know any of this. For the most part human knowledge is not individual; it is social.

CONFLICTS OF BELIEF

When I was a child my mother had a chart taped to the wall of a room shared by my brother and me. The chart represented the history of life on Earth; each *kind* of life was represented by a colored band. At different times in the earth's history different kinds of life predominated, single-celled life, then aquatic, then amphibians, then dinosaurs, then mammals. I took it for granted that this chart that my mother had put on the wall of the room represented the actual history of life on Earth. I never questioned it.

But other people were learning other things from their families, incompatible with what I was learning from mine. Many grow up learning that the stories of creation in Genesis represent a literal account of the history of life on Earth. Many of my students learned this; we meet. Trusting our families, we each believe what we were told growing up.

What is true about the history of life is true about many other things. Not just morality or sports teams (although those too) but other things as well: Was Thomas Jefferson or Abraham Lincoln a racist? Was Stalin a brutal butcher? These last two questions demonstrate how many questions of history are intertwined with political questions. And most of us soon encounter people whose understanding of important historical issues, events, and processes is significantly different from our own.

What are we to do when we realize that others disagree with us? We all—let us suppose—grew up trusting those who care for us. Now we find that others were brought up differently and came in this way (through trust) to different beliefs. If we leave the situation at that, we are just two people who think differently, and that is the end of the matter. Is there an alternative? We may choose not to associate with people who think differently from us because being around them makes us uncomfortable, makes us think about things we would rather not think about.

CONFLICT AND STEPPING BACK FROM OUR BELIEFS

Here I will describe the process of *stepping back* from what we believe. Hence I want to consider both the difficulty and some reasons for stepping back from our own beliefs. Let us consider again the example of two people, A and B, one brought up to believe a literal version of Genesis's six day account of the origins of the universe and the other brought up to believe that life underwent long evolutionary processes of change that scientists can study and understand.

Person A was brought up to believe a six day account of origins. Person B was brought up to believe that life had a long natural history. Each of them (and each of us) looks at the world from her own point of view. That is inevitable. But there is more. Each of them (and each of us) looks at the world from a social point of view, a point of view shared with others. But "others" doesn't mean "all others." Specifically for each of us there are people whose views of ourselves and the world are particularly important to us—let us call this our reference group. This group is often our family or very close friends or others whom we may trust. We care about what they think and about what they think of us more than we care about what strangers think. We form a sense of who we are—as perhaps a son or daughter, as a sister or brother, as a parent, as a Christian or Muslim, as an intellectual, rapper, or poet, as a Democrat or communist—from others, our reference group, who help us to define what it means to be a good son or a good daughter (and similarly for the other categories). These categories become central to our *identities*, our sense of who we are. These relationships with others are also central to our identities as is the *trust* we have for those in our reference group. We look at the world from our personal point of view but also from the social point of view of those whom we trust.

All of this is fine until A and B meet. What happens when they meet can be this: A and B, coming from very different reference groups and hence social worlds, *reject the possibility* of friendship, communication, and learning from one another. Perhaps that is most common; perhaps not. All of us find comfort from those whose view of the world is like our own, and many find it difficult to sustain friendships with those who think very differently from them about the most profound issues of life, about morality, religion, and politics. Hence, many say, you shouldn't argue about those things.

But suppose A and B have enough trust in one another and a recognition of the humanity of the other that they strive for a *broader social point of view*, one that can include both of them. That may not require them to change those beliefs that are in conflict, but it may suggest that they *step back* from those beliefs. By "stepping back" I mean thinking *about* our beliefs. For example, we might ask where beliefs come from and why different people have different beliefs. When we ask such questions we are not thinking from *inside* our own beliefs but thinking *about* our beliefs, as if they were anyone's beliefs.

When A and B have beliefs that are in conflict and they both step back from their beliefs, they can come to a realization: *we can't both be right; one of us must be wrong.* Stepping back from their beliefs doesn't necessarily demand that people change the beliefs that lead them into conflict, but it may lead them to try to find a common ground at some level. How is that possible? One way that may be possible is that people step back from their beliefs to *ask further questions about which they might agree.* For example, each could ask, "How did I come to believe the things I came to believe?" And, if the account I just gave of things is right, each could come to recognize that both their beliefs and the beliefs of the other arose from their trust in those who raised and cared for them and who now serve as their reference group. So while they would not be any closer to agreement about Genesis and evolution, they would have found common ground on something by stepping back from their beliefs. They will agree that, for both, belief arises from trust. They will have found a way in which they are alike. This is a philosophical agreement.

STEPPING BACK: SHOULD WE ALWAYS
PRACTICE EPISTEMIC MODESTY?

Let us discuss a different conflict: C believes that in particular cases of
medical crisis that affected her or family members God has intervened
in the course of nature to cause something to happen that would not
have happened naturally. D regards these same cases as unexplained
phenomena which should be included in the total sum of cases
researchers should engage in trying to understand the *natural* course
of the disease. So for C the cases are miraculous interventions in nature
that science could not possibly explain as the result of natural causes,
while for D they represent puzzles which, now or in the future, we may
solve through a deeper understanding of how healing may occur naturally. C says she knows why the people recovered from their conditions.
D says she does not know but that we should try to investigate what
might have caused recovery.

In my paper "Miracles and Research" I defended D's position and
called it "epistemic modesty": when encountered with an exception,
a rare and unusual case of recovery from disease, regard that case as
a puzzle that one does not understand ("I don't know why that happened") rather than an event whose cause one already understands.

Certainly C and D disagree about epistemic modesty. And perhaps
they can agree that they disagree about whether epistemic modesty is
always a virtue. For example, C might say to D, "To say you don't know,
when you are presented with a clear case of God's grace, is to fail to
honor God. It is sin." And D can agree with C that this is a possible way
of understanding their disagreement. So while they will continue to
disagree about what they should believe, they might, by standing back,
agree that they disagree about whether epistemic modesty is a virtue in
this case. D thinks it is a proper scientific virtue while C thinks it is a
failure to honor God.

To put the point in another way, when D says she does not know
why the recovery occurred, she is being modest. But C believes that
to think you do not know is a sinful lack of honor to God's power and
willingness to heal and hence a prideful arrogance (not epistemic arrogance but a sin of pride in what human's might be able to learn and
know through the advancement of science). It is, for C, a lack of proper
humility before God.

Now suppose we identify the virtue of epistemic modesty with critical
thinking. That is, suppose we think of critical thinking as refusing to

believe something unless the evidence is such that it would persuade any reasonable, open-minded person who looked into it that it is probably true. Then for C, to insist that we always be critical thinkers, that we always withhold belief until we have such clear, compelling evidence of what caused something that it would persuade any investigator, is to fail to have a proper faith in God's power and to do Him honor. But then can't C and D agree that they disagree about *whether it is always good to be a critical thinker*? They can be understood to disagree about the proper scope of critical thinking and epistemic modesty.

BUT WE CAN'T BOTH BE RIGHT

Now, however, consider the conflict between A and B about the literal truth of the story of creation in Genesis. Although A and B can agree that they disagree because they grew up trusting different people and different authorities, it still leaves a conflict about whether the story in Genesis is true. Both A and B, stepping back from their beliefs, should realize: *we can't both know the truth; one of us must be wrong.* Now what do we do? One possibility, mentioned earlier, is to cease to be friends. Another is to acknowledge the conflict but decide not to discuss it: to each his own. But this last seems, to me, to be unsatisfactory because we both know that one of us (or both) must be wrong.

It makes a difference what we do once we become aware of these conflicts. It seems to me one line of thought is natural. We realize that there is something *accidental* about our believing what we do. Had we been brought up in a different family or a different country or a different religion, we likely would have different beliefs. We realize that the thought "these beliefs come from *my* parents (or family)" *cannot give us a reason to think our beliefs true and those of others false.* These thoughts can and should lead us to *epistemic modesty*, to modesty about what it is we think we know.[15]

---

15 Some might use the word "skepticism" for what I am calling "modesty." And they would not be wrong, for "skepticism" can mean simply a requirement for strong supporting evidence to justify belief—belief that will itself be somewhat provisional: "worthy of belief until new information may show us otherwise." But in philosophy the word "skepticism" has often been used to refer to what is also called Pyrrhonism, doubting everything, even the reality of the material world itself. I did not want to confuse the virtue of recognizing that we may be wrong and that we need a way of deciding whether we are right or wrong with this more radical traditional philosophical view. Hence my use of "modesty."

Epistemic modesty is not, however, simply shrugging our shoulders and saying, "Hey, I don't know; I was taught one thing, others something else; who knows who is right?" I assume a desire to know. The desire to know is a virtue. It is natural to humans. It is present in every young child who has not had it driven out of them by fear or humiliation. Young children are very curious, filled with the human love of learning.

Something frequently happens in childhood to change that, to cause students to associate schoolwork and learning with shame and pain rather than with the natural following of our own curiosity. I referred earlier to alienation in students, where they cease to believe what they read or are taught. Some lack confidence that they can figure things out themselves. Some people stop loving to learn and to think. That is a bad thing. It denies or harms our humanity. To be human is to be searching to know, to discover, to think, to learn. This does not necessarily mean being a philosopher—study of philosophy is but one expression of this love of thinking; it doesn't even mean loving to learn in the sense of the academic arts and sciences. Some express their love of thinking in music, painting, sculpture, quilting; others in analyzing human relationships and problems; others in practical crafts such as building and repairing things; others in running a business; I don't mean to be partisan to what most engages me.

Even if your interests do not lie primarily with philosophical questions, it seems to me that you, my reader, should share with me the desire to know the answer when our beliefs conflict. If you do, then you will soon realize that we need a way of deciding, when beliefs conflict, which belief is right.

There are two methods that make sense to me, and, in combination, this is the path I recommend as the path of epistemic modesty. One method is to think things through to try to figure out what makes sense but without doing further investigation of the facts or of what others have discovered. This essay is an attempt to demonstrate how much can be accomplished simply by thinking clearly (I know, not much— but that doesn't mean nothing at all).[16] The other method combines the first method with investigation, what Peirce called "the method of science." Whatever we call it, scientific investigation has to be done in combination with thinking clearly about what we find and what it shows.

---

16   Alec Fisher's *The Logic of Real Arguments*, second edition (Cambridge: Cambridge University Press, 2004) is a text for philosophy classes which tries to show how some intellectual issues can be resolved through careful thinking.

Before going on, I must say a word about science and alienation. I think much science education is awful. Students come away hating science because science becomes just another area where people are telling us what to think. I don't think that is what science is, but I think that many students come away from school with that experience of science education. Science *really* is *you* thinking, investigating, and then arguing with others about the meaning of what you have found. In science *you, not the teacher, are the authority.* But that is not how science is usually taught. If it were taught better, everyone would realize that science is about you investigating things.

However, investigating does not mean that we can rely only on personal experience. We are social learners and, for us, looking and seeing often means looking into what others have discovered. But ultimately we have to come back to the careful, skeptical, thoughtful inquiry into the world around us that has come to be called "science."

But there are problems, and they come back to sources. If science requires us to believe others, we seem to be back to the problem of whom we trust.

SOCIAL KNOWLEDGE

Human knowledge is social. Modern epistemology derived from Descartes, who understood knowledge as something that the *individual* could attain by being clear in his own mind. But gains in human knowledge over the past several hundred years have come largely from the social organization of scientific research. Scientists form communities where they communicate, pursue research, and share research results and theoretical interpretations of their meanings. The literature is filled with controversy and disagreement as well as with specific replicable experimental or observational results.

At bottom science as a social process of inquiry and criticism rests on both trust and modesty. Chemists trust one another's research results; there is the element of trust. But, wait; when a surprising result is reported, don't other chemists seek to replicate it? Isn't that a lack of trust? Yes and no. It is really epistemic modesty. Don't trust until the result has been checked and confirmed. But in the end the cooperative work of a community of chemists or geologists rests on trust. After all, not everyone carries out the replication. And when research results are reported that replicate and confirm the original result, readers trust that result. In the end we have to believe others.

It is pretty obvious, when you think about it, that without believing others, without trust at the bottom of things, you would not know much of anything, not your name, where you live, or where you went to school. Believing others is part of human experience. As individuals we know very little. Collectively we know much more than we used to. The development of collective knowledge depends on trust.

It also depends on the epistemic modesty, skepticism, that is organized into scientific research. This skepticism makes scientific research more than just a bunch of beliefs. These are social beliefs that have withstood scrutiny, questioning, and efforts to show that they are wrong. When many are trying to show that a result or interpretation of the data is wrong, and every effort leads to further support for that result or interpretation, the process increases our confidence that the result or interpretation is right. That is why science works as social knowledge.

COMMUNITIES OF TRUST

Here scientific research is different from religious belief. Religious disagreements are not resolved in favor of one religious doctrine and against another by inquiry and rational disputation. Religious worldviews remain plural; they do not converge toward a single shared view. While there is still much disagreement within scientific communities, including disagreement on important matters, issues do get resolved and settled. Communities move toward agreement, imperfectly, but they do move in that direction.

I know that many students belong to communities of trust that do not include trust of science. I just argued that scientific communities of trust are more worthy of our trust because skepticism is built into the practice of the community. A scientist contributes to the community by showing that someone else's work has flaws or is inconclusive or is not as good a theory as an alternative. Religious and other communities of trust often are not worthy of trust: some religious communities believe in weeping icons, but we are never allowed to investigate the natural causes of the "weeping." These "communities of trust" ask us to believe things that have not stood up to skeptical questioning. If the community does not share practices, such as the ones scientists share, of checking the statements of others to insure that they are true, then the community is not worthy of trust. Based on whether the community in which I was embedded is worthy of trust, I would decide whether to believe what I had been told.

I have proposed that what makes a community worthy of trust is that it shares practices of organized skepticism as science does. But suppose someone is part of a religious community of trust with a different standard of what makes a community worthy of trust (the criterion for trustworthiness may be, for example, that it devotes itself to advancing the faith); then that person will reject my view of what makes a community worthy of trust. Fair enough. We may be at an impasse. Or perhaps not. We will be at an impasse if someone is part of only one community of trust or of communities which share only one single standard for trustworthy communication. But most of us are part of multiple communities of trust. Their plurality gives us the ability to compare communities and ask whether some are more trustworthy than others. When we do this, perhaps we will realize that a community that organizes scrutiny of each person's ideas into its practices is most worthy of trust.

CONCLUSION

Some of my students seem quite discouraged about the prospects of using their own intelligence to deal with questions that are important to us. I would like to change that attitude, but I am not sure how. I could say to them what I believe: "Use your mind to think, to question, to investigate, to wonder, and to determine what makes sense to you. When you do that you will discover the joys of using your own intelligence." But then I would be telling them something, and why should they trust me?[17]

---

17   This paper has benefited from criticism by (and encouragement from) Adam Elga.

SECTION IV

RELIGIOUS BELIEFS
AND
CRITICAL SCRUTINY

INTRODUCTION

The central question raised in this anthology is how we should decide whether an idea is worthy of belief. Clifford proposed that we should withhold belief unless we have sufficient evidence. This principle is particularly problematic when applied to people's deepest religious (and perhaps political) convictions. In this section we explore whether evidence is relevant to the acceptability of religious and other similar deep life-governing convictions.

   The first selection is from a talk given by Richard Dawkins, who is by training a biologist. His arguments come fast and furious, and he moves quickly from one to another. He argues or asserts that (1) when it comes to religion people usually believe what their parents believe; (2) they have no evidence for their religious beliefs; (3) many, including non-believers, hold that religious belief is a matter of faith but "faith is the great cop-out, the great excuse to evade the need to think and evaluate evidence"; (4) some think we should suspend judgment about the existence of God, but that makes no more sense than suspending judgment about the existence of the tooth fairy; (5) complex life forms are thought by many religious thinkers to be statistically improbable and therefore require God as their cause, while evolution shows how complexity can arise step by step; in contrast, an omnipotent God is very improbable. Dawkins can be interesting because he raises so many issues. Perhaps the most interesting problem he poses is this: many people hold that their particular religious convictions are uniquely true (and that other faiths are false), but how can that confidence be justified if there are many religious convictions and there is no evidence to show that one faith is the true faith?

In "The Will to Believe"—written as a reply to Clifford's "The Ethics of Belief"—William James develops a sustained argument that it is permissible to embrace our religious convictions (or any belief) when both belief and non-belief appeal to the mind as possibly correct, when the decision is forced (for example, either we believe it or we don't), and when the choice is momentous (it makes an important difference what we believe). James argues that all these conditions are met in the case of the "religious hypothesis" and hence that our passional nature may rightly move us to religious belief when intellectual grounds cannot determine when belief is justified. To insist on always withholding belief in such situations would, James argues, irrationally elevate our desire to avoid error over our desire to believe the truth.

Richard Feldman makes an important criticism of James's argument. James had pointed out that there may be goods that are available to those who believe the truth but are unavailable to those who suspend judgment (suspending judgment seems to be Clifford's recommendation). Feldman replies that there may also be goods associated with *disbelief* (in God); so there are three relevant alternatives (belief, disbelief, and suspension of judgment) not two, as James suggests. When a hypothesis and its negation are equally probable, given the evidence, the epistemically correct response is to withhold judgment, not to believe either the hypothesis or its negation. He concludes by acknowledging that there may be other justifications (besides sufficient evidence) for arriving at belief, but that they have little to do with James's argument. In the course of making his argument Feldman distinguishes "epistemic" wrongness from a more general idea that something is wrong; he says that a belief is epistemically wrong when it is "wrong from a purely rational (or perhaps 'objective') point of view." Allen Wood's essay (that follows) does not distinguish epistemic wrongness from other sorts. Are there different sorts of wrongness? Is it clear what epistemic wrongness is?

Allen Wood's "Belief Can Be Right or Wrong" gives a robust defense of Clifford's Principle. He explicates two of Clifford's arguments. First, the standards we adopt for arriving at belief influence those around us; human progress is advanced when everyone adopts a responsible approach to belief, one that requires that we base our beliefs on adequate evidence; when we believe without such evidence, we impede progress and harm humanity generally. Here Wood argues that believing beyond evidence has important bad consequences, a conclusion I had suggested Clifford may not have defended adequately. Do you think Wood does better? Second, Wood argues that there is a connection between our standards for coming to belief and our personal integrity (being honest with ourselves); integrity requires us to form beliefs based on evidence and to act on beliefs we sincerely hold. When we form beliefs in other ways, we are not honest with ourselves. In this second argument, Wood defends Clifford's Principle on grounds that do not depend on questionable speculations about the consequences of violating it. Perhaps surprisingly, Wood closes with some remarks that imply that the connection between Clifford's Principle and religious faith are complicated by the difficult question of what constitutes adequate reason for religious belief.

Hilary Putnam's discussion of the notes from Wittgenstein's lectures on religion argues that somehow believers and non-believers talk past one another but that it is hard to say how they are failing to "connect" with one another. Religious convictions are very firmly held; they seem to reflect a picture that "regulates for all in one's life." (Of course, while believers construct good lives and conceptions of themselves grounded in their faith, disbelievers may also construct a conception of how to live grounded in a naturalist worldview that implies disbelief.) Moreover, if our religious convictions represent a picture that regulates our lives, then they may have little to do with belief. This interesting idea takes the discussion in a whole new direction and may suggest that the emphasis on *belief*—in the ways in which we may believe scientific theories to be true—misleads us when we are concerned with religious convictions.

From "A Scientist's Case against God"[1]
Richard Dawkins

As a Darwinian, something strikes me when I look at religion. Religion shows a pattern of heredity which I think is similar to genetic heredity. The vast majority of people have an allegiance to one particular religion. There are hundreds of different religious sects, and every religious person is loyal to just one of these.

Out of all the sects in the world, we notice an uncanny coincidence: the overwhelming majority just happen to choose the one their parents belonged to. Not the sect that has the best evidence in its favour, the best miracles, the best moral code, the best cathedral, the best stained-glass, the best music: when it comes to choosing from the smorgasbord of available religions, their potential virtues seem to count for nothing compared to the matter of heredity.

This is an unmistakeable fact; nobody could seriously deny it. Yet people with full knowledge of the arbitrary nature of this heredity, somehow manage to go on believing in their religion, often with such fanaticism that they are prepared to murder people who follow a different one.

Truths about the cosmos are true all around the universe. They don't differ in Pakistan, Afghanistan, Poland, or Norway. Yet we are apparently prepared to accept that the religion we adopt is a matter of an accident of geography.

It you ask people why they are convinced of the truth of their religion, they don't appeal to heredity. Put like that it sounds too obviously stupid. Nor do they appeal to evidence. There isn't any, and nowadays the better educated admit it. No, they appeal to faith. Faith is the great cop-out, the great excuse to evade the need to think and evaluate evidence. Faith is belief in spite of, even perhaps because of, the lack of evidence. The worst thing is that the rest of us are supposed to respect it: to treat it with kid gloves.

If a slaughterman doesn't comply with the law in respect of cruelty to animals, he is rightly prosecuted and punished. But if he complains that his cruel practices are necessitated by religious faith, we back off apologetically and allow him to get on with it. Any other position that

---

1 This is an edited version of a speech that Dawkins gave at the Edinburgh International Science Festival on 15 April 1992, published in *The Independent*, 20 April 1992.

someone takes up can expect to be defended with reasoned argument. But faith is immune. Faith is allowed not to justify itself by argument. Faith must be respected; and if you don't respect it, you are accused of violating basic human rights.

Even those with no faith have been brainwashed into respecting the faith of others. When so-called Muslim community leaders go on the radio and advocate the killing of Salman Rushdie, they are clearly committing incitement to murder—a crime for which they would ordinarily be prosecuted and possibly imprisoned. But are they arrested? They are not, because our secular society respects their faith, and sympathizes with the deep hurt and insult to it.

Well, I don't. I will respect your views if you can justify them. But if you justify your views only by saying you have faith in them, I shall not respect them.

I want to end by returning to science. It is often said ... that although there is no positive evidence for the existence of a God, nor is there evidence against His existence. So it is best to keep an open mind and be agnostic.

At first sight that seems an unassailable position, at least in the weak sense of Pascal's wager.[2] But on second thoughts it seems a cop-out, because the same could be said of Father Christmas and tooth fairies. There may be fairies at the bottom of the garden. There is no evidence of it, but you can't *prove* that there aren't any, so shouldn't we be agnostic with respect to fairies?

The trouble with the agnostic argument is that it can be applied to anything. There is an infinite number of hypothetical beliefs we could hold which we can't positively disprove. On the whole, people don't believe in most of them, such as fairies, unicorns, dragons, Father Christmas, and so on. But on the whole they do believe in a creative God, together with whatever particular baggage goes with the religion of their parents.

I suspect the reason is that most people ... nevertheless have a residue of feeling that Darwinian evolution isn't quite big enough to explain everything about life. All I can say as a biologist is that the feeling

---

2   [Pascal's wager refers to an argument by the French philosopher and mathematician Blaise Pascal, which can be summarized roughly as follows: Either the tenets of Christian faith are true or false. If false, then there is little that is gained or lost in either believing them or not believing them. However, if they are true, then if I believe them, I am rewarded with eternal bliss while if I disbelieve them I suffer eternal damnation. Therefore, it is rational to believe the tenets of Christian faith. PG]

disappears progressively the more you read about and study what is
known about life and evolution.

I want to add one thing more. The more you understand the significance of evolution, the more you are pushed away from the agnostic
position and towards atheism. Complex, statistically improbable things
are by their nature more difficult to explain than simple, statistically
probable things.

The great beauty of Darwin's theory of evolution is that it explains
how complex, difficult to understand things could have arisen step by
plausible step, from simple, easy to understand beginnings. We start our
explanation from almost infinitely simple beginnings: pure hydrogen
and a huge amount of energy. Our scientific, Darwinian explanations
carry us through a series of well-understood gradual steps to all the
spectacular beauty and complexity of life.

The alternative hypothesis, that it was all started by a supernatural
creator, is not only superfluous; it is also highly improbable. It falls
foul of the very argument that was originally put forward in its favour.
This is because any god worthy of the name must have been a being of
colossal intelligence, a supermind, an entity of enormous sophistication
and complexity. In other words, an entity of extremely low statistical
probability—a very improbable being.

Even if the postulation of such an entity explained anything (and we
don't need it to), it still wouldn't help because it raises a bigger mystery
than it solves.

Science offers us an explanation of how complexity (the difficult)
arose out of simplicity (the easy). The hypothesis of God offers no
worthwhile explanation for anything, for it simply postulates the difficult to explain and leaves it at that. We cannot prove that there is no
god, but we can safely conclude that He is very, very improbable indeed.

From "The Will to Believe"[3]
William James

... I have brought with me to-night something like a sermon on justification by faith to read to you,—I mean an essay in justification *of* faith, a
defense of our right to adopt a believing attitude in religious matters,

---

3   This is an edited version of James's address to the Philosophical Clubs of Yale
and Brown Universities, published in *The New World*, June, 1896. Some sections have
been removed.

in spite of the fact that our merely logical intellect may not have been coerced. 'The Will to Believe,' accordingly, is the title of my paper ....

1 [OPTIONS: LIVING, FORCED, AND MOMENTOUS]

Let us give the name of *hypothesis* to anything that may be proposed to our belief; and just as the electricians speak of live and dead wires, let us speak of any hypothesis as either *live* or *dead*. A live hypothesis is one which appeals as a real possibility to him to whom it is proposed .... [D]eadness and liveness in an hypothesis are not intrinsic properties, but relations to the individual thinker. They are measured by his willingness to act. The maximum of liveness in an hypothesis means willingness to act irrevocably. Practically, that means belief; but there is some believing tendency wherever there is willingness to act at all.

Next, let us call the decision between two hypotheses an *option*. Options may be of several kinds. They may be—1, *living* or *dead*; 2, *forced* or *avoidable*; 3, *momentous* or *trivial*; and for our purposes we may call an option a *genuine* option when it is of the forced, living, and momentous kind.

1.   A living option is one in which both hypotheses are live ones. If I say to you: "Be a theosophist[4] or be a Mohammedan,"[5] it is probably a dead option, because for you neither hypothesis is likely to be alive. But if I say: "Be an agnostic or be a Christian," it is otherwise: trained as you are, each hypothesis makes some appeal, however small, to your belief.

2.   Next, if I say to you: "Choose between going out with your umbrella or without it," I do not offer you a genuine option, for it is not forced. You can easily avoid it by not going out at all. Similarly, if I say, "Either love me or hate me," "Either call my theory true or call it false," your option is avoidable. You may remain indifferent to me, neither loving nor hating, and you may decline to offer any judgment as to my theory. But if I say, "Either accept this truth or go without it," I put on you a forced option, for there is no standing place outside of the alternative. Every dilemma based on a complete logical

---

4   [Theosophy was a nineteenth-century fringe religious-mystical movement. PG]
5   [That is, a Muslim. PG]

disjunction, with no possibility of not choosing, is an option of this forced kind.

3.   Finally, if I were Dr. Nansen and proposed to you to join my North Pole expedition, your option would be momentous; for this would probably be your only similar opportunity, and your choice now would either exclude you from the North Pole sort of immortality altogether or put at least the chance of it into your hands. He who refuses to embrace a unique opportunity loses the prize as surely as if he tried and failed.... [T]he option is trivial when the opportunity is not unique, when the stake is insignificant, or when the decision is reversible if it later prove unwise. Such trivial options abound in the scientific life. A chemist finds an hypothesis live enough to spend a year in its verification: he believes in it to that extent. But if his experiments prove inconclusive either way, he is quit for his loss of time, no vital harm being done.

It will facilitate our discussion if we keep all these distinctions well in mind.

II [MOST BELIEFS ARE NOT MATTERS OF WILL]

The next matter to consider is the actual psychology of human opinion. When we look at certain facts, it seems as if our passional and volitional nature lay at the root of all our convictions. When we look at others, it seems as if they could do nothing when the intellect had once said its say. Let us take the latter facts up first.

Does it not seem preposterous on the very face of it to talk of our opinions being modifiable at will? Can our will either help or hinder our intellect in its perceptions of truth? Can we, by just willing it, believe that Abraham Lincoln's existence is a myth, and that the portraits of him in McClure's Magazine are all of some one else? Can we, by any effort of our will, or by any strength of wish that it were true, believe ourselves well and about when we are roaring with rheumatism in bed, or feel certain that the sum of the two one-dollar bills in our pocket must be a hundred dollars? We can *say* any of these things, but we are absolutely impotent to believe them; and of just such things is the whole fabric of the truths that we do believe in made up,—matters of fact, immediate or remote, as Hume said, and relations between ideas, which are either there or not there for us if we see them so, and which if not there cannot be put there by any action of our own.

In Pascal's *Thoughts* there is a celebrated passage known in literature as Pascal's wager. In it he tries to force us into Christianity by reasoning as if our concern with truth resembled our concern with the stakes in a game of chance. Translated freely his words are these: You must either believe or not believe that God is—which will you do? Your human reason cannot say. A game is going on between you and the nature of things which at the day of judgment will bring out either heads or tails. Weigh what your gains and your losses would be if you should stake all you have on heads, or God's existence: if you win in such case, you gain eternal beatitude; if you lose, you lose nothing at all. If there were an infinity of chances, and only one for God in this wager, still you ought to stake your all on God; for though you surely risk a finite loss by this procedure, any finite loss is reasonable, even a certain one is reasonable, if there is but the possibility of infinite gain. Go, then, and take holy water, and have masses said; belief will come and stupefy your scruples.... Why should you not? At bottom, what have you to lose?

You probably feel that when religious faith expresses itself thus, in the language of the gaming-table, it is put to its last trumps.[6] Surely Pascal's own personal belief in masses and holy water had far other springs; and this celebrated page of his is but an argument for others, a last desperate snatch at a weapon against the hardness of the unbelieving heart. We feel that a faith in masses and holy water adopted willfully after such a mechanical calculation would lack the inner soul of faith's reality; and if we were ourselves in the place of the Deity, we should probably take particular pleasure in cutting off believers of this pattern from their infinite reward. It is evident that unless there be some pre-existing tendency to believe in masses and holy water, the option offered to the will by Pascal is not a living option....

The talk of believing by our volition seems, then, from one point of view, simply silly. From another point of view it is worse than silly, it is vile. When one turns to the magnificent edifice of the physical sciences, and sees how it was reared; what thousands of disinterested moral lives of men lie buried in its mere foundations; what patience and postponement, what choking down of preference, what submission to the icy laws of outer fact are wrought into its very stones and mortar; how absolutely

---

6   [That is, down to its last option, in trouble. PG]

impersonal it stands in its vast augustness,—then how besotted and con-
temptible seems every little sentimentalist who comes blowing his voluntary smoke-wreaths, and pretending to decide things from out of his private dream! ... And that delicious *enfant terrible* Clifford writes: "Belief is
desecrated when given to unproved and unquestioned statements for
the solace and private pleasure of the believer.... Whoso would deserve
well of his fellows in this matter will guard the purity of his belief with
a very fanaticism of jealous care, lest at any time it should rest on an
unworthy object, and catch a stain which can never be wiped away.... If
[a] belief has been accepted on insufficient evidence [even though the
belief be true, as Clifford on the same page explains] the pleasure is a
stolen one.... It is sinful because it is stolen in defiance of our duty to
mankind. That duty is to guard ourselves from such beliefs as from a
pestilence which may shortly master our own body and then spread to
the rest of the town.... It is wrong always, everywhere, and for every one,
to believe anything upon insufficient evidence."

III [MOST BELIEFS ARE SOCIAL AND COME FROM OUR PASSIONAL NATURE]

All this strikes one as healthy, even when expressed, as by Clifford, with
somewhat too much of robustious pathos in the voice. Free-will and
simple wishing do seem, in the matter of our credences, to be only
fifth wheels to the coach. Yet if any one should thereupon assume that
intellectual insight is what remains after wish and will and sentimental
preference have taken wing, or that pure reason is what then settles our
opinions, he would fly quite as directly in the teeth of the facts.

It is only our already dead hypotheses that our willing nature is
unable to bring to life again. But what has made them dead for us is for
the most part a previous action of our willing nature of an antagonistic
kind. When I say "willing nature," I do not mean only such deliberate
volitions as may have set up habits of belief that we cannot now escape
from,—I mean all such factors of belief as fear and hope, prejudice and
passion, imitation and partisanship, the circumpressure of our caste
and set. As a matter of fact we find ourselves believing, we hardly know
how or why.... Here in this room, we all of us believe in molecules and
the conservation of energy, in democracy and necessary progress ... all
for no reasons worthy of the name. We see into these matters with no
more inner clearness, and probably with much less, than any disbeliever
in them might possess. His unconventionality would probably have

some grounds to show for its conclusions; but for us, not insight, but the *prestige* of the opinions, is what makes the spark shoot from them and light up our sleeping magazines of faith. Our reason is quite satisfied, in nine hundred and ninety-nine cases out of every thousand of us, if it can find a few arguments that will do to recite in case our credulity is criticized by some one else. Our faith is faith in some one else's faith, and in the greatest matters this is most the case. Our belief in truth itself, for instance, that there is a truth, and that our minds and it are made for each other,—what is it but a passionate affirmation of desire, in which our social system backs us up? We want to have a truth; we want to believe that our experiments and studies and discussions must put us in a continually better and better position towards it; and on this line we agree to fight out our thinking lives. But if a ... sceptic asks us *how we know* all this, can our logic find a reply? No! certainly it cannot. It is just one volition against another,—we are willing to go in for life upon a trust or assumption which he, for his part, does not care to make.

As a rule we disbelieve all facts and theories for which we have no use. Clifford's cosmic emotions find no use for Christian feelings.... This very law which the logicians would impose upon us—if I may give the name of logicians to those who would rule out our willing nature here— is based on nothing but their own natural wish to exclude all elements for which they, in their professional quality of logicians, can find no use.

Evidently, then, our non-intellectual nature does influence our convictions. There are passional tendencies and volitions which run before and others which come after belief, and it is only the latter that are too late for the fair; and they are not too late when the previous passional work has been already in their own direction. Pascal's argument, instead of being powerless, then seems a regular clincher, and is the last stroke needed to make our faith in masses and holy water complete. The state of things is evidently far from simple; and pure insight and logic, whatever they might do ideally, are not the only things that really do produce our creeds.

IV [PASSIONAL NATURE AND BELIEF]

Our next duty, having recognized this mixed-up state of affairs, is to ask whether it be simply reprehensible and pathological, or whether, on the contrary, we must treat it as a normal element in making up our minds. The thesis I defend is, briefly stated, this: *Our passional nature not only lawfully may, but must, decide an option between propositions, whenever it is a*

genuine option that cannot by its nature be decided on intellectual grounds; for
to say, under such circumstances, "Do not decide, but leave the question open,"
is itself a passional decision,—just like deciding yes or no,—and is attended
with the same risk of losing the truth. The thesis thus abstractly expressed
will, I trust, soon become quite clear. But I must first indulge in a bit
more of preliminary work.

V [EMPIRICIST BELIEF IN TRUTH]

... [T]he faith that truth exists, and that our minds can find it, may be
held in two ways. We may talk of the *empiricist* way and of the *absolutist*
way of believing in truth. The absolutists in this matter say that we not
only can attain to knowing truth, but we can *know when* we have attained
to knowing it; while the empiricists think that although we may attain it,
we cannot infallibly know when. To *know* is one thing, and to know for
certain *that* we know is another. One may hold to the first being possible
without the second; hence the empiricists and the absolutists, although
neither of them is a sceptic in the usual philosophic sense of the term,
show very different degrees of dogmatism in their lives.

If we look at the history of opinions, we see that the empiricist tendency has largely prevailed in science, while in philosophy the absolutist tendency has had everything its own way. The characteristic sort of
happiness, indeed, which philosophies yield has mainly consisted in the
conviction felt by each successive school or system that by it bottom-certi-
tude had been attained. "Other philosophies are collections of opinions,
mostly false; *my* philosophy gives standing-ground forever,"—who does
not recognize in this the key-note of every system worthy of the name?
A system, to be a system at all, must come as a *closed* system, reversible in
this or that detail, perchance, but in its essential features never!...

We slouchy modern thinkers dislike ... to talk in set terms at all; but
at bottom our own state of mind is very much like [the dogmatists']
whenever we uncritically abandon ourselves: You believe in objective
evidence, and I do. Of some things we feel that we are certain: we know,
and we know that we do know. There is something that gives a click
inside of us.... The greatest empiricists among us are only empiricists
on reflection: when left to their instincts, they dogmatize like infallible
popes. When the Cliffords tell us how sinful it is to be Christians on
such "insufficient evidence," insufficiency is really the last thing they
have in mind. For them the evidence is absolutely sufficient, only it

makes the other way. They believe so completely in an anti-christian order of the universe that there is no living option: Christianity is a dead hypothesis from the start.

VI [EMPIRICIST CONCEPTION OF TRUTH]

But now, since we are all such absolutists by instinct, what in our quality of students of philosophy ought we to do about the fact? Shall we espouse and indorse it? Or shall we treat it as a weakness of our nature from which we must free ourselves, if we can?

I sincerely believe that the latter course is the only one we can follow as reflective men. Objective evidence and certitude are doubtless very fine ideals to play with, but where on this moonlit and dream-visited planet are they found? I am, therefore, myself a complete empiricist so far as my theory of human knowledge goes. I live, to be sure, by the practical faith that we must go on experiencing and thinking over our experience, for only thus can our opinions grow more true; but to hold any one of them—I absolutely do not care which—as if it never could be reinterpretable or corrigible, I believe to be a tremendously mistaken attitude, and I think that the whole history of philosophy will bear me out....

No concrete test of what is really true has ever been agreed upon.... To claim that certain truths now [meet the test of what is really true] is simply to say that when you think them true and they *are* true, then their evidence is objective, otherwise it is not. But practically one's conviction that the evidence one goes by is of the real objective brand, is only one more subjective opinion added to the lot. For what a contradictory array of opinions have objective evidence and absolute certitude been claimed! The world is rational through and through,—its existence is an ultimate brute fact; there is a personal God,—a personal God is inconceivable; there is an extra-mental physical world immediately known,—the mind can only know its own ideas; a moral imperative exists,—obligation is only the resultant of desires; a permanent spiritual principle is in every one,—there are only shifting states of mind; there is an endless chain of causes,—there is an absolute first cause; an eternal necessity,—a freedom; a purpose,—no purpose; a primal One,—a primal Many; a universal continuity,—an essential discontinuity in things; an infinity,—no infinity. There is this,—there is that; there is indeed nothing which some one has not thought absolutely true, while his neighbor deemed it absolutely false; and not an absolutist among them seems ever to have considered that the trouble may all the time be essential, and that the intellect, even with truth directly in its grasp, may have no infallible signal for knowing whether it be truth or no ....

But please observe, now, that when as empiricists we give up the doctrine of objective certitude, we do not thereby give up the quest or hope of truth itself. We still pin our faith on its existence, and still believe that we gain an ever better position towards it by systematically continuing to roll up experiences and think. Our great difference from the scholastic lies in the way we face. The strength of his system lies in the principles, the origin ... of his thought; for us the strength is in the outcome, the upshot.... Not where it comes from but what it leads to is to decide. It matters not to an empiricist from what quarter an hypothesis may come to him: he may have acquired it by fair means or by foul; passion may have whispered or accident suggested it; but if the total drift of thinking continues to confirm it, that is what he means by its being true.

VII [WHICH IS PRIMARY, AVOIDING ERROR OR FINDING TRUTH?]

One more point, small but important, and our preliminaries are done. There are two ways of looking at our duty in the matter of opinion,—ways entirely different, and yet ways about whose difference the theory of knowledge seems hitherto to have shown very little concern. *We must know the truth*; and *we must avoid error*,—these are our first and great commandments as would-be knowers; but they are not two ways of stating an identical commandment, they are two separable laws. Although it may indeed happen that when we believe the truth *A*, we escape as an incidental consequence from believing the falsehood *B*, it hardly ever happens that by merely disbelieving *B* we necessarily believe *A*. We may in escaping *B* fall into believing other falsehoods, *C* or *D*, just as bad as *B*; or we may escape *B* by not believing anything at all, not even *A*.

Believe truth! Shun error!—these, we see, are two materially different laws; and by choosing between them we may end by coloring differently our whole intellectual life. We may regard the chase for truth as paramount, and the avoidance of error as secondary; or we may, on the other hand, treat the avoidance of error as more imperative, and let truth take its chance. Clifford, in the instructive passage which I have quoted, exhorts us to the latter course. Believe nothing, he tells us, keep your mind in suspense forever, rather than by closing it on insufficient evidence incur the awful risk of believing lies. You, on the other hand, may think that the risk of being in error is a very small matter when compared with the blessings of real knowledge, and be ready to be duped many times in your investigation rather than postpone indefinitely the chance of guessing true. I myself find it impossible to go with Clifford. We must remember that these feelings of our duty about either truth or error are in any case only expressions of our passional life. Biologically considered, our minds are as ready to grind out falsehood as veracity, and he who says, "Better go without belief forever than believe a lie!" merely shows his own preponderant private horror of becoming a dupe. He may be critical of many of his desires and fears, but this fear he slavishly obeys. He cannot imagine any one questioning its binding force. For my own part, I have also a horror of being duped; but I can believe that worse things than being duped may happen to a man in this world: so Clifford's exhortation has to my ears a thoroughly fantastic sound. It is like a general informing his soldiers that it is better to keep out of battle forever than to risk a single wound. Not so are victories either over enemies or over nature gained. Our errors are surely not such awfully solemn things. In a world where we are so certain to incur them in spite of all our caution, a certain lightness of heart seems healthier than this excessive nervousness on their behalf. At any rate, it seems the fittest thing for the empiricist philosopher.

VIII [BELIEF AND SCIENCE]

And now, after all this introduction, let us go straight at our question. I have said, and now repeat it, that not only as a matter of fact do we find our passional nature influencing us in our opinions, but that there are some options between opinions in which this influence must be regarded both as an inevitable and as a lawful determinant of our choice.

I fear here that some of you my hearers will begin to scent danger, and lend an inhospitable ear. Two first steps of passion you have indeed had to admit as necessary,—we must think so as to avoid dupery, and we must think so as to gain truth; but the surest path to those ideal consummations, you will probably consider, is from now onwards to take no further passional step.

Well, of course, I agree as far as the facts will allow. Wherever the option between losing truth and gaining it is not momentous, we can throw the chance of *gaining truth* away, and at any rate save ourselves from any chance of *believing falsehood*, by not making up our minds at all till objective evidence has come. In scientific questions, this is almost always the case; and even in human affairs in general, the need of acting is seldom so urgent that a false belief to act on is better than no belief at all. Law courts, indeed, have to decide on the best evidence attainable for the moment, because a judge's duty is to make law as well as to ascertain it, and (as a learned judge once said to me) few cases are worth spending much time over: the great thing is to have them decided on *any* acceptable principle, and got out of the way. But in our dealings with objective nature we obviously are recorders, not makers, of the truth; and decisions for the mere sake of deciding promptly and getting on to the next business would be wholly out of place. Throughout the breadth of physical nature facts are what they are quite independently of us, and seldom is there any such hurry about them that the risks of being duped by believing a premature theory need be faced. The questions here are always trivial options, the hypotheses are hardly living (at any rate not living for us spectators), the choice between believing truth or falsehood is seldom forced. The attitude of sceptical balance is therefore the absolutely wise one if we would escape mistakes....

I speak, of course, here of the purely judging mind. For purposes of discovery such indifference is to be less highly recommended, and science would be far less advanced than she is if the passionate desires of individuals to get their own faiths confirmed had been kept out of the game.... The most useful investigator, because the most sensitive observer, is always he whose eager interest in one side of the question is balanced by an equally keen nervousness lest he become deceived.... Let us agree, however, that wherever there is no forced option, the dispassionately judicial intellect with no pet hypothesis, saving us, as it does, from dupery at any rate, ought to be our ideal.

The question next arises: Are there not somewhere forced options in our speculative questions, and can we (as men who may be interested at least as much in positively gaining truth as in merely escaping dupery) always wait with impunity till the coercive evidence shall have arrived? It seems *a priori* improbable that the truth should be so nicely adjusted to our needs and powers as that. In the great boarding-house of nature, the cakes and the butter and the syrup seldom come out so even and leave the plates so clean. Indeed, we should view them with scientific suspicion if they did.

IX [FORCED OPTIONS I: MORAL AND
OTHER PRACTICAL QUESTIONS]

Moral questions immediately present themselves as questions whose solution cannot wait for sensible proof. A moral question is a question not of what sensibly exists, but of what is good, or would be good if it did exist. Science can tell us what exists; but to compare the *worths*, both of what exists and of what does not exist, we must consult not science, but what Pascal calls our heart. Science herself consults her heart when she lays it down that the infinite ascertainment of fact and correction of false belief are the supreme goods for man.... The question of having moral beliefs at all or not having them is decided by our will. Are our moral preferences true or false, or are they only odd biological phenomena, making things good or bad for *us*, but in themselves indifferent? How can your pure intellect decide? If your heart does not *want* a world of moral reality, your head will assuredly never make you believe in one .... Some men (even at the student age) are so naturally cool-hearted that the moralistic hypothesis never has for them any pungent life, and in their supercilious presence the hot young moralist always feels strangely ill at ease.... Yet, in the inarticulate heart of him, he clings to it that he is not a dupe, and that there is a realm in which (as Emerson says) all their wit and intellectual superiority is no better than the cunning of a fox. Moral scepticism can no more be refuted or proved by logic than intellectual scepticism can. When we stick to it that there *is* truth (be it of either kind), we do so with our whole nature, and resolve to stand or fall by the results. The sceptic with his whole nature adopts the doubting attitude; but which of us is the wiser, Omniscience only knows.

Turn now from these wide questions of good to a certain class of questions of fact, questions concerning personal relations, states of mind between one man and another. *Do you like me or not?*—for example. Whether you do or not depends, in countless instances, on whether I meet you half-way, am willing to assume that you must like me, and show you trust and expectation. The previous faith on my part in your liking's existence is in such cases what makes your liking come. But if I stand aloof, and refuse to budge an inch until I have objective evidence, until you shall have done something apt, ... ten to one your liking never comes. How many women's hearts are vanquished by the mere sanguine insistence of some man that they *must* love him! he will not consent to the hypothesis that they cannot. The desire for a certain kind of truth

here brings about that special truth's existence; and so it is in innumer-
able cases of other sorts. Who gains promotions, boons, appointments,
but the man in whose life they are seen to play the part of live hypotheses, who discounts them, sacrifices other things for their sake before
they have come, and takes risks for them in advance? His faith acts on
the powers above him as a claim, and creates its own verification.

... There are, then, cases where a fact cannot come at all unless a
preliminary faith exists in its coming. *And where faith in a fact can help
create the fact,* that would be an insane logic which should say that faith
running ahead of scientific evidence is the 'lowest kind of immorality'
into which a thinking being can fall. Yet such is the logic by which our
scientific absolutists pretend to regulate our lives!

X [FORCED OPTIONS II: RELIGIOUS BELIEF]

In truths dependent on our personal action, then, faith based on desire
is certainly a lawful and possibly an indispensable thing.

But now, it will be said, these are all childish human cases, and have
nothing to do with great cosmical matters, like the question of religious
faith. Let us then pass on to that. Religions differ so much in their
accidents that in discussing the religious question we must make it very
generic and broad. What then do we now mean by the religious hypothesis? Science says things are; morality says some things are better than
other things; and religion says essentially two things.

First, she says that the best things are the more eternal things, the
overlapping things, the things in the universe that throw the last stone,
so to speak, and say the final word. "Perfection is eternal,"—this phrase
of Charles Secrétan seems a good way of putting this first affirmation of
religion, an affirmation which obviously cannot yet be verified scientifically at all.

The second affirmation of religion is that we are better off even now
if we believe her first affirmation to be true.

Now, let us consider what the logical elements of this situation are *in
case the religious hypothesis in both its branches be really true.* (Of course, we
must admit that possibility at the outset. If we are to discuss the question at all, it must involve a living option. If for any of you religion be a
hypothesis that cannot, by any living possibility be true, then you need
go no farther. I speak to the "saving remnant" alone.) So proceeding,
we see, first, that religion offers itself as a *momentous* option. We are supposed to gain, even now, by our belief, and to lose by our non-belief, a

certain vital good. Secondly, religion is a *forced* option, so far as that good goes. We cannot escape the issue by remaining sceptical and waiting for more light, because, although we do avoid error in that way *if religion be untrue*, we lose the good, *if it be true*, just as certainly as if we positively chose to disbelieve. It is as if a man should hesitate indefinitely to ask a certain woman to marry him because he was not perfectly sure that she would prove an angel after he brought her home. Would he not cut himself off from that particular angel-possibility as decisively as if he went and married some one else? Scepticism, then, is not avoidance of option; it is option of a certain particular kind of risk. *Better risk loss of truth than chance of error,*—that is your faith-vetoer's exact position. He is actively playing his stake as much as the believer is; he is backing the field against the religious hypothesis, just as the believer is backing the religious hypothesis against the field. To preach scepticism to us as a duty until 'sufficient evidence' for religion be found, is tantamount therefore to telling us, when in presence of the religious hypothesis, that to yield to our fear of its being error is wiser and better than to yield to our hope that it may be true. It is not intellect against all passions, then; it is only intellect with one passion laying down its law. And by what, forsooth, is the supreme wisdom of this passion warranted? Dupery for dupery, what proof is there that dupery through hope is so much worse than dupery through fear? I, for one, can see no proof; and I simply refuse obedience to the scientist's command to imitate his kind of option, in a case where my own stake is important enough to give me the right to choose my own form of risk. If religion be true and the evidence for it be still insufficient, I do not wish, by putting your extinguisher upon my nature (which feels to me as if it had after all some business in this matter), to forfeit my sole chance in life of getting upon the winning side—that chance depending, of course, on my willingness to run the risk of acting as if my passional need of taking the world religiously might be prophetic and right.

All this is on the supposition that it really may be prophetic and right, and that, even to us who are discussing the matter, religion is a live hypothesis which may be true. Now, to most of us religion comes in a still further way that makes a veto on our active faith even more illogical. The more perfect and more eternal aspect of the universe is represented in our religions as having personal form. The universe is no longer a mere *It* to us, but a *Thou*, if we are religious; and any relation that may be possible from person to person might be possible here. For instance, although in one sense we are passive portions of the universe, in another we show a curious autonomy, as if we were small active centers on our own account. We feel, too, as if the appeal of religion to us were made to our own active good-will, as if evidence might be forever withheld from us unless we met the hypothesis half-way. To take a trivial illustration: just as a man who in a company of gentlemen made no advances, asked a warrant for every concession, and believed no one's word without proof, would cut himself off by such churlishness from all the social rewards that a more trusting spirit would earn—so here, one who should shut himself up in snarling logicality and try to make the gods extort his recognition willy-nilly, or not get it at all, might cut himself off forever from his only opportunity of making the gods' acquaintance. This feeling, forced on us we know not whence, that by obstinately believing that there are gods (although not to do so would be so easy both for our logic and our life) we are doing the universe the deepest service we can, seems part of the living essence of the religious hypothesis. If the hypothesis *were* true in all its parts, including this one, then pure intellectualism, with its veto on our making willing advances, would be an absurdity; and some participation of our sympathetic nature would be logically required. I, therefore, for one, cannot see my way to accepting the agnostic rules for truth-seeking, or willfully agree to keep my willing nature out of the game. I cannot do so for this plain reason, that *a rule of thinking which would absolutely prevent me from acknowledging certain kinds of truth if those kinds of truth were really there, would be an irrational rule.* That for me is the long and short of the formal logic of the situation, no matter what the kinds of truth might materially be.

I confess I do not see how this logic can be escaped. But sad experience makes me fear that some of you may still shrink from radically saying with me ... that we have the right to believe at our own risk any hypothesis that is live enough to tempt our will. I suspect, however, that if this is so, it is because you have got away from the abstract logical point of view altogether, and are thinking (perhaps without realizing it) of some particular religious hypothesis which for you is dead. The freedom to "believe what we will" you apply to the case of some patent superstition; and the faith you think of is the faith defined by the schoolboy when he said, "Faith is when you believe something that you know ain't true." I can only repeat that this is misapprehension.... [T]he freedom to believe can only cover living options which the intellect of the individual cannot by itself resolve; and living options never seem absurdities to him who has them to consider. When I look at the religious question as it really puts itself to concrete men, and when I think of all the possibilities which both practically and theoretically it involves, then this command that we shall put a stopper on our heart, instincts, and courage, and *wait*—acting of course meanwhile more or less as if religion were *not* true—till doomsday, or till such time as our intellect and senses working together may have raked in evidence enough—this command, I say, seems to me the queerest idol ever manufactured in the philosophic cave.... If we had an infallible intellect with its objective certitudes, we might feel ourselves disloyal to such a perfect organ of knowledge in not trusting to it exclusively, in not waiting for its releasing word. But if we are empiricists, if we believe that no bell in us tolls to let us know for certain when truth is in our grasp, then it seems a piece of idle fantasticality to preach so solemnly our duty of waiting for the bell. Indeed we *may* wait if we will—I hope you do not think that I am denying that—but if we do so, we do so at our peril as much as if we believed. In either case we *act*, taking our life in our hands. No one of us ought to issue vetoes to the other, nor should we bandy words of abuse. We ought, on the contrary, delicately and profoundly to respect one another's mental freedom: then only shall we bring about the intellectual republic; then only shall we have that spirit of inner tolerance without which all our outer tolerance is soulless, and which is empiricism's glory; then only shall we live and let live, in speculative as well as in practical things....

If we decide to leave the riddles unanswered, that is a choice; if we waver in our answer, that, too, is a choice: but whatever choice we make, we make it at our peril. If a man chooses to turn his back altogether on God and the future, no one can prevent him; no one can show beyond reasonable doubt that he is mistaken. If a man thinks otherwise and acts as he thinks, I do not see that any one can prove that *he* is mistaken. Each must act as he thinks best; and if he is wrong, so much the worse for him....

"Clifford's Principle and James's Options"[7]
Richard Feldman

1. A well-known principle in the debate over the ethics of belief is William K. Clifford's famous dictum:

It is wrong always, everywhere, and for anyone, to believe anything upon insufficient evidence. (1879, p. 183)

---

7 This article was originally published in *Social Epistemology* 20 (March 2006), pp. 19-33. It is reprinted here, with some revisions, with permission from the author.

William James disputed this principle, claiming that there are certain cases in which it is not wrong to believe things based on insufficient evidence. In this essay, I will examine James's response to Clifford.

Two things about Clifford's claim require explanation. One concerns exactly how to understand the word "wrong" as it is used in this principle. In the first part of this essay I will take the claim to be that it is "epistemically" wrong to believe on insufficient evidence. To say that a belief is epistemically wrong is to say that it is wrong from a purely rational (or perhaps "objective") point of view. Toward the end, I will consider some other interpretations.

A second question about Clifford's claim concerns what counts as "insufficient evidence." There is a reading of his words that makes his claim wholly trivial. If "sufficient evidence" just is enough evidence to make belief on that evidence not wrong, then Clifford's claim is completely uncontroversial. I will not enter into any discussion of what Clifford actually had in mind. Instead, I will make use of the idea that one's evidence concerning a proposition can either support the proposition, support the negation of that proposition, or equally support the proposition and its negation. When the evidence is equally divided in this way, I will say, following Chisholm (1989, p. 9), that the evidence is *counterbalanced*. I take Clifford's claim to be that when one's evidence supports the negation of a proposition or is counterbalanced, then one has insufficient evidence to believe that proposition. Thus, I take Clifford's principle to be:

  C. It is epistemically wrong to believe a proposition when one's evidence fails to support that proposition.

For present purposes, the key implication of (C) is that it is epistemically wrong to believe a proposition when one's evidence concerning it is counterbalanced.

2. The interpretation of Clifford's view just described is adequate to make his view conflict with a plausible interpretation of William James's famous claim:

  Our passional nature not only lawfully may, but must, decide an option between propositions, whenever it is a genuine option that cannot by its nature be decided on intellectual grounds; for to say, under such circumstances, "Do not decide, but leave the question open," is itself a passional decision,—just like deciding yes or no,—and is attended with the same risk of losing the truth. (1956, p. 11)

Several things about James's claim require explanation. These include what a "genuine option" is, what it is to "decide an option," what it is to be unable to decide an option on "intellectual grounds," what a "passional decision" is, and what it means to say that one "lawfully may" decide an option in a particular way. I will explain these ideas in the next three sections.

3. The term "genuine option" is a clearly explained technical term in James's work. He says that an option is "a genuine option when it is of the forced, living, and momentous kind." (p. 3) An *option* is a decision between believing one or another of two hypotheses. *Hypotheses*, he says, are propositions that are candidates for being believed. An option is a *living* option for a person when both hypotheses have at least "some appeal" to the person. An option is *forced* when one cannot avoid selecting one of the alternatives.[8] An option is *momentous* when a great deal turns on one's decision. And, as noted, an option is *genuine* when it is living, forced, and momentous.

One point of clarification is needed. James says that an option is a choice between two hypotheses. But he illustrates the idea of an unforced option with "Either love me or hate me," (p. 3) which is not a matter of hypotheses (propositions to be believed) at all. It is a choice between two attitudes. And he says that a forced option is illustrated by "Either accept this truth or go without it." (p. 3) But here there are not two hypotheses put forward for belief but rather a pair of potential attitudes toward one proposition. (I take "going without" a proposition to be either disbelieving it or suspending judgment—having no opinion—about it.) It will be easiest to accommodate these examples by broadening what counts as an option. We can say that one is confronted with an option when one has a choice between two alternatives. These alternatives can be cognitive attitudes toward hypotheses or emotional states or behaviors, although only cognitive attitudes will be under discussion here. And alternatives can be different attitudes toward the same proposition, as in James's example of a forced option, or the same attitude (e.g., belief) toward different propositions.

---

8 I do not assume that one voluntarily selects one of the alternatives. In particular, I do not assume that forming a belief is something that we can do voluntarily.

I take *deciding* an option to be simply adopting one of the alternatives that constitutes the option. In the cases that are of central concern here, it will be adopting an attitude toward a proposition.

4. In the passage quoted above James suggests that some options cannot be decided on *intellectual grounds*. The idea is that there is no intellectual basis—no evidence or arguments—that provides a good basis for selecting among the alternatives that constitute the option. The evidence then provides no intellectual basis for a choice. Such cases may include those in which one is deciding about believing a proposition and one's evidence concerning that proposition is counterbalanced.

James says that in some cases, when we cannot decide an option on intellectual grounds, we lawfully may make a passional decision. I take a *passional decision* to be a decision made on the basis of one's passions, i.e., one's desires and preferences. I will sometimes describe passional decisions as "non-intellectual decisions."

5. James says that we *lawfully may* make a passional decision when there are no intellectual grounds to make the decision. I take him to mean that such a passional decision is not wrong. Initially, I will take this to mean that these decisions are not epistemically wrong. This interpretation will help to make James's claim conflict most clearly with (C). Toward the end, I will consider alternative interpretations of James's idea.

6. Thus, I take James's key claim to be that it is not epistemically wrong to adopt, on a passional basis, one of the alternatives constituting a genuine option when it is not an intellectually decidable option. The intended implication of all of this is that it is not always epistemically wrong to believe a proposition constituting such an option when one's evidence is counterbalanced.

7. James contends that the conditions listed in his principle apply in the case of "the religious hypothesis." I will assume that the specific hypothesis is the proposition that God exists. Let us call the option we face when deciding about religious belief "the religious option." I will follow him by making the religious option the focus of my discussion, but my point is primarily about Clifford's principle and James's objection, and not about religious belief itself.

On this interpretation, James's argument relies on the idea that the religious option is not intellectually decidable. I will assume for the present discussion that the evidence for and against the existence of God is perfectly counterbalanced. Whether that is actually true is, of course, a matter of considerable controversy. Whether James accepted it is a matter of historical scholarship into which I will not enter. It is, however, an assumption that makes James's view interesting and relevant to (C). Without it, it appears that his stated principle does not apply to the case.[9]

It may be that for some of us, the religious option is not momentous. For some, the hypothesis or its denial may have no appeal and thus the option may not be living. Set such people aside. Let us assume that, for at least some people, the religious option is momentous and living. For the remainder of this paper, I will be speaking only of people for whom these conditions are true.

8. Using the concepts previously described, it is relatively easy to formulate the argument James proposed. I set it out here in excruciating detail.

James's Argument

1. The evidence for and against the existence of God is counterbalanced.
2. The religious option is live and momentous.
3. The religious option is forced.
4. Therefore, the religious option is not decidable on intellectual grounds. [(1), Def. of "the religious option," Def. of "not decidable on intellectual grounds"]
5. Therefore, the religious option is a genuine option. [(2), (3), Def. of "genuine option"]

---

9 I assume in this discussion that options are intellectually undecidable only when the evidence is counterbalanced. One might think that evidence only slightly favoring one hypothesis or the other is also not enough to decide the option. With little or no modification, everything in this paper can accommodate this more inclusive view about which options cannot be intellectually decided. It will be simpler to proceed by ignoring this complication.

6. If an option is genuine and not decidable on intellectual grounds, then it is not epistemically wrong to decide it on non-intellectual grounds. [James's Principle]
7. Therefore, it is not epistemically wrong to decide the religious option on non-intellectual grounds. [(4), (5), (6)]
8. Therefore, it is not epistemically wrong to believe that God exists. [(7), Def. of "the religious option," Def. of "decide an option"]
9. Therefore, the evidence for the proposition that God exists is not sufficient. [(1), Def of "not sufficient"]
10. Therefore, it is not epistemically wrong to believe that God exists and the evidence for the proposition that God exists is not sufficient. [(8), (9)]

The conclusion provides a falsifying instance of Clifford's principle. I am accepting (1) for the sake of argument. The argument is intended to be about people for whom (2) is true. Thus, I will not question these premises. I will discuss (3) and (4) below. Given the definitions, (5) does follow from the prior steps. (6) is just a restatement of James's key principle, (7) applies that principle to the present case, and (8) draws out the consequence of that application. (9) is a simple consequence of the assumption stated in (1). (10) is the conjunction of (8) and (9).

9. Evaluation of James's Argument depends in large part on exactly what the religious option is. I have said that this is the option we face when deciding about religious belief. However, there is more than one way to specify this option.

If the religious option is the decision between believing that God exists and believing that God does not exist, then, given our assumptions, (4) does follow from (1) and the option is not intellectually decidable. However, a problem for James's Argument emerges immediately. The religious option, as just described, is not a forced option since we are not forced to either believe that God exists or believe that God does not exist. Suspending judgment is a third alternative. So if this is the religious option, then (3) is false.

James himself makes a similar point with respect to other examples early in his essay. He says that the option between going with your umbrella or going without it is not forced, since you can choose not to go at all. (p. 3) Analogously, he might agree, the religious option as just described is not forced. He suggests, however, that we conceive of the religious option as the decision between believing that God exists and not believing that God exists. (p. 26) In this case the option is forced and (3) is true. It may seem that this solves the problem. I will argue that it merely introduces a new problem.

10. If the religious option is the choice between believing that God exists and not believing that God exists, and evidence concerning the existence of God is counterbalanced, then the option is intellectually decidable. (4) does not follow from (1). The key point to notice is that the non-belief option can be carried out in two ways: by disbelieving and by suspending judgment. Since, on our assumption, the evidence is counterbalanced, the intellect can decide the case. It decides in favor of suspending judgment, and thus in favor of not believing.

It will be useful to describe the situation in a slightly different way. Instead of limiting options to just two alternatives, we can imagine options with more alternatives. The notion of a genuine option can still be understood in essentially the same way. We can therefore think of ourselves as having a three-way option with respect to the hypothesis that God exists: we can believe it, we can suspend judgment about it, and we can disbelieve it. This is a forced option. It is also an intellectually decidable option, given our assumption about the evidence. Suspending judgment is the preferred choice. Reconceiving of the option as having only two alternatives—believe or do not believe— does not change things in any significant way.

11. One might object at this point, arguing that since the "do not believe" alternative does not specify how it will be implemented, it is wrong to think that there are intellectual grounds for favoring this option. However, this objection is mistaken. Compare the following case, which involves actions rather than beliefs. Suppose that you have a serious allergic reaction to chocolate. You are given a choice for dessert: chocolate cake, chocolate ice cream, or nothing. We can think of this as a three-way option and agree that it is a forced option. Given standard background assumptions, such as a desire to avoid foods to which you have a serious allergic reaction, the option can clearly be decided in favor of no dessert. Suppose we reconceive the case as a two-way option, the alternatives being having chocolate cake and not having chocolate cake. The option can be intellectually decided in favor of

the latter alternative. Nothing changes by subsuming two of the three alternatives under a broader category and reducing the number of alternatives to two.

12. In effect, then, my contention is that James's Argument rests on an equivocation. On one way of conceiving the religious option, it is not forced and therefore not genuine. On another, it is intellectually decidable (given the assumption about the evidence). Thus, either (3), as well as (5), is false or (4) does not follow from (1) (and is false). On no interpretation is the argument sound.

13. It is worth noting that I have objected to James's Argument without calling into question James's principle, (6). In fact, my contention is that the conditions in the antecedent of his principle do not apply to the case under discussion. And the point generalizes. Any decision about believing a proposition can be considered as a two-way option where the alternatives are believing the proposition and disbelieving the proposition. Such cases can be intellectually undecidable. However, suspending judgment is always an alternative. Hence, believe or disbelieve options are never forced. The cases can be redescribed as three-way options, where suspending judgment is one of the alternatives. These forced options are intellectually decidable in favor of this third alternative whenever the evidence is counterbalanced. (When the evidence is not counterbalanced, it will favor either believing or disbelieving.) The cases can also be thought of as two-way options in which the alternatives are believing the proposition and not believing it. However, this option is also intellectually decidable in favor of the non-belief option whenever the evidence is counterbalanced, and in favor of believing when the evidence supports the proposition and in favor of non-belief when the evidence supports its negation. There just are no cases of the sort James needs to make his objection to Clifford work.

14. Readers familiar with James's essay may object that he anticipated all of this when he defends his claim that the religious option is forced. He writes:

> We cannot escape the issue by remaining skeptical and waiting for more light, because, although we do avoid error in that way *if religion be untrue,* we lose the good, *if it be true,* just as certainly as

if we positively chose to disbelieve. It is as if a man should hesitate indefinitely to ask a certain woman to marry him because he was not perfectly sure that she would prove an angel after he brought her home. (p. 26)

I take "remaining skeptical and waiting for more light" to be analogous to suspending judgment. So the idea here seems to be that disbelieving and suspending judgment are not relevantly different, just as hesitating indefinitely about marriage and choosing not to marry do not differ in any way that matters. (This requires taking "hesitating indefinitely" to be hesitating so long that the chance to marry is gone.)

One aspect of James's marriage analogy may distract us from the central point. Surely the man he describes would be foolish to hesitate if all that is holding him back is his not being "perfectly sure" that the marriage will prove to be successful. Being "perfectly sure" of the outcome is a far higher standard and not the one at issue in the case of belief on the basis of counterbalanced evidence.

To develop a closer analogy to the religious option, imagine a case in which the man's evidence is counterbalanced between the proposition that marriage will make his life better and the proposition that it will make his life worse. As he is deciding what to do, for all relevant purposes, there will be no difference between hesitating indefinitely and deciding not marry.[10] In each case, he ends up not married to the woman. No other consequences are relevant to our consideration of the case.[11] He has only two real choices.

It is worth noting that attitudes toward risk do not affect this case. Riskiness does not favor one alternative over the other here: each alternative is risky. Nor will it help to say that it is better to seek good than to avoid harm. Each alternative has its potential good features and its potential harms.

---

10   I assume that we are not to complicate the story by worrying about the possibility that if he chooses not marry this woman, he will then possibly meet someone else, whereas if he hesitates indefinitely he will spend the rest of his life considering only this one potential spouse.

11   In limiting consideration to "practical purposes," I set aside considerations having to do with the ongoing unpleasantness the man may experience by failing to make a decision. I consider only the factors having to do with being married or not being married. Also, throughout discussion of this example, I ignore considerations having to do with the possibility that his marriage proposal will be rejected.

Waiting for more evidence may seem like a good idea in such a case. However, to wait forever is, in effect, to decide against marriage. Perhaps, then, one should simply make a choice, and neither choosing to marry nor choosing not to marry would be unreasonable. Thus, it seems reasonable to make a decision without having evidence to support it.

This line of reasoning might be thought to defend James's Argument from my objection. The two-way option involving believing and disbelieving is not intellectually decidable and, contrary to my claim, it is a forced option since suspending judgment is not a genuine third alternative. This is because it really does not differ from disbelieving. If this is correct, then the argument through line (5) can be sustained after all. The rest of the argument goes through as before.

15. The claim that there is no real difference between disbelieving and suspending judgment is incorrect.[12] This can be seen by noting a key difference between beliefs and actions. When one is deciding about performing an action, one can either do it or not do it. Hesitating forever is the same as not doing it. When one is considering a proposition, one can believe it, disbelieve it (i.e., believe its negation), or suspend judgment. It is true that both disbelieving and suspending judgment entail not believing. But there still is a real difference between disbelieving and suspending judgment: when one disbelieves, one does believe the negation whereas when one suspends judgment, one does not believe the negation. Thus, suspending judgment does not play the same role in the religious example that hesitating plays in the marriage example. In the religious belief case, there really are three different end states, whereas in the marriage example there really are only two different end states. Hesitating indefinitely does coincide with not marrying, whereas suspending judgment does not similarly coincide with disbelieving.

Another way to argue for this point begins by noting that the three-way religious option includes two different actions, believing that God exists and believing that God does not exist. James thinks that suspending judgment is, for all relevant purposes, the same as believing that God does not exist since by suspending judgment "we lose the good (of

---

12 Mavrodes (1963) takes up this same aspect of James's argument. Several of my points overlap significantly with points developed in that extremely useful paper.

believing that God exists), *if it be true*, just as certainly as if we positively chose to" believe that God does not exist. However, one could just as well say that for all relevant purposes, suspending judgment and believing that God exists are the same since by suspending judgment "we lose the good (of believing that God does not exist), *if it be true*, just as certainly as if we positively chose to" believe that God exists. Suspending judgment no more amounts to the same thing as believing that God exists than it amounts to believing that God does not exist.

When it comes to an action, one can do it or not. There isn't a third alternative. When it comes to belief, there always is a third alternative.

16. The marriage example does not indicate any good way to defend the version of James's Argument formulated above, but it may suggest a way to revise the argument in the light of my objection. The lesson to be drawn from the marriage example is that hesitating indefinitely is not required. In a case in which one's evidence about which outcome is best is evenly split, it is not wrong to make a choice. Similarly, one might think, when a belief is associated with crucial decisions about how one will live one's life, suspending judgment may not be the required option even if the evidence is counterbalanced. In the religious case, either one lives a religious life, with all the attendant goods, or one does not. There really isn't a middle ground. Of course, one can choose the purely non-religious life, perhaps one governed by a complete acceptance of a rational, scientific outlook. To choose neither is to be left adrift, with no larger world-view guiding one's life. That might seem to be the worst of all options.

James says things that seem to support such a view. He says that our goals in believing are to "Believe truth! Shun error!" (p. 18) But he places a greater emphasis on believing truths. He rejects in a number of places such things as "*Better risk loss of truth than chance of error*" and he writes:

> *a rule of thinking which would absolutely prevent me from acknowledging certain kinds of truth if those kinds of truth were really there, would be an irrational rule.* (p. 28)

In the cases with counterbalanced evidence, we will be prevented from acknowledging (believing) certain truths, and living the life that goes with them, if we adhere to Clifford's principle.

We might capture the idea here by revising James's key principle. The new idea is that when one's evidence is counterbalanced and the option is momentous because of its impact on one's life, it is not wrong to believe (or to disbelieve). That is,

> 6a.   If an option to believe P or disbelieve P is momentous and is not decidable on intellectual grounds, then it is not epistemically wrong to decide it on non-intellectual grounds.

A revised argument, making use of (6a), could easily be constructed.[13] We can grant that the option involving believing that God exists and believing that God does not exist is momentous and is not decidable on intellectual grounds. Thus, if (6a) is correct, James's conclusion is correct.

The view just described may get some apparent support by considering another case in which the evidence about a choice of actions is counterbalanced.[14] Suppose that I come to a fork in the road and have no information about which path leads to my destination. It is very important that I get there. Given suitable details about the situation, it may be that waiting is the worst option. It's better to just pick one path. At least then I have some chance of arriving at my destination. But either path is just as good a choice as the other. Choosing either path is reasonable. I think that this view about actions is correct. Similarly, then, one might think that momentous choices involving beliefs can properly be decided without there being evidential support for one's choice.

It is worth noting that the fork in the road example again makes vivid a key difference between action and belief. It is clear, I think, that I should not believe, as I proceed along my chosen path, that I have chosen the correct path. I should suspend judgment about which path is best, even as I take one. Once again, suspending judgment remains a good alternative in this case, whereas inaction is not. But this serves to highlight the striking thing about the momentousness of the religious option. In that case it is, allegedly, belief itself that is crucial, and not associated actions. In the fork in the road example, it was crucial that

---

13   The revised argument would omit the step involving the premise that this is a forced option.
14   The marriage example could be used here as well. But I think that a fresh example will be helpful.

I go along one of the paths. It did not much matter what I believed. In the religious option, believing itself makes all the difference. This may seem to suggest that believing here should be considered an action and that it can be reasonable, in spite of the counterbalanced evidence. Picking an attitude is like a picking a path in my example.

17. If (6a) is true, then momentousness makes a significant *epistemic* difference. However, what makes the religious option momentous is the practical significance of religious belief. This makes (6a) highly implausible. From a purely epistemic perspective, where this has to do with trying to believe truths and trying to avoid believing falsehoods, and perhaps also with trying to have knowledge and reasonable belief, there is nothing better about believing important propositions whose evidence is counterbalanced than believing insignificant propositions whose evidence is counterbalanced. In each case, an honest appraisal of the situation requires acknowledging that one has no reason to believe or to disbelieve, and suspending judgment is the epistemically proper response. In such cases, believing *is* epistemically wrong.

18. One might reply that the argument so far overlooks a key element of James's thought. The religious option illustrates the idea that having a belief can have enormous practical significance. It can dramatically affect the quality of one's life. Considered as a practical option, it may be that it is better in such a case to commit oneself than it is to suspend judgment. Whether suspending judgment on such an important topic as the existence of God really has serious negative consequences is difficult to say. However, it is worth exploring the implications of this idea for James's argument. Let us concede, then, that there are practical benefits that may come from belief. It can affect the quality of one's life.

To determine the implications of this concession for James's Argument and Clifford's principle, it will be helpful to examine some alternative uses of the word "wrong." A plausible view is that there are many different kinds of wrongness or, alternatively, that there are many senses of the word "wrong." Thus, things can be morally wrong, or prudentially wrong, or epistemically wrong. Perhaps there is also such a thing as "all-things-considered" (or "overall") wrongness. Things can be evaluated differently along these different dimensions. Thus, something might be morally wrong but not prudentially wrong. Perhaps

James's idea is that given all the relevant factors, it is not overall wrong to believe in the cases under consideration. Thus, his principle may be:

> 6b.   If an option to believe P or disbelieve P is momentous and is not decidable on intellectual grounds, then it is not all-things-considered wrong to decide it on non-intellectual grounds.

To use (6b) in James's argument, the rest of the argument must be revised to be about all-things-considered wrongness, and not epistemic wrongness. To make the resulting conclusion conflict with Clifford's thesis, that thesis must also be revised along similar lines. And it may be that Clifford did intend to make a claim about all-things-considered wrongness. It is notable that he emphasizes alleged social harms that come from believing on the basis of insufficient evidence.

19. If James's central point has to do with the quality of life considerations associated with belief, and his claim is that evidential factors can be outweighed by non-intellectual factors in overall evaluations, then his argument is curiously complex and indirect. There are plenty of cases in which people will cause themselves or the world to be better if they believe things without sufficient supporting evidence. The evidence in such cases need not be counterbalanced; it can even go against the beneficial belief. One simple example will establish the point clearly. A person in a treacherous situation who optimistically believes, against the evidence, that he will survive surely may benefit from that belief. Though Clifford may stridently disagree, it is hard to see any sensible basis for the claim that a potentially life-saving belief in such a situation must be all-things-considered wrong. It is easy to make up many more examples in which the practical benefits of belief are significant even if there is little or no supporting evidence. If these non-epistemic evaluations of belief make sense, then beliefs are wrong or not wrong depending upon how these collective factors add up. So if the point is that beliefs that are not supported by one's evidence need not be wrong in these other (non-epistemic) ways, then the point is well-taken. However, *all* the machinery James introduces is completely irrelevant to his argument. Nothing about intellectually undecidable options or forced options or momentous options is needed to make that point. Nothing about the relative importance of the twin goals of believing truths and avoiding falsehoods plays a role in the argument. Nothing concerning the alleged irrationality of rules that could prevent believing a true proposition enters into

the argument. The point is just that these other factors can outweigh evidential considerations in these overall evaluations. Sometimes, we are better off if we believe something without sufficient evidence.

20. My conclusion is thus as follows. There are a variety of ways in which we can understand the idea of "wrongness" that the debate is about. One possibility is that it is about epistemic wrongness, where this depends upon failures to pursue truth or knowledge in epistemically proper ways. On this construal, James's point is that it is not epistemically wrong to believe on insufficient evidence. I think that if this is his view, then his view has not been defended well. There are no genuine options that are intellectually undecidable, and thus no cases to which James's Principle, (6), applies. Therefore, the argument I have extracted from his essay is not sound. A revised argument making use of (6a) can be formulated, but I claim that (6a) is false.

Another possibility is that James's point is that it is not prudentially, morally, or all-things-considered wrong to believe on insufficient evidence. If that is his point, then I think that he is right. But his argument is needlessly complex, invoking concepts such as genuine options and intellectual undecidability, that play no crucial role. He need only have pointed out that sometimes a person, or society, is better off when someone believes something on insufficient evidence. That there are cases of that sort is beyond serious debate, even if Clifford thought otherwise. Whether such considerations resolve the religious option in a way that would meet with James's approval is a question I will not attempt to address here. The general theoretical considerations he develops in his essay do not establish that they do.

REFERENCES

Chisholm, Roderick, *Theory of Knowledge* 3rd Edition (Englewood Cliffs, NJ: Prentice Hall, 1989).

Clifford, W.K., "The Ethics of Belief," originally printed in *Contemporary Review* (1877) and reprinted in Clifford's *Lectures and Essays* (London: MacMillan, 1879).

James, William, "The Will to Believe," in *The Will to Believe and Other Essays in Popular Philosophy* (New York: Dover Publications, 1956). (Originally published by David McKay, 1911).

Mavrodes, George I., "James and Clifford on 'The Will to Believe'," *The Personalist* 44 (1963).

Believing Can Be Right or Wrong[15]
Allen Wood

Many people seem to think that what you believe is simply "up to you" or "your own business"—and they infer from this that believing can't be a matter of morality or ethics. Or else they think that it can't be a matter of morality or ethics because it is *not* up to you at all—because, that is, we simply have our beliefs, whatever they are, getting them from our environment, our upbringing, or wherever, and can't change them just by deciding to. But a little reflection should quickly get us beyond both these shallow points of view. Maybe beliefs themselves are not (or aren't often) directly voluntary, but the ways we form and maintain them—by looking for evidence or not looking for it, considering it or not considering it, letting ourselves be swayed by irrational factors or resisting their influence—are often up to us. And although what we believe may be "our own business" in the sense that no one has a right to *force* you to profess beliefs you don't hold, or manipulate your beliefs by brainwashing, this does not mean it cannot be a matter of your own personal morality what you believe, just as no one has a right to force you to help out a friend in need, but you still may be blameworthy if you are too selfish and stingy ever to help anyone. You have a moral responsibility to help people, even if no one has a right to force you to do it or punish you for not doing it. And it might be—I think it is—the same with beliefs. Even though no one has any business dictating your beliefs to you and punishing you if you don't believe what they think you should, you still have a moral responsibility to form the right beliefs, to reach them in the right ways, on the right grounds, and not to let yourself form or hold on to your beliefs from the wrong motives.

The basic principle of the ethics of belief was stated by the nineteenth-century scientist and philosopher William Kingdon Clifford: "It is wrong always, everywhere and for anyone to believe anything upon insufficient evidence." Clifford's Principle (as I will call it) is here stated only in terms of the wrongness of positive beliefs. But I think the spirit of the Principle applies more broadly: You should believe what evidence or rational argument justifies your believing, and with the strength that evidence or argument justifies it; and you should doubt or disbelieve only what evidence or argument justifies your doubting or disbelieving, and to the extent that they justify it. We could put it this way, using the

_____

15   This essay was written for this volume and is published here for the first time.

words of a different philosopher, David Hume: We should always "proportion our belief to the evidence." And we should also not let other factors besides rational argument and evidence that may influence us—such as wishful thinking, self-complacency, prejudice, partisanship or social conformity, fear or laziness—determine what we believe.

Deciding what the evidence or argument justifies in these matters is not a question of ethics, but of what philosophers call "epistemology" or "theory of knowledge." And it may depend on your particular situation whether or not you have any reason to form a belief about something at all, how much you need to inquire to form a justified belief, and what standards of evidence you should apply in deciding what is justified. For instance, I may have no reason to form any belief about the safety of a certain medication being considered for treatment of a disease that neither I nor anyone I know happens to suffer. But a scientist employed by the FDA may have a professional responsibility to form a well-founded belief about this, based on established procedures for testing drugs. Here is a clear case where it can also be wrong to form a belief on the wrong grounds. If the scientist decides a drug is safe without testing it because he is too lazy to test it, or because the manufacturer has offered him money to decide it is safe, then this is clearly a belief formed on the wrong grounds. And we can also see how Clifford's Principle applies to this case: For that belief would not only be an epistemological mistake, but it could also be a serious moral wrong (even a violation of the law), if it led the scientist to approve an unsafe drug for sale to sick people.

Clifford thought his Principle is based chiefly on the same kinds of considerations that are at work in this example: Holding beliefs that are not justified by the evidence (or more generally, not apportioning your belief to the evidence) is wrong because you owe it to other people to believe as the evidence justifies and not to hold beliefs merely for your own pleasure, comfort, or convenience. Clifford imagines the owner of a ship which is about to depart for a foreign shore with many poor emigrant families on board. It is an old ship, showing a few signs that it might not be seaworthy. But it has made voyages safely before, and the owner knows it would cost him a lot of money to have it inspected and repaired. Such worries about the soundness of his ship trouble him; if he gives in to them, he will feel unhappy, and if he acts on them he will have to spend a lot of money. So he quashes these doubts, trusting in God's Providence (which cannot fail to look after all those poor people), and he watches the ship depart with a light heart and good wishes for all those on board. And then, Clifford's story concludes, the ship owner later collects his insurance money when the ship goes down in mid-ocean and tells no tales. Here, as in the case of the scientist working for the FDA, it looks as if someone has a moral (maybe even a legal) duty to inquire, to form beliefs based on the evidence, and not believe only what it is pleasant or advantageous to believe.

The most famous challenge to Clifford's Principle is one offered by the American philosopher William James, who holds that we have a moral right to believe at our own risk whatever may tempt our will, whatever may motivate our beliefs—hopes and fears, prejudice and partisanship, social pressure or any other factors belonging (in James's words) to "our passional nature." The crucial phrase here, however, seems to be "at our own risk." James does not seem to want to defend the convenient but harmful beliefs of our corrupt FDA scientist or Clifford's ship owner. James is interested mainly in defending religious beliefs that are based not on the evidence but (in the words of the title of James's famous essay) on the will to believe. James seems to think that religious beliefs (at least the ones he wants to defend) will never pose any harm to others, but he argues that they may very well benefit believers—by making their lives more pleasant, more meaningful, comforting them when adversity threatens them with cosmic despair or encouraging them when they set out on some great enterprise whose success (judged by the evidence) is doubtful, but which they will not put their hearts into unless they believe it will succeed. James thinks that it is irrational for Clifford to want to forbid us beliefs that can do no harm but may do a great deal of good.

I think Clifford has a good response to this line of argument, however. He questions whether there are any beliefs that we hold only at our own risk, and that pose no danger to others if they are held on the wrong grounds. Beliefs that ground some project or enterprise, for instance, must be based on the evidence if we are to be sure that the project will be good either for ourselves or others. We can't let our "passional nature" dictate beliefs about what will be beneficial or harmful to others and then pretend to justify holding those beliefs on "passional" grounds by citing our belief, based on those grounds and not on the evidence, that they cannot harm others. Clifford argues that the very habit of believing on grounds other than the evidence is harmful to others, and should be forbidden on that ground alone, even if there were some short-run benefit to us, or even to others, from holding a belief from that corrupt habit. Humanity, according to Clifford, constitutes a collective community of belief and of actions based on belief. These beliefs tend toward truth, and the actions toward well-being, only if both the beliefs of the community, and those of its individual members, on which the beliefs of the community are based, are formed in accordance with the habit of believing according to the evidence rather than of holding beliefs that cater to the private satisfaction of the believer. To argue that it might be harmless, or even beneficial, to get in the habit of holding some beliefs (for instance, James's religious ones) based on wishful thinking, convenience, prejudice, or social conformity, and to defend those beliefs on those grounds, is like arguing that it might be justified for a judge to get in the habit of taking bribes from people appearing before him in exchange for favorable verdicts, because there might be some benefit to him, and he might have ruled the same way anyhow, in which case there would be no harm to anyone else. The obvious objection here is that the judge would be corrupting the judicial process on whose impartiality everyone depends. Likewise, Clifford argues that those who believe without sufficient evidence are corrupting the collective human activity of inquiring, communicating, and forming beliefs, which we all need if society is to make progress in its knowledge, and to flourish on the basis of this knowledge.

Clifford's argument here, though sound as far as it goes, seems to me in danger of making claims that exceed what it can establish. I think the argument shows that there is an important point of view from which we can always see something wrong with believing not on the evidence but for pleasure, convenience, or supposed advantage. But Clifford ought to acknowledge that this point of view is much more important in some circumstances than others, and that having regard to other people's interests is a much more important consideration in favor of his Principle in some cases than it is in others. Not every belief on insufficient evidence is equally likely to corrupt the social process of inquiry and communication. Scientists falsifying their data out of laziness or professional ambition, or policemen letting their prejudices rather than the evidence dictate whom they charge with a crime, are doing more vital harm to social processes of inquiry than an old person clinging to a superstition they were taught as a child, which may make no difference in anyone's life but their own.

It might even be argued that short-term advantages involved in holding beliefs we can know are relatively harmless to others (even if they are wrong) might justify making exceptions to Clifford's strict insistence that belief on insufficient evidence is wrong "always, everywhere, and for anyone." It is wrong to break a promise, but perhaps in unusual

cases a great benefit (or avoidance of harm) justifies making an exception to the moral rule against promise-breaking. The same might be
thought true of Clifford's Principle, to the extent that it rests on the
interests of others. We shouldn't try to push this point too far, though.
If it is true that there are always in principle exceptions to any moral
principle, it is also true that people are sadly inclined to use this fact
to make exceptions when they shouldn't. It is all too easy to deceive
yourself into thinking that "in this case" the benefits of lying, breaking
a promise, believing on insufficient evidence justify breaking the rule,
and "in this case" no harm will come from it. So we should not be too
quick to argue that Clifford's Principle has exceptions because the pet
beliefs we want to hold "from our passional nature" are held merely "at
our own risk" and do more good than harm.

I think there is a second, entirely different reason behind Clifford's
Principle, and this reason gives us no room at all for making exceptions
to it. Clifford's Principle rests on the demand that we be honest with
ourselves, that we not lie to ourselves, and even that we not participate
in accepted cultural practices that systematically involve people (individually or collectively) lying to themselves. I do not think it is possible to
violate Clifford's Principle without being dishonest with yourself. This is
because there is a *conceptual link* between holding a belief and responding to evidence regarding it. Beliefs are states of a person which mediate
between the person's perceptions of the world and their reasoning about
these perceptions, and their standing disposition to respond actively to
the world, including dispositions to reason from other evidence, seek it
out, and so on. A belief performs its function as a belief when it involves
an honest and rational assessment of the evidence, and also represents
a wholehearted disposition to act on the content of the belief. When
people hold beliefs not supported by an honest and rational response
to the evidence, they can do so only by substituting non-rational and
non-evidential factors (such as wishful thinking), and this necessarily
involves dishonesty and self-deception. When, conversely, people do
not respond to their situation as their professed beliefs imply that they
should, this is also a case of dishonesty—it is what we call 'hypocrisy'.

These two forms of dishonesty often go together. When people form
beliefs not supported by the evidence but held from other motives,
these beliefs are not held honestly, and as a result the person is also
apt to act hypocritically in relation to the belief. For instance, consider
someone who thinks that the only reason to behave honestly is fear of
burning in Hell, but their belief in Hell is held not because there is

good evidence for the existence of Hell, but because they have been brought up and pressured to believe in Hell or because they wish there were a Hell (at least for their enemies). In that case, their belief in Hell is apt to be dishonestly held, and they are also likely to be hypocritical and unreliable in dealing honestly with others.

Reasons for following Clifford's Principle that are based on the good of others apply more in some cases than in others. But reasons based on being honest with yourself apply in all cases equally. It is never right to lie to yourself or to be dishonest with yourself. I have heard people argue, however, that there could be exceptions here too. Suppose I have cancer, and my chances of recovery are known to improve if I believe that I will recover, but go down if I do not. Shouldn't I try to believe I will recover, irrespective of the evidence?

Here is what I say about this argument: If your doctor or relatives know these facts, that might lead them to think that they should withhold certain things from you or even lie to you, so that you are likely to live longer. Whether this kind of paternalistic dishonesty is justified is an interesting issue, but it is not an issue involved in Clifford's Principle. You can't possibly raise the same issue about yourself in the same way. When you talk about 'trying to believe' here, you must mean trying to deceive yourself. I don't deny that people can try to do this, but how likely is it to work, if they know they are trying to believe a lie? And even if they succeed, isn't it degrading? What good is a life based on a lie—a lie that you yourself know is a lie? But here's a further thought: Suppose I have good evidence for believing that if I believe I will recover, then I will recover. Doesn't this in effect mean that if I believe I will recover, then I also have good evidence that I will recover? If so, my belief does not violate Clifford's Principle after all. But then there is no need to make an exception to Clifford's Principle to allow it.

Clifford thought that his Principle was especially applicable to religious beliefs. Religious people seem often to agree with him, when they dispute Clifford's Principle or seek ways around it. But I do not necessarily agree with Clifford (or with these religious people) that Clifford's Principle necessarily condemns religious belief. I do not think it is clear what epistemic standards (standards of proof or evidence) apply to religious beliefs. I accept the claim that some religious people make, that these standards may not be the same as for scientific beliefs. Clearly some religious beliefs are better off, regarding the evidence, than others. Those systems of religious belief that require us to hold wildly implausible beliefs about history—stories about miracles that so defy the known laws of nature that testimony in their favor necessarily lacks historical credibility, or to deny what we are told by the sciences of astronomy, paleontology, and evolutionary biology—these religious systems are worse off—regarding the evidence, hence regarding Clifford's Principle—than those religious systems that do not demand that we believe in defiance of all the evidence. I also don't say that even religious people whose beliefs clearly violate Clifford's Principle are, as individuals, necessarily *dishonest people*. It may be that they are instead caught up in cultural patterns of dishonesty, for which religious traditions and institutions, more than individuals, should bear the blame. So I leave it up to particular religious people themselves to decide whether their faith violates Clifford's Principle. All I say is this: To the extent that it does, it is morally wrong.

From "Wittgenstein on Religious Belief"[16]
Hilary Putnam

I shall begin by discussing Wittgenstein's three Lectures on Religious Belief. We do not have the full text of these lectures; what we have are notes taken by one of the people who was present. But these notes are a valuable source nonetheless. For one thing, in these lectures Wittgenstein's students sometimes make objections or make suggestions as to what Wittgenstein should say; and Wittgenstein's refusal to accept what his students thought he should say tells us a great deal about Wittgenstein's philosophy, and about the ways in which even the best of his students were tempted to misinterpret it.

I was first led to study the published notes on the Lectures on Religious Belief by their subject, of course, but as I studied them and thought about them it came to seem to me more and more that besides the interest they have for anyone who has thought about the subject of religious language and religious belief, they also have great interest for anyone who is interested in understanding the work of the later Wittgenstein. They were given, in fact, in a transitional period, the summer of 1938, when Wittgenstein's later views were in development, and they by no means bear their meaning on their sleeve. Even if we had the full text of what Wittgenstein said in that room in Cambridge in

16   "Wittgenstein on Religious Belief," reprinted by permission of the publisher from *Renewing Philosophy* (Cambridge, MA: Harvard University Press, 1992) by Hilary Putnam, pp. 141-52, 154. Copyright 1992 by the President and Fellows of Harvard College.

1938, I suspect we would be deeply puzzled by these lectures; as it is, we have only twenty-one printed pages of notes summarizing three lectures.

The first of the three lectures sets the interpretative problem before us. What Wittgenstein says in this first lecture is very much contrary to received opinion in linguistic philosophy, and there is an obvious problem as to how it is to be understood. In this lecture, Wittgenstein considers a number of religious utterances, not utterances about God, but about the afterlife, or the Last Judgment, such as "an Austrian general said to someone, 'I shall think of you after my death, if that should be possible'." (Wittgenstein says, "We can imagine one group would find this ludicrous, another who wouldn't.") Again, Wittgenstein imagines someone asking him if he believes in a Last Judgment, and on the first page of the published notes Wittgenstein says, "Suppose I say that the body will rot, and another says 'No. Particles will rejoin in a thousand years, and there will be a Resurrection of you.'" Wittgenstein's comment is "If some said: 'Wittgenstein, do you believe in this?' I'd say: 'No.' 'Do you contradict the man?' I'd say: 'No' ... Would you say: 'I believe the opposite,' or 'There is no reason to suppose such a thing'? I'd say neither." In short—and perhaps this is the only thing that is absolutely clear about these lectures—Wittgenstein believes that the religious man and the atheist talk past one another.

I remember that the first time I had lunch with a great student of comparative religion, Wilfrid Cantwell Smith, Smith said to me that when the religious person says "I believe there is a God" and the atheist says "I don't believe there is a God" they do not affirm and deny the same thing. We shall see that Wittgenstein makes the same point later in his lectures. Religious discourse is commonly viewed (by atheists) as pre-scientific or "primitive" discourse which has somehow strangely—due to human folly and superstition—managed to survive into the age of the digital computer and the neutron bomb. Wittgenstein (and Smith) clearly believe no such thing. Wittgenstein's picture is not that the believer makes a claim and the atheist asserts its negation. It is as if religious discourse were somehow incommensurable, to employ a much-abused word. But there are many theories of incommensurability, and the problem is to decide in what way Wittgenstein means to deny the commensurability or homophony[17] of religious and non-religious discourse.

17   [Homophony means words that sound the same but have different meanings, such as "bank" the financial institution and "bank" the edge of a river or stream.

The first lecture provides us with a number of clues. When a question is an ordinary empirical question, the appropriate attitude is often not to say "I believe" or "I don't believe," but to say, "probably not" or "probably yes" or possibly "I'm not sure." Wittgenstein uses the example of someone's saying "There is a German aeroplane overhead." If Wittgenstein were to reply, "Possibly I'm not so sure," one would say that the two speakers were "fairly near." But what if someone says "I believe in a Last Judgment" and Wittgenstein replies "Well, I'm not so sure. Possibly"? Wittgenstein says, "You would say that there is an enormous gulf between us." For a typical non-believer, the Last Judgment isn't even a possibility.

I don't think that Wittgenstein is denying that there is a state of mind in which someone on the verge of a religious conversion might suddenly stop and say, "What if there is a Last Judgment?" But I think that Wittgenstein would deny that this is at all like "Possibly there is a German airplane overhead."

Wittgenstein distinguishes religious beliefs partly by what he calls their unshakeability. Speaking again of the man who believes in a Last Judgment, Wittgenstein says: "But he has what you might call an unshakeable belief. It will show, not by reasoning or by appeal to ordinary grounds for belief, but rather by regulating for in [sic] all his life. This is a very much stronger fact—forgoing pleasures, always appealing to this picture. This in one sense must be called the firmest of all beliefs, because the man risks things on account of it which he would not do on things which are by far better established for him. Although he distinguishes between things well-established and not well-established."

In understanding these remarks I think it is important to know that although Wittgenstein presents himself in these lectures as a non-believer, we know from the other posthumous writings published as *Culture and Value* that Wittgenstein had a deep respect for religious belief, that he thought a great deal about religious belief, especially about Christianity, and that in particular he paid a great deal of attention to the writings of Kierkegaard, and especially to the *Concluding Unscientific Postscript*. The man who has an unshakeable belief in the Last Judgment and lets it regulate for all his life, although he is very

---

Here Putnam means that believers and non-believers use the same words but don't mean the same thing by them. Putnam's problem is to make clear exactly how they are "not the same" in meaning. PG]

willing to admit that the Last Judgment is not an established fact, sounds like a Christian after Kierkegaard's own heart. Yet Kierkegaard himself wrote that faith "has in every moment the infinite dialectic of uncertainty present with it." It would be ludicrous to suppose that inner struggles with the issue of religious belief are something that Wittgenstein did not know. When he takes the unshakeableness of a religious belief as one of its characteristics, he does not mean that a genuine religious belief is always and at every moment free from doubt. Kierkegaard spoke of faith as a state in which one cannot permanently stay. But I think that Kierkegaard would agree with Wittgenstein— and that Wittgenstein is here agreeing with Kierkegaard—that religious belief "regulates for all" in the believer's life, even though his religious belief may alternate with doubt. In this respect it is different from an empirical belief. If I confidently believe that a certain way is the right way to build a bridge, then I will set out building the bridge that way. If I come to have doubts, I will not go on building the bridge in that way (unless I am a crooked contractor); I will halt the construction and run further tests and make calculations.

Wittgenstein uses the following example:

Suppose you had two people, and one of them, when he had to decide which course to take, thought of retribution and the other did not. One person might, for instance, be inclined to take everything that happened to him as a reward or punishment, and another person doesn't think of this at all.

If he is ill, he may think: "What have I done to deserve this?" This is one way of thinking of retribution. Another way is, he thinks in a general way whenever he is ashamed of himself: "This will be punished."

Take two people, one of whom talks of his behaviour and of what happens to him in terms of retribution, the other one does not. These people think entirely differently. Yet, so far, you can't say they believe different things.

[Wittgenstein adds] It is this way: if someone said: "Wittgenstein, you don't take illness as a punishment, so what do you believe?"— I'd say: I don't have any thoughts of punishment.

There are, for instance, these entirely different ways of thinking first of all—which needn't be expressed by one person saying one thing, another person another thing.

I think we take this example in the wrong way if we suppose that the person who thinks of his life in terms of retribution is supposed to be what we ordinarily call a religious believer. The example doesn't depend on whether he is or isn't. What Wittgenstein means to bring out by the example is that one's life may be organized by very different pictures. And he means to suggest that religion has more to do with the kind of picture that one allows to organize one's life than it does with expressions of belief. As Wittgenstein says, summing up this example, "What we call believing in a Judgement Day or not believing in a Judgement Day—The expression of belief may play an absolutely minor role."

Wittgenstein also contrasts the basis upon which one forms empirical beliefs and the basis upon which one forms religious beliefs. "Reasons look entirely different from normal reasons" in the religious case. "They are, in a way, quite inconclusive." He contrasts two cases: a person who believes that something that fits the description of the Last Judgment will in fact happen, years and years in the future, and who believes this on the basis of what we would call scientific evidence, and a person who has a religious belief which "might in fact fly in the face of such a forecast and say 'No. There it will break down.'" Wittgenstein says that if a scientist told him that there would be a Last Judgment in a thousand years, and that he had to forgo all pleasures because of such a forecast, that he, Wittgenstein, "wouldn't budge." But the person whose belief in such a forecast was religious and not scientific "would fight for his life and not to be dragged into the fire. No induction. Terror. That is, as it were, part of the substance of the belief."

The quoted passages give some sense of the texture of these notes. What seems most important in this first lecture is the repeated claim that the relation between Wittgenstein (who thoroughly conceals his own struggle with or against religious belief in these lectures) and the believer is not one of contradiction:

> If you ask me whether or not I believe in a Judgement Day, in the sense in which the religious people have belief in it, I wouldn't say: "No. I don't believe there will be such a thing." It would seem to me utterly crazy to say this.
>
> And then I give an explanation: "I don't believe in ...," but then the religious person never believes what I describe.
>
> I can't say. I can't contradict that person.

In one sense, I understand all he says—the English words "God," "separate," etc. I understand. I could say: "I don't believe in this," and this would be true, meaning I haven't got these thoughts or anything that hangs together with them. But not that I could contradict the thing.

... If Wittgenstein is not saying one of the standard things about religious language—for example, that it expresses false pre-scientific theories, or that it is non-cognitive, or that it is emotive, or that it is incommensurable—then what is he saying and how is it possible for him to avoid all of these standard alternatives? Still more important, how does he think we, including those of us who are not religious (and I don't think Wittgenstein himself ever succeeded in recovering the Christian faith in which he was raised, although it was always a possibility for him that he might), are to think about religious language? What sort of a model is Wittgenstein offering us for reflection on what is always a very important, very difficult, and sometimes very divisive part of human life?...

One concern of Wittgenstein's in the first two lectures is to contrast superstition and credulity—which often coexist with religion, to be sure—with religious belief in his sense. (Again, the parallelism with Kierkegaard is striking.) In the first lecture, the example of superstition is a Catholic priest who tries to offer scientific arguments for the truths of religion. Wittgenstein's comment is:

I would definitely call O'Hara unreasonable. I would say, if this is religious belief, then it's all superstition.

But I would ridicule it, not by saying it is based on insufficient evidence. I would say: here is a man who is cheating himself. You can say: this man is ridiculous because he believes, and bases it on weak reasons.

In the second lecture, Wittgenstein says:

Suppose I went to somewhere like Lourdes in France. Suppose I went with a very credulous person. There we see blood coming out of something. He says: "There you are, Wittgenstein, how can you doubt?" I'd say: "Can it only be explained one way? Can't it be this or that?" I'd try to convince him that he'd seen nothing of any

consequence. I wonder whether I would do that under all circumstances. I certainly know that I would under normal circumstances.
   "Oughtn't one after all to consider this?" I'd say: "Come on.
Come on." I would treat the phenomenon in this case just as I
would treat an experiment in a laboratory which I thought badly
executed.

Wittgenstein is concerned to deny any continuity at all between what
he considers religious belief and scientific belief. When there is a continuity, and only when there is a continuity, Wittgenstein is willing to use
words like "ridiculous," "absurd," "credulous," "superstition."
   To come back to the question of incommensurability. An example
might seem to be afforded by Wittgenstein's own thought experiment at the beginning of the first lecture, of imagining two people
of whom the first one says "I believe in a Last Judgement" and the
second (whom Wittgenstein imagines to be himself) says "Well, I'm
not so sure. Possibly." Here Wittgenstein does say "It isn't a question
of my being anywhere near him, but on an entirely different plane,
which you could express by saying: 'You mean something altogether
different, Wittgenstein.'"... In the notes we have of the first lecture, it
is Wittgenstein's imaginary interlocutor who says [this]. Wittgenstein
replies to his imaginary interlocutor, "The difference might not show
up at all in any explanation of the meaning."
   Something lovely happens here. Wittgenstein is often charged with
simple-mindedly equating use and meaning. Yet here he imagines an
interlocutor who plays the role of the stock "Wittgenstein" and proposes
to say that the words "I believe in a last Judgement" have a different
meaning in the two uses (one is, of course, completely imaginary), and
the real Wittgenstein reminds the stock "Wittgenstein" that we don't use
the word "meaning" that way, that is, that the difference in these two uses
is not something that we would ordinarily call a difference in meaning.
   Wittgenstein says something more about this toward the end of the
same lecture. He points out that as an educated person who has read
(and, as we know, has thought deeply about) the religious classics there
is a very good sense in which he knows what the religious person means,
although there is another sense in which Wittgenstein is inclined to say
"I don't know whether I understand him or not": "If Mr. Lewy [Cassimir
Lewy, one of the students present at these sessions] is religious and
says he believes in a Judgement Day, I won't even know whether to say

I understand him or not. I've read the same things as he's read. In a most important sense, I know what he means." Wittgenstein immediately goes on to ask, "If an atheist says: 'There won't be a Judgement day,' and another person says there will, do they mean the same?—Not clear what the criterion of meaning the same is. They might describe the same things. You might say, this already shows that this means the same."

So Wittgenstein is warning us against supposing that talk of "meaning the same" and "not meaning the same" will clarify anything here. In a perfectly ordinary sense of meaning the same, we might say that they do mean the same (although Wittgenstein is still inclined to say "I don't even know whether I should say that I understand him or not"); and to dismiss the question whether words mean the same, that is, whether the sentence means the same, as of no help here, is precisely to dismiss "incommensurability" talk. That the two speakers are not able to communicate *because* their words have different "meanings" is precisely the doctrine of incommensurability....

What then is Wittgenstein saying? I believe that what Wittgenstein (in company with Kierkegaard) is saying is this: that religious discourse can be understood in any depth only by understanding the form of life to which it belongs. What characterizes that form of life is not the expressions of belief that accompany it, but a way—a way that includes words and pictures, but is far from consisting in just words and pictures—of living one's life, of regulating all of one's decisions. Here the believer, Kierkegaard, would add something that Wittgenstein does not say, but that I think he would agree with: namely, that a person may think and say all the right words and be living a thoroughly non-religious life. Indeed, Kierkegaard insists that a person may think he or she is worshipping God and really be worshipping an idol. (I suspect that this is one of the reasons that Kierkegaard is so much hated by fundamentalists. For Kierkegaard an authentically religious form of life is characterized by a constant concern that one not replace the idea of God with a narcissistic creation of one's own; and this concern expresses itself in uncertainty as much as in certainty. For Kierkegaard, to be absolutely sure you are "born again" is a sign that you are lost.) What Kierkegaard and Wittgenstein have in common is the idea that understanding the words of a religious person properly—whether you want to speak of understanding their "meaning" or not—is inseparable from understanding a religious form of life, and this is not a matter of "semantic theory," but a matter of understanding a human being....

SECTION V: EPILOGUE

WHAT
SHOULD
I BELIEVE?

BY THE TIME WE START TO THINK ABOUT WHAT WE *should* BELIEVE, WE already have many beliefs to think about. Our beliefs come from many sources, but mostly from other people. Of course some of our beliefs come from our experience, but even our experience depends on what we learn from others: I have seen New York, but it was the sign or the map or another person (or a combination of these) that assured me that it was New York that I was seeing. (Elizabeth Anscombe makes this point.) Our knowledge and belief are social in this way. We may get beliefs from our parents, from school, from church, from our reading, including what we read on the internet, from television and the movies, and from what our friends tell us.

Often what we are told in one place does not fit with what we are told in another, or the things others tell us may not fit with what we actually experience. There is a conflict.

The problem of what I should believe arises from this conflict and from our reflecting on what to do when different sources of belief do not mesh. The readings in this book have focused on the natural sciences and on communities of religious faith and practice as sources of belief and on the conflict between them, particularly about the history of life on earth.

We started with the proposals of Peirce and Clifford that beliefs should be grounded in scientific investigation and that we should believe only what is supported by sufficient evidence. For some people this principle defines what critical belief is.

To get clearer about what "sufficient evidence" might be we considered what makes scientific thought persuasive. Science involves constant criticism of the "received opinions" (what most folks in science believe to be true); when scientific ideas can be justified in the face of this constant criticism, this gives us more confidence that those ideas are true.

Is scientific method then the method of critical thinking? Feyerabend proposed that there was no such thing as "scientific method." He argued for this by developing Galileo's defense of the Copernican theory that the earth moves. Feyerabend argued that in fact the theory *did not* fit observations. Observations were distorted by bad physical theory which had become part of the common sense of the time. To advance science Galileo had to *reinterpret* observations to fit the theory. Scientific method requires that the theory fit observations, but that principle would have retarded science. But no one would advance the principle "reinterpret observations to fit your theory" as a *general* account of scientific method (though it worked in this case). So we have no method of proceeding which will advance science. Even if Feyerabend overstated what he had shown—even if he only showed that the observations were open to *alternative*, (at the time) *equally plausible* interpretations—he still seems to have shown that the "obvious" methodological principle that the theory must fit the observations is useless in some instances.

If the "method of science" is the same as "thinking critically," then we may have no adequate theory of what critical thinking is. Could Feyerabend's method (finding examples where "obviously correct" principles of scientific method don't work or are inconclusive) be extended to textbook accounts of what is correct critical thinking? I suspect that it can. If no one can tell us what the "correct" method of thinking is, we have to rely on what makes sense to us, and that is what I recommend (and appealed to in my own paper on evolution)— what makes sense of the evidence, when that evidence is developed in detail (that is what makes it science, not just the *a priori* method).

We then came to consider how many of our beliefs are derived from what others tell us. We considered first Hume's and Clifford's view that we should believe others only when we have evidence that what they tell us is likely to be true. But in Elizabeth Anscombe's words Hume holds that "we believe in the truth of testimony because we perceive the testimony and we have (well! often have) found testimony and truth to go together! The view needs only to be stated to be promptly rejected. It was always absurd, and the mystery is how Hume could ever have entertained it." While some have tried to defend a more sophisticated version of the Humean approach, I agree with Anscombe that the project is likely to be hopeless. We are stuck with the fact that we must believe others—not always, but believing others is the default unless we have reason to doubt what they say. But people we listen to often disagree. So we are often in a situation of having to work out whom we should believe.

This brings us to the question of religious belief, the final section of the anthology. Here the central question is whether critical belief, belief that can be defended in the face of doubt, is appropriate in all situations. William James says "no," that critical belief has a place in science and other matters, but that in many practical endeavors and in our religious life, we may be better off if we believe beyond what the evidence can justify. To obtain the good of a religious life (and other practical goods) James holds that we must believe.

Richard Feldman points out, however, that there are three options, not two, when it comes to particular religious convictions: to believe, to disbelieve, or to suspend judgment. While there may be goods that come with belief that are lost if we disbelieve or suspend judgment, there are also goods that come with each of the other two (different good for disbelief and for suspension of judgment), goods that we lose if we believe in God. Allen Wood adds that we are dishonest with ourselves and undermine our own integrity when we believe anything for any reason except the reason that the evidence shows it to be true. Thus, he believes, Clifford's principle is vindicated.

Putnam questions the connection between the holding of a belief because of the evidence for it and a way of life; he holds that religious convictions are not captured by words expressing beliefs based on the evidence for them. Putnam agrees with what he interprets Wittgenstein to be saying, that "religion has more to do with the kind of picture that one allows to organize one's life than it does with expressions of belief." In the rest of this epilogue I will investigate these two ideas from Putnam's essay: (1) that there is a "disconnect" between the language in which religious people express their convictions and the language of beliefs based on evidence and (2) that a picture by which we organize our lives may not have an obvious connection to our beliefs.

Putnam writes:

> When [Wittgenstein] takes the unshakeableness of a religious belief as one of its characteristics, he does not mean that a genuine religious belief is always and at every moment free from doubt. Kierkegaard spoke of faith as a state in which one cannot permanently stay. But I think that Kierkegaard would agree with Wittgenstein—and that Wittgenstein is here agreeing with Kierkegaard—that religious belief "regulates for all" in the believer's life, even though his religious belief may alternate with doubt.

Putnam thinks that religious conviction is unlike "empirical belief" in this regard. He follows this passage with an example of how, in the case of an empirical belief, doubts would be resolved. He asks us to imagine someone who comes to have doubts that he is building a bridge correctly; in that case "I will not go on building the bridge in that way (unless I am a crooked contractor); I will halt the construction and run further tests and make calculations." Putnam is imagining a case where there are well-established ways to resolve doubt about the right way to build the bridge.

Based on this case Putnam draws a contrast between the uncertainty inherent in religious belief that "regulates for all in one's life" and the doubts that arise about "empirical beliefs," doubts that we resolve through investigation. I am skeptical of this contrast.

In many cases of what seem to be "empirical beliefs" we may have to live with doubts when we have no established method to resolve them. Suppose I am building a bridge and have doubts whether I am doing it correctly but also have no way to discover how to build it except to build it as best I can and then see how it works (as would be true if this were the first effort to build a bridge to span a chasm). Practical problems of how we are to conduct our lives are often like that: we have doubts about how to handle marital problems or to organize a class, but we forge ahead, do the best we can, and evaluate the results. Since there may be no way of knowing except by giving it a try, living with uncertainty can be part of life, religious or not.

Uncertainty that exists in a marriage or classroom can also be present in our life as a whole; we may have doubts about the "picture we may allow to organize our lives." Not everyone organizes their life by a picture, and some people who are not conventionally religious do so. A professor may organize her life, or much of it, by a picture of contributing to philosophy or the arts, through teaching and writing. Speaking personally, as a political activist I have striven to organize my life by a picture of how my life might contribute to a future without racial injustice or any comparable form of oppression or disadvantage (my book *How to Make Opportunity Equal* describes what a society without disadvantage might look like).[1] But such a life, if lived honestly, may have, in Kierkegaard's words, an "infinite dialectic of uncertainty," or at least unresolved uncertainty about one's contributions to philosophy or to a future without racial injustice.

Yet evidence is relevant to the picture that organizes one's life. Pessimistic accounts of human nature—ones that hold that sexism or ethnocentrism are "in our genes"—are relevant to the validity of the picture by which an egalitarian political activist organizes her life; they must be engaged and answered. Hence I disagree with Putnam that there is a clear contrast between a religious life—where irresolvable doubts are inherent—and "empirical beliefs" where there are clear methods of resolving doubts. Rather the problem is options that are, in James's words, momentous and forced: we choose how to live our lives, but we never have enough knowledge to be assured that, had we known more, we would have chosen the same life. Yet, we may engage evidence and argument that would either vindicate or undermine the picture that regulates our lives. While evidence and argument are relevant, we still live with uncertainty.

Living with doubt is often necessary for another, really quite simple, reason. What James means by an option is a choice between *two* alternatives. Feldman points out that when it comes to belief, even in the case of propositions (statements) that can be only either true or false, there are three options: believe it true, believe it false, suspend judgment. When it comes to how to live our lives, there are many more options. Even though not all possible ways of living one's life (as a Christian, a philosopher, an egalitarian, a feminist—obviously the list could be extended indefinitely) will seem "alive" to any of us, there may be *many*,

---

1   *How to Make Opportunity Equal: Race and Contributive Justice* (Oxford: Blackwell [now Wiley-Blackwell], 2007).

certainly often more than one, ways of living that do seem to be real possibilities to us. The choice is forced. Which life will make me happiest, which will allow me to do the most good or to contribute the most to society or to my family? These questions are *relevant* to my choice. But the more the options, the less the probability (assuming other things are equal) that the option I choose is the best one.

It is, *in principle*, possible to know the answers to questions such as which life might do the most good for humanity or for me or my family, and surely the evidence can speak to them. For example, Mill observed that people who consciously strive for their own happiness are not happy. Tim Kasser has reviewed evidence that striving for material affluence tends to be associated with alienation and dysfunction.[2] Evidence that egalitarian social norms work well in traditional foraging societies seems to show that human nature is not inherently adapted to social hierarchy and that egalitarian society is possible. The point of the last several paragraphs is that while I typically will not have enough evidence to justify belief that the life I have chosen is the best one to advance my goals, evidence is still relevant to our choice of how to live. I choose and live with uncertainty. Therefore, *contra* Putnam, evidence can vindicate or undermine a picture that organizes a person's life, and, relatedly, living with insufficient evidence is not peculiar to the religious life.

If we cannot know—or even have adequate reason to believe—that the life we live will achieve the goals for which we strive (for example, can't be certain that a life devoted to a family will succeed in raising one's children well or that a life devoted to egalitarian justice will actually contribute to that end), how are we to justify our lives? To justify a devotion to parenting does a parent have to have sufficient evidence to believe that his children will turn out well? Does an anti-racist activist have to know that a non-racist society will exist some day? These are the goals for which we may strive, and, related to them, there may be a picture (of oneself as a parent or activist) of how one's life may contribute to those goals. Do we have to believe that these goals *will* be realized, or only something weaker? Do we have to know that our lives advance these goals, or only something weaker?

In his essay *Perpetual Peace* and in some other historical writings Immanuel Kant distinguishes between the sort of evidence required to justify his own hope for a world of peaceful and just relations between

---

2   *The High Price of Materialism* (Cambridge, MA: MIT Press, 2002).

nations and the sort of evidence required to come to a conclusion based on evidence. Kant believed that the means to peace must be to act from the moral law. But would acting from the moral law lead to a world of perpetual peace? Kant believed it would; he thought that history worked through the human passions to promote peace. He gives three ways that history is moving toward peace: our selfish inclinations lead to conflicts between citizens *within* nations that make clear the need for republican self-government; conflicts *between* nations teach us the need for universal principles and peaceful relations among states; the desire for enrichment through commerce requires peaceful relations among nations. How certain does he feel about whether there will be peace? He writes that "nature guarantees perpetual peace by the mechanism of the human passions. Certainly she does not do so with sufficient certainty for us to predict the future in any theoretical sense, but adequately from a practical point of view, making it our duty to work toward this end." So Kant is recognizing two kinds of justification for belief, one that is satisfactory for theoretical reason and a weaker justification that is sufficient to create, for Kant, a practical duty. Practical duties require only enough evidence to establish reasonable hope.

Commitment to raising one's children or to egalitarian justice requires sufficient evidence that the goals one strives for—children who become moral adults or a society of egalitarian justice—are possible, enough evidence that we may reasonably hope for them. Reasonable hope also is required that one's particular life advances that goal. I need a *reasonable hope* that, by the actions of my life, I may help to achieve those ends. Evidence is relevant to these hopes, and rationally evidence can either sustain or undermine them. But I don't have to have enough evidence to justify, as a statement of fact about the future, that my children will turn out well or that my parenting will contribute to their turning out well; that there will be an egalitarian society or that my life will contribute to that goal. The evidence must be enough that I can *believe in* my own life and believe that it is reasonable to strive for the goals that guide it. That does not mean, however, that I have enough evidence to say that I *believe that* that those goals will be achieved or that my life will advance them. Hence, on this Kantian view I have defended, belief in one's own life and the picture that organizes it is consistent with epistemic modesty and doxastic conservatism (being conservative about what we believe).

Kant's distinction between the evidence sufficient for theoretical justification and that sufficient for practical justification is not the distinction Putnam makes. Perhaps it articulates part of what he was thinking when he contrasted the sort of uncertainty that characterizes the religious life and the uncertainty that may characterize empirical belief. However, I have argued that the contrast between justifying a belief and justifying a picture that organizes one's life applies to many lives which are not conventionally religious.

Putnam writes that "religion has more to do with the kind of picture that one allows to organize one's life than it does with expressions of belief." Some religions—Judaism is an example (and Putnam is an observant Jew)—do not emphasize doctrine but observance of law. Here a personal anecdote may help. A few years ago I attended my niece's *bat mitzvah* at a conservative Jewish congregation: one was not to enter the sanctuary without a head covering; many there wore prayer shawls and rocked during prayer; the *Torah* was removed from its ark and the rabbi led a procession through the congregation where many kissed their prayer shawls and touched it to the *Torah*. During the service the rabbi delivered a sermon. During the course of the year, they had read the entire *Torah* and had come again to the beginning of *Genesis*; hence the topic of the sermon was the first words of the *Torah* usually translated into English as "In the beginning God created the heavens and the earth." The rabbi discussed three interpretations of these words. In the most common English version they meant that God existed from eternity and, at a particular time, created the heavens and the earth. But, she assured us, there were other interpretations which were part of Jewish tradition. On one God and the heavens and earth were separate but coterminous in time. In another, God was not really separate from creation; rather speaking of God and speaking of the creation were two ways of speaking about the same thing. All three interpretations of these words were valid within the Jewish tradition. On this view, then, belief in God does not necessarily imply belief in a God separate from the natural world. This anecdote should illustrate the meaning of a non-doctrinal religion. It would seem, then, that being a Jew may be compatible with not believing anything which goes beyond the evidence. Observant practices, such as covering one's head in the sanctuary, may not imply anything about belief.

All of this suggests that there are ways of living—some which are not religious in the usual sense, others which are—that do not depend on much by way of beliefs and are compatible with epistemic modesty and doxastic conservatism. But a religion without very strong beliefs might be incompatible with many faith traditions. Some Christian traditions, in particular, put great emphasis on the specifics of belief and on doctrine. Some traditions interpret scripture as answering questions that others of us might think can only be answered (if they can be answered at all) by scientific investigation.

Some religious communities resist dialogue with those outside the community who have beliefs contrary to their own. For example, some religious beliefs deriving from Genesis conflict with scientific accounts, and there is no dialogue between the two communities. Given the separateness of these communities, it may be impossible to resolve the disagreements and issues raised in this anthology. Or perhaps this anthology can help us to speak to one another.

INDEX

Using 0,3685 tons of Rolland Enviro100 Print instead of virgin fibres paper reduces your ecological footprint of:

Trees: 6
Waste: 771 lbs
Water: 6,097gal
Energy: 10 MMBTU
Greenhouse gases: 2,004 lbs
Smog: 6 lbs   [3]